Defining Cinema

Rutgers Depth of Field Series

Charles Affron, Mirella Jona Affron, Robert Lyons, Series Editors

Edited and with an introduction by
Peter Lehman

Defining
Cinema

Rutgers
University
Press

New Brunswick,
New Jersey

Library of Congress Cataloging-in-Publication Data

Defining cinema / edited and with an introduction by Peter Lehman.
    p.   cm. — (Rutgers depth of field series)
   Includes bibliographical references and index.
   ISBN 0-8135-2301-X (alk. paper). — ISBN 0-8135-230281 (pbk. :
alk. paper)
   1. Motion pictures—Philosophy. I. Lehman, Peter. II. Series.
PN1995.D38 1997
791.43'01—dc21   97-7710
                                               CIP

Manufactured in the United States of America

For Eleanor

Acknowledgments

The idea for this volume originated with Charles Affron and Mirella Affron. I thank them for the idea, and for their confidence in me as the right editor for the project. I am grateful to Edward Branigan for his insightful comments on the first draft of my introduction. Melanie Magisos was, once again, a careful reader of my work and, as always, it is much better as a result.

Defining Cinema

Peter Lehman

Introduction: What Is Film Theory?

In an oft-quoted line, Supreme Court Justice Potter Stewart once re-marked of pornography, "I don't know what it is, but I know it when I see it." Although many members of the general public would no doubt nod in agreement with this "seeing is believing" mentality, such a position is in-adequate for a film theorist. It is analogous to saying, "I don't know what realism is, but I know a realistic movie when I see one." Theorists demand a much more rigorous approach to these types of judgments. Both the na-ture of "seeing" and the nature of "believing" are very complex areas of in-vestigation for theorists; there is nothing simple about them.

This volume is an anthology of essays by five major film theorists, each of which is coupled with a commentary by a film scholar. In this in-troductory essay, referring to pornography and realism, I indicate why film theory is important and what some of its major concerns are. I then define the components of a theory and introduce the theorists included in this volume, placing them within the history of film theory. Finally, I draw some distinctions between the classical theorists represented in this vol-ume and contemporary theory.

Let us return for the moment to pornography. Many people think pornographic films can be defined fairly simply. For example, some define them as films made with the intent of sexually arousing the spectator. Unlike Justice Potter's remark, at least this approach gives us criteria that we can test. But how helpful are these criteria?

Unfortunately, not very. First of all, even if someone intends to sexually arouse the spectator, how can we determine that that is all they intend? Some filmmakers may have unconscious motives of which they are not aware, meaning even *they* don't know what they intend. Nor for that matter is it clear how one would define a sexually aroused spectator in such a manner that only pornography as opposed to art would cause such arousal. And even if we had a definition of what it meant to be a sex-ually aroused spectator, many spectators might not be consciously aware of whether or not they were in such a state.

Let us take one other definition of pornography as an example. Some people think that something is pornographic if it lacks any socially redeeming value. But such a definition may be useless since nothing may fit that definition. Linda Williams has shown, for example, how early silent stag films served the social function of providing male bonding within the context of "smokers" or bachelors' parties. One can imagine labeling this function as disgusting, adolescent, mysogynistic, and the like, but that is different from saying there is no social meaning or value. Sexually explicit films can have multiple socially redeeming values that have nothing to do with the intentions of the filmmakers. Some viewers, for example, may find the films educational by virtue of learning about new aspects of sexuality. Indeed, some marriage counselors and medical professionals recommend porn tapes to their patients and clients. Within such a context the tapes are serving a much different function than they would at a bachelor party screening. But both functions have a significant element that certainly could be defined as socially redeeming value, be it friendship among men or marital bliss among couples.

I use the example of pornography here for several reasons. It grabs attention since nearly everyone in our society has his or her own definition of pornography and an accompanying strong feeling about whether it should be banned or protected as free speech. If we apply systematic, rigorous thought to the topic of pornography, however, we quickly discover that it is much more complex than we had realized. Such is the case with all aspects of film theory.

Definitions of what is pornographic also shift strongly over time, suggesting that pornography cannot be simply located in a work. Changing societal criteria affect whether a work will be classified as pornographic. Such shifts prove that what is pornographic is at least in part determined not by intrinsic features of a work but, rather, by changing social and legal definitions.

Finally, pornography of necessity raises gender issues. Indeed, a cliché of pornography is that it exploits women for the pleasure of men. Pornography has been targeted by anti-porn feminists who claim that it oppresses women, but it has also been defended by other feminists as affording women important opportunities to address issues of female sexuality and desire as well as the opportunity to analyze historically shifting aspects of male sexuality within patriarchy.

Let us switch now from pornography to realism. Just like Justice Stewart believed he knew pornography when he saw it, most of us think we know realism when we see it. Notice, incidentally, that to believe in the ease of making these distinctions is to believe in their importance. If we did not think it was important to recognize pornography, we wouldn't do so. So if we all think we know that some films are realistic and some aren't, we must believe that the distinction is of some significance. But what if no films are or can be realistic? What if, on close examination, it makes no sense to believe that films can in any meaningful sense be simply like real life? How much like real life? Whose life and when?

It is not uncommon at the end of a movie to hear someone say he or she didn't like it because it wasn't realistic. Here we have an example of one possible importance of the distinction between realistic and unrealistic films: some might think a movie better if it is realistic. In this case, their beliefs about realism affect their judgments about how good or bad films are. This shows us that there is frequently a connection between our beliefs about different aspects of cinema. We connect, in other words, what we think we see, what we think when seeing it, and what we finally think after seeing it. If, on the one hand, we believe we know a pornographic film when we see one, we may feel comfortable censoring such films. If, on the other hand, we are unsure about the distinction between art and pornography, we are less likely to support censorship, believing that important works might get censored in the process. Similarly, if we believe we know a realistic film when we see one, we may judge such films superior to unrealistic films. If, however, we believe that realism is only an illusion or perhaps a judgment made by a social class, and a dangerous or at least oppressive one at that, we are unlikely to value it as a criterion for judging good films.

No doubt, just like we all think we know if a film is realistic or not or whether or not it is good, we all think we know what a camera is. But let us not be too quick to dismiss the question, "What is a camera?" Indeed, what is a movie? What is a projector? What is a screen? What is a spectator? Most of us would think that only an alien from outer space could ask such questions. But in addition to space aliens there is another category of people who ask such questions—film theorists. The rest of us think we know what a movie is when we see it and that is adequate for our purposes. And everyone knows what a camera is, right? In fact, most of us have used one and surely if we've used one, we know what it is. Or do we? Edward Branigan, one of the contributors to this volume, has published a provocative conference paper entitled "What Is a Camera?" The paper was first delivered to a group of professional film academicians who presumably knew just as well as the rest of the population about the physical objects that we use to take snapshots of our family vacations or of the related physical objects used to make movies. But Branigan's point was precisely that such a simple, common definition of a camera obscures the fact that at least eight different assumptions underlie theoretical accounts of them within film theory. For some theorists, a camera may record the physical world while for others it constructs and shapes a unique world of its own. A joke helps bring these issues into focus.

A sailor whose ship was in port in Spain was walking down the street when he thought he recognized Pablo Picasso. When he approached the man, he discovered that indeed he was the famous artist. Like most of us, it seems this sailor knew what was good and what was bad and willingly offered his opinion to Picasso. "I don't like your paintings," he said, "because they aren't realistic." "What do you think is realistic?" the artist asked the sailor. "This picture of my girlfriend," he said, reaching into his pocket and producing a photograph. Picasso looked at it carefully and handed it back to the sailor, remarking, "She's very pretty, but awfully small."

This joke turns on the inadequacy of the simple belief that a photographic record of the world is like the world. Obviously, the sailor's girlfriend is really much larger than her image in the photograph and, just as obviously, Picasso knows this and speaks facetiously. But Picasso's comment on her beauty also suggests that we accept some aspects of photographs as revealing some truth about the physical world. The photograph conveys enough information about the woman that Picasso concludes that she conforms to his or his culture's definition of beautiful. When presented with photographs of spouses and children they have never seen, people commonly remark on their appearance (e.g., a daughter looks like her mother, a wife is beautiful, a husband is handsome, etc.). Clearly, we accept some aspects of photographs as containing a likeness.

Theorists probe these issues in a rigorous, philosophical manner. In what way, if any, can we say a photograph resembles what it represents? The world, for example, is three-dimensional but photographs are two-dimensional. As aestheticians such as Nelson Goodman have shown using the criterion of resemblance, when we look at a photograph we would conclude it resembles all the other photographs we have ever seen more than its subject matter (e.g., a building). Photographs, in other words, resemble other photographs more closely than they resemble anything else in the world. So, as the above joke indicates, the resemblance must only apply to certain features of the photograph (e.g., the woman's beauty) rather than others (e.g., her size).

But even this is much more complicated than it seems. Hollywood directors and cinematographers commonly use the expression "The camera loves her face" when referring to a photogenic actress. They also readily acknowledge, however, that the only way they can discover whether or not the camera loves someone's face is by conducting a screen test. Looking at the face as it actually appears, in other words, will not yield the answer. That even these professionals must look at a represented image to confirm their hunches indicates that photographic images do not merely resemble their subjects; they are also different from them. A thin face might look heavy, for example, while a well-shaped face might look shapeless. Cheekbones might disappear or be accentuated. Or perhaps with one kind of lighting and lens the former will happen and with another kind of lighting and lens the latter will happen. If that is the case, then lighting and lenses shape the representation rather than simply record the face as it appears in "real life."

Film theorists rigorously question and examine every aspect of cinema in this fashion. But certainly the phrase "every aspect" is rather all-encompassing. How can we more carefully define and categorize the various aspects of film theory? What issues must one address to earn the title of a "film theorist"? As we have already seen, it is not enough to simply identify movies as good or bad, realistic or unrealistic, pornographic or artistic, and so on. People making such snap judgments are like our sailor who knows what he likes but is hardly an art theorist.

In the introduction to his book *The Major Film Theorists*, Dudley Andrew, a contributor to this collection, has claimed that "every question about film falls under at least one of the following headings: raw material, methods and techniques, forms and shapes, purpose or value" (7). Edward Branigan in his essay in this volume suggests that the questions theorists ask address ontology, epistemology, aesthetics, ideology, and truth. Like Andrew and Branigan, I think it is important to address these issues and will do so briefly using three of the terms Branigan employs: ontology, epistemology, and aesthetics. Those terms do not, of course originate with Branigan. They are part of a long-standing philosophical tradition. What is important is that we systematically organize our thoughts, questions, and investigations about cinema. Whether we have three, four, or five categories, or what we call the categories, is of less importance.

Ontology deals with the nature of being. In terms of film theory, ontology addresses the conditions of being of such aspects of cinema as the camera and the world of which it is a part. This includes the manner in which light rays are reflected from objects, enter the lens of the camera, leave an impression on the chemically sensitive strip of film, and so on. Cinema, in other words, includes an elaborate physical apparatus involving film stocks, cameras, projectors, screens—the list is extensive. Much like a theory of literature has to consider the nature and reality of language, a theory of cinema has to consider the nature and reality of the elaborate physical apparatus without which there would be no movies.

But how do we know what it is we have seen when we have seen a movie? This question takes us from ontology to epistemology. Epistemology deals with the nature of knowledge. When we leave a movie theater after watching a film like *Jurassic Park*, we presume we know what it is "about." For most of us, feature films are "about" their story and, for that reason, if a friend asks what a movie was about we recount the highlights of the story. Few of us would start describing camera positions and movements or other highlights of visual style, though we could (indeed, some theorists would say we should). As this simple example shows, films are "about" different things to different people. How do we come to *know* what a film is about? When we talk about the story of a film, how do we *know* what that story is? We do not, after all, simply see a story unfolding before our eyes when we watch a movie. How we gain knowledge of the story and what we think the film is about is the province of epistemology.

When we talk to a friend after seeing a movie, we are just as likely to be asked whether we liked the movie as we are to be asked what it was about. Or perhaps like the sailor who accosted Picasso, we simply feel a need to readily tell others what kinds of movies we like and why we like them (e.g., they are "realistic"). When we say a movie was great or that it was awful, we have moved from the realm of epistemology to the realm of aesthetics. Aesthetics involves making distinctions among films and value judgments about them.

There is a saying in our culture that "everyone is a critic," and there certainly is no shortage of people happy to tell us which movies they like and don't like and which movies are good or bad. Indeed, it appears we are a society of aesthetic experts. There is no equivalent saying in our culture that everyone is a theorist, and for good reason. Indeed, this curious state of affairs helps us understand what a theory is and what distinguishes a theorist from a critic, though critics may be theorists and theorists may be critics.

Let us turn once again to our hapless sailor who helps make this distinction crystal clear: he is a critic and not a theorist. Many would no doubt point out that he is not a good critic, but that is a different matter. He has an aesthetic that employs the following logic: good art is realistic art in that what it represents looks like the world as we know it; Picasso's paintings, at least the ones he's familiar with, don't look like the real world; therefore, Picasso is not a good artist. This aesthetic, however, is simply asserted much like some moviegoers only like movies with happy endings. Why art should represent the physical world as we know it, or why movies should make us feel good with their happy endings, is never questioned or examined in relation to anything else—it is simply asserted as self-evident.

In other words, nearly everyone has an aesthetic but very few people have integrated that aesthetic within a theory. At the other extreme, a complete theory addresses and integrates all three areas of ontology, epistemology, and aesthetics. If a true theorist such as André Bazin has an aesthetic that values long takes with moving camera and depth of field, it will logically stem from his ontology and epistemology. Bazin, in other words, will value those features because he conceives of the camera as having a special link with the physical world that enables it to make a record of the world and he believes that if the spectator perceives the world within the spatial and temporal continuity of long takes with moving camera and depth of field, he or she will respond differently than if he or she perceives the world through many brief shots with many edits and shallow focus. In other words, Bazin's ontology grants the photographic image a special link to the physical world; his epistemology claims that spectators gain their knowledge of that world differently if perceived via certain techniques that respect spatial and temporal continuity; and his aesthetic champions those films that employ such techniques over other styles.

The example of Bazin here serves another purpose beyond that of illustrating what a true theory consists of; it introduces the work of someone who is generally agreed upon by scholars to be one of the most important film theorists of all time. Film theory has a history and that history helps explain the contents and organization of this volume, which has a fairly simple design: it pairs an essay by a film theorist with a new essay about that theorist's work written by a film scholar. The theorists I have chosen are Sergei Eisenstein, André Bazin, Siegfried Kracauer, Noël Burch, and Christian Metz. A word about this selection is in order.

It is, to say the least, not an original lineup. Dudley Andrew and Robert Eberwein, two of the scholars who have contributed new essays to this volume, have written books surveying film theory and both have included Eisenstein, Bazin, and Metz in their books. Indeed, Robert Eberwein's *A Viewer's Guide to Film Theory and Criticism* discusses the work of all five of the theorists under consideration in this volume. Similarly, in his book *Mystifying Movies: Fads and Fallacies in Contemporary Film Theory*, Noël Carroll, another contributor to this volume, devotes extensive attention to the work of Christian Metz. This points to the fact that there is an agreed-upon tradition within film theory that certain figures have defined the field. Stated another way, there is a film theory canon and any volume or course attempting to introduce people to the field will inevitably return over and over again to the same figures. Before pursuing the implications of this, I want to briefly introduce and contextualize Eisenstein, Bazin, Kracauer, Burch, and Metz and place them within the history of film theory.

Classical film theory has traditionally been divided into two camps: formalists and realists. Eisenstein is nearly always recognized as the leading formalist theorist and Bazin and Kracauer are similarly recognized as the leading realist theorists. Starting in the late sixties, as we shall see with Burch and Metz, this simple opposition is called into question.

Although there has been no clear-cut historical progression from one school to the other, Noël Carroll, in *Philosophical Problems of Classical Film Theory*, makes the observation that early theories of cinema tended to be formalist since at the time of the origin of cinema there was a great deal of question about whether this mechanical form of reproduction was an "art" form. In order to rush to the defense of cinema as an art form worthy of serious critical attention, theorists had to emphasize the differences between film "art" and simple mechanical reproduction of reality. Their arguments, in other words, emphasized how film form uniquely shaped and transformed resemblances to the physical world into a whole new artistic arena. By the time of the post–World War II years, when the major realist theories emerged, cinema had been established as a legitimate art form for decades. No longer needing to prove cinema's worthiness, these theorists emphasized the closeness between cinema and reality.

Sergei Eisenstein was a Russian filmmaker and theorist who began making silent films in the Soviet Union in the twenties following the revolution, and continued into the forties. The span of his career included the avant-garde, revolutionary period, which was followed by the Stalinist socialist realist period and the transition from silent to sound cinema. Although Eisenstein always remained a formalist in his various filmmaking styles and theories, both changed significantly over the years.

The fact that Eisenstein was a filmmaker as well as a theorist points to another significant aspect of the history of film theory: some major theorists like Eisenstein and Burch have also been filmmakers, and some like Bazin and Metz have not. The distinction is important, I think, not because filmmakers know more about cinema than non-filmmakers but, rather, because they bring a different perspective. The history of film theory is one that benefits from the combined perspectives of insiders and outsiders. Indeed, Vance Kepley's essay on Eisenstein concludes by emphasizing his legacy not as a pure theorist but, rather, as a theoretically informed filmmaker.

It is perhaps no coincidence that French theorist André Bazin's career began almost exactly when Eisenstein's ended—the late forties. Bazin's career, tragically cut short by his premature death, did not span the varying historical epochs that Eisenstein's did and accordingly his theories did not change as much. He began as a strong realist and remained one throughout his career. In addition to Carroll's above-noted observation about the development of film theory, we should also consider the manner in which artists and critics typically rebel against the previous generation's work. Given that Eisenstein had been such a major influence, it is hardly surprising that Bazin should, in part, rebel against him. Similarly, Annette Michelson has shown how Noël Burch's theory, discussed below, must be positioned in response to a then-current Bazinian orthodoxy.

By the time Bazin began his work, he could react to the many established styles of filmmaking, including Soviet montage of which Eisenstein had been a part and several new trends such as postwar Italian cinema (the films of Roberto Rosselini and Vittorio De Sica). Finally, the war itself points to the importance of historical and cultural events other than those confined to the world of cinema in understanding the development of film theory. Dudley Andrew's essay on Bazin does precisely that by acknowledging the perspective of a contemporary scholar informed by important new developments in digital technology that threaten a whole new definition of the photographic image than that current at the time of Bazin's work.

That the major postwar theorists were profoundly affected by the war in terms of how they thought about cinema is nowhere more evident than with Siegfried Kracauer. The title of Kracauer's first film book, *From Caligari to Hitler*, points to the importance of World War II in his work. He had been a newspaper reporter in Germany who left for the United States after Hitler's rise to power. Kracauer's importance as a theorist, however, rests primarily on his 1960 book *The Redemption of*

Physical Reality. It is this work that Noël Carroll analyzes in his essay in this volume.

Noël Burch was a formalist when he wrote *Theory of Film Practice*, which originally was published in France in 1969. But his formalism grew out of a rejection of the conventional formalist–realist split in film theory. As Vance Kepley explains in his essay, Eisenstein's formalism places a strong emphasis on montage and the style of his films rests on the editing together of comparatively brief shots. Bazin's realism valued long-held shots with moving camera and depth of field, a technique that he found admirably employed in the films of Jean Renoir. By the late sixties, montage had become heavily identified with formalism and long takes with moving camera and depth of field with realism. The styles seemed theoretically irreconcilable until Burch rethought cinema in such a radical manner that his aesthetics could logically praise both Renoir's long takes and Eisenstein's montages of brief shots.

Burch was able to accomplish this by not accepting the underlying assumptions that particular cinematic stylistic features were necessarily identified with either realism or formalism. Rather than align himself with any single style of filmmaking, Burch inventoried and defended all the possibilities of cinema as long as they were used in a complex and structurally unified manner. He is a formalist who seeks the aesthetic value and complexity in any style, be it one heavily reliant on editing or on long takes. Unlike Bazin, Burch admired Renoir's camerawork not because it was realistic but because it was aesthetically complex in a manner dependent on cinematic form.

In his essay, Edward Branigan points out the importance of the concept of "zero" in Burch's work. One of the many meanings of zero that Branigan identifies is Burch's labeling of the classical Hollywood style of filmmaking (sometimes referred to as the invisible style) as the zero-degree style of filmmaking. Burch condemned this style because it uses a predictable and limited range of techniques, none of which challenge the viewer. In short, the style is much too simple. The Hollywood filmmakers he admires are the ones who created some spatial and temporal complexity in their work.

From my perspective, zero has an additional meaning. Burch, in a metaphorical sense, returned to zero before formulating his film theory. He cast off the realist–formalist opposition and started anew from zero, developing a new formalist approach to cinema broad enough to encompass all styles. But *Theory of Film Practice* was only the beginning of Burch's ongoing productive career as a film theorist, and the changes he underwent help position the work of Christian Metz, our final theorist.

Burch had no sooner published his book in 1969, than he began to have second thoughts about his formalist position. The late sixties in France and elsewhere was a period of political turmoil. Protest against U.S. involvement in the Vietnam War, a new women's movement, and labor disputes in France leading to a major strike provided a social climate that made Burch retract his nonjudgmental approach of inventorying all possible cinematic styles from a purely aesthetic point of view. Film styles, he now believed, were part of larger cultural ideologies.

France in the late sixties was a vital intellectual center which, led by such luminaries as Claude Lévi-Strauss, Roland Barthes, Louis Althusser, and Jacques Lacan, gave rise to new schools of thought such as structuralism and semiotics alongside new interpretations of Marx and Freud. It is within this climate that Christian Metz made his contribution to film theory. As Robert Eberwein shows, Metz's work initially emphasized structural semiotics, then shifted to include a Lacanian psychoanalytic perspective. The incorporation of psychoanalytic theory into film theory characterized an influential development in the field throughout the seventies and into the mid-eighties. But that was accompanied by the manner in which feminist film theory, led by Laura Mulvey's groundbreaking article "Visual Pleasure and Narrative Cinema," used psychoanalytic theory for its purposes. And it is here that I want to refer back to the gender issues I raised earlier with my pornography example.

The topic of this book is what is frequently called "classical film theory." As I already mentioned, that theory involves a canon and that canon has been comprised of white males. This itself points to something that should be historically contextualized. Classical film theory developed prior to feminist theory. Film theory currently includes important work on race, class, gender, and sexual orientation by women, people of color, and gays and lesbians. The work of these theorists has totally redefined the field and, indeed, Noël Burch and Christian Metz are pivotal figures who have bridged the gap between these traditions. Although the philosophical tradition of understanding theories in terms of ontology, epistemology, and aesthetics has proven extremely useful for the study of classical film theory, contemporary theorists have emphasized an additional category—that of ideology.

If, in some sense then, the classical tradition of film theory is dated, why study it? Although at first glance this might seem like a reasonable question, it is based on dangerous assumptions. The history of film theory reveals, not surprisingly, that there is no simple chronological progression toward the "truth" or a "right answer." If theory were that simple, then it would make perfect sense to simply start with current work and forget about the difficulty of learning the work of all those past theorists who were "wrong." Indeed, film theory might be less a matter of right and wrong than of usefulness. And as soon as one raises the question of how useful a theory is, the related question of "Useful for whom?" must be answered.

It is a matter of historical record, for example, that Freudian and Lacanian psychoanalytic theory was extremely useful to seventies and eighties feminist film theorists. Yet that theory is itself under attack at the moment by a new school of film theory led by David Bordwell. In

Making Meaning and "Contemporary Film Studies and the Vicissitudes of Grand Theory," Bordwell has mounted a comprehensive attack on the dominant forms of seventies, eighties, and nineties film theory, that influenced first by French Marxist, psychoanalytic, semiotic theory and then by cultural studies. But one of the reasons that Bordwell has been able to mount such an effective critique is that he has a superb grasp of the entire history of film theory. Thus, he can formulate new directions with reference to the limitations of his predecessors.

We can never stop questioning current models of theory by presuming a simple progress in theory. It is clear in the nineties that much of the feminist film theory of the seventies and eighties, for example, paid little or no attention to race, sexual orientation, or class, presuming a white, middle-class, heterosexual position. Hence the methods of that theory are not extremely useful to, for example, a black, working-class, lesbian theorist. Ironically, that is also one of the criticisms being leveled against the Bordwellian school. Quite simply, Bordwell is interested in other issues and will find other theoretical approaches more useful to his purposes. No theories exist outside such a context of use value to someone, and just as we must understand the theories, we must understand the uses to which those theories are put. No theory can be all-inclusive and simply right. As such, there will never be an end to film theory as long as people care about the subject. Cinema will never *be defined*. As the title of this volume suggests, *defining cinema* is an ongoing process. And those wishing to make a major contribution to it will have to understand its history as well as its current moment.

This volume addresses a major tradition within that history. It would be folly to presume that however profound their contribution, one tradition of white male theorists could *define cinema*. The defining process not only includes a plurality of voices but ever-new generations of voices with new and frequently urgent agendas shaped by historical, social, and cultural conditions. This does not mean that there is nothing of lasting value in the works of major theorists. None of them may possess the simple truth, but only by studying them do we prevent the need for rediscovering the wheel or prevent ourselves from blindly rushing down dead-end streets.

As all the essays in this volume attest, film theory is a vital area of ongoing debate. Within such a climate, scholars attack, defend, or simply probe and explicate the nuances of varying theories, and the scholars in this book demonstrate the full range of these positions. At the extremes, we find Dudley Andrew's impassioned defense of André Bazin and Noël Carroll's sharp critique of Siegfried Kracauer. Although Edward Branigan's reading of Burch is more of an explication than an attack or defense, it clearly assumes the position that understanding the nuances of Burch's complex theory is of profound value to contemporary film scholars. Somewhat similarly, Vance Kepley demonstrates the value of

Eisenstein's theory in relation to his own work and his considerable legacy as a filmmaker who has influenced the course of film history. Perhaps Robert Eberwein's careful tracing of Metz's complex career most fully approximates a nonjudgmental explication that wishes to neither overtly defend nor attack its subject but, rather, attempts to make clear its many facets.

Each theorist is represented in this volume with a selection which, though limited in length, is a representative example of his important work. As such the reader has the opportunity to test the claims and arguments made in the following commentaries. While the theories themselves should not be seen as simply right or wrong, the positions of the commentators should also be interrogated. One can learn a great deal about Bazin from Dudley Andrew, for example, and yet take a much more critical view of Bazin than Andrew does. Or, one can learn a great deal about Kracauer from Noël Carroll and take a much more positive view of him than Carroll does. These essays in other words should stimulate the reader to question and argue back as well as nod his or her head in agreement. In short, these provocative couplings of major theorists with commentary by scholars is an invitation to join in the intellectual vitality of classical film theory. Without such theory, we are left to fall back on empty platitudes such as "I don't know what pornography is, but I know it when I see it" or "That was a great movie because it was realistic."

WORKS CITED

Andrew, Dudley. 1976. *The Major Film Theorists: An Introduction.* New York: Oxford University Press.

Bordwell, David. 1996. "Contemporary Film Studies and the Vicissitudes of Grand Theory." In *Post-Theory: Reconstructing Film Studies.* Ed. David Bordwell and Noël Carroll. Madison: University of Wisconsin Press.

———. 1989. *Making Meaning: Inference and Rhetoric in the Interpretation of Cinema.* Cambridge, Mass.: Harvard University Press.

Branigan, Edward. 1984. "What Is a Camera?" In *Cinema Histories, Cinema Practices.* Ed. Patricia Mellencamp and Philip Rosen. Los Angeles: American Film Institute.

Carroll, Noël . 1988. *Mystifying Movies: Fads and Fallacies in Contemporary Film Theory.* New York: Columbia University Press.

———. 1988. *Philosophical Problems of Classical Film Theory.* Princeton, N.J.: Princeton University Press.

Eberwein, Robert T. 1979. *A Viewer's Guide to Film Theory and Criticism.* Metuchen, N.J.: Scarecrow.

Goodman, Nelson. 1968. *Languages of Art.* New York: Bobbs-Merrill.

Michelson, Annette. 1973. "Introduction." In *Theory of Film Practice* by Noël Burch. New York: Praeger.

Mulvey, Laura. 1975. "Visual Pleasure and Narrative Cinema." *Screen* 16, no. 3 (Autumn): 6–18.

Williams, Linda. 1989. *Hard Core: Power, Pleasure, and the "Frenzy of the Visible."* Berkeley: University of California Press.

ANNOTATED BIBLIOGRAPHY

Andrew, Dudley. 1976. *The Major Film Theories: An Introduction.* New York: Oxford University Press.

An analysis of classical film theory, including formalism (Hugo Münsterberg, Rudolph Arnheim, Sergei Eisenstein, and Béla Balázs), realism (Siegfried Kracauer and André Bazin), and semiology (Christian Metz).

Carroll, Noël. 1988. *Philosophical Problems of Classical Film Theory.* Princeton, N.J.: Princeton University Press.

A philosophical critique of classical film theory with chapters on Rudolf Arnheim, André Bazin, and V. F. Perkins.

———. 1988. *Mystifying Movies: Fads and Fallacies in Contemporary Film Theory.* New York: Columbia University Press.

A critique of contemporary film theory with a chapter on psychoanalysis that includes Christian Metz.

Eberwein, Robert T. 1979. *A Viewer's Guide to Film Theory and Criticism.* Metuchen, N.J.: Scarecrow.

An introductory survey of film theory and criticism that includes discussion of Vachel Lindsay, Hugo Münsterberg, Lev Kuleshov, V. I. Pudovkin, Sergei Eisenstein, Béla Balázs, Rudolf Arnheim, André Bazin, Siegfried Kracauer, and Christian Metz.

Eisenstein

The Montage of Film Attractions

These thoughts do not aspire to be manifestos or declarations, but they do represent an attempt to gain at least some understanding of the bases of our complex craft.

If we regard cinema as a factor for exercising emotional influence over the masses (and even the Cine-Eyes, who want to remove cinema from the ranks of the arts at all costs, are convinced that it is), we must secure its place in this category and, in our search for ways of building cinema up, we must make widespread use of the experience and the latest achievements in the sphere of those arts that set themselves similar tasks. The first of these is, of course, theater, which is linked to cinema by a common (identical) basic material—the *audience*—and by a common purpose—*influencing this audience in the desired direction* through a series of calculated pressures on its psyche. I consider it superfluous to expatiate solely on the intelligence of this kind of approach to cinema and theater since it is obvious and well founded from the standpoint both of social necessity (the class struggle) and of the very nature of these arts that deliver, because of their formal characteristics, a series of blows to the consciousness and emotions of the audience. Finally, only an ultimate aspiration of this sort can serve to justify diversions that give the audience real satisfaction (both physical and moral) as a result of fictive collaboration with what is being shown (through motor imitation of the action by those perceiving it and through psychological "empathy"). If it were not for this phenomenon which, incidentally, alone makes for the magnetism of theater, circus, and cinema, the thoroughgoing removal of accumulated forces would proceed at a more intense pace and sports clubs would have in their debt a significantly larger number of people whose physical nature had caught up with them.

Thus cinema, like theater, makes sense only as "one form of pressure." There is a difference in their methods, but they have one basic device in common: the montage of attractions, confirmed by my theater work in Proletkult and now being applied by me to cinema. It is this path

"The Montage of Film Attractions" [1924] appears in *S. M. Eisenstein, Selected Works*, vol. 1, *Writings 1922–34*, ed. and trans. Richard Taylor (London: BFI Publishing and Bloomington and Indianapolis: Indiana University Press, 1988), 39–58.

that liberates film from the plot-based script and for the first time takes account of film material, both thematically and formally, in the construction. In addition, it provides criticism with a method of objective expertise for evaluating theater or film works, instead of the printed exposition of personal impressions and sympathies spiced with quotations from a run-of-the-mill political report that happens to be popular at a particular moment.

An attraction is in our understanding any demonstrable fact (an action, an object, a phenomenon, a conscious combination, and so on) that is known and proven to exercise a definite effect on the attention and emotions of the audience and that, combined with others, possesses the characteristic of concentrating the audience's emotions in any direction dictated by the production's purpose. From this point of view a film cannot be a simple presentation or demonstration of events: rather it must be a tendentious selection of, and comparison between, events, free from narrowly plot-related plans and molding the audience in accordance with its purpose. (Let us look at *Cine-Pravda* in particular: *Cine-Pravda* does not follow this path—its construction takes no account of attractions—but "grabs" you through the attraction of its themes and, purely superficially, through the formal mastery of its montage of separate sequences, which by their short footage conceal the "neutral" epic "statement of facts.")

The widespread use of all means of influence does not make this a cinema of polished style but a cinema of action that is useful to our class, a class cinema due to its actual formal approach because attractional calculation is conceivable only when the audience is known and selected in advance for its homogeneity.

The application of the method of the montage of attractions (the comparison of facts) to cinema is even more acceptable than it is to theater. I should call cinema "the art of comparisons" because it shows not facts but conventional (photographic) representations (in contrast to "real action" in theater, at least when theater is employing the techniques we approve of). For the exposition of even the simplest phenomena cinema needs comparison (by means of consecutive, separate presentation) between the elements that constitute it: montage (in the technical, cinematic sense of the word) is fundamental to cinema, deeply grounded in the conventions of cinema and the corresponding characteristics of perception.

Whereas in theater an effect is achieved primarily through the psychological perception of an actually occurring fact (e.g., a murder),[1] in cinema it is made up of the juxtaposition and accumulation, in the audience's psyche, of associations that the film's purpose requires, associations that are aroused by the separate elements of the stated (in practical terms, in "montage fragments") fact, associations that produce, albeit tangentially, a similar (and often stronger) effect only when taken as a whole. Let us take that same murder as an example: a throat is gripped, eyes bulge, a knife is brandished, the victim closes his eyes, blood is spattered on a wall, the victim falls to the floor, a hand wipes off the knife—each fragment is chosen to "provoke" associations.

An analogous process occurs in the montage of attractions: it is not in fact phenomena that are compared but chains of associations that are linked to a particular phenomenon in the mind of a particular audience.[2] (It is quite clear that for a worker and a former cavalry officer the chain of associations set off by seeing a meeting broken up and the corresponding emotional effect in contrast to the material that frames this incident, will be somewhat different.) I managed to test quite definitively the correctness of this position with one example where, because what I should call this law had not been observed, the comic effect of such a well-tried device as the alogism fell flat. I have in mind the place in *The Extraordinary Adventures of Mr. West in the Land of the Bolsheviks*, where an enormous lorry is pulling a tiny sledge carrying Mr. West's briefcase. This construction can be found in different variants in any clown's act—from a tiny top hat to enormous boots. The appearance of such a combination in the ring is enough. But, when the whole combination was shown on the screen in one shot all at once (even though it occurred as the lorry was leaving the gates so that there was a short pause—as long as the rope joining the lorry to the sledge), the effect was very weak. Whereas a real lorry is immediately perceived in all its immensity and compared to a real briefcase in all its insignificance and (for comic effect) it is enough to see them side by side, cinema requires that a "representation" of the lorry be provided first for long enough to inculcate the appropriate associations—and then we are shown the incongruous light load. As a parallel to this I recall the construction of an analogous moment in a Chaplin film, where much footage is spent on the endlessly complicated opening of the locks on a huge safe[3] and it is only later (and apparently from a different angle) that we are shown the brooms, rags, and buckets that are hidden inside it. The Americans use this technique brilliantly for characterization—I remember the way Griffith "introduced" the "Musketeer," the gang-leader in *Intolerance*: he showed us a wall of his room completely covered with naked women and then showed the man himself. How much more powerful and more cinematic this is, we submit, than the introduction of the workhouse supervisor in *Oliver Twist* in a scene where he pushes two cripples around: he is shown through his deeds (a purely theatrical method of sketching character through action) and not through provoking the necessary associations.

From what I have said it is clear that the center of gravity of cinema effects, in contrast to those of theater, lies not in directly *physiological* effects, although a purely *physical* infectiousness can sometimes be attained (in a chase, with the montage of two sequences with movements running against the shot). It seems that there has been absolutely no study or evaluation of the purely physiological effect of montage irregularity and rhythm and, if it has been evaluated, this has only been for its role in narrative illustration (the tempo of the plot corresponding with the material being narrated). "We ask you not to confuse" the montage of attractions and its method of comparison with the usual montage parallelism used in the exposition of a theme such as the narrative principle in *Cine-Pravda*, where the audience has first to guess what is going on and then become "intellectually" involved with the theme.

The montage of attractions is closer to the simple contrasting comparisons (though these are somewhat compromised by *The Palace and the Fortress*, where the device is naively revealed) that often produce a definitely powerful emotional effect (chained legs in the ravelin and a ballerina's feet). But we must point out that in *The Palace and the Fortress* (from which this example comes) any dependence on comparison in the construction of the shots for this sequence was completely ignored: their construction does not assist association but disrupts it and it enters our consciousness through literary rather than visual means. For example, Nechayev, seen from the waist up and with his back to the camera, hammers on a barred door and the prison warder, seen in long shot somewhere in a corner by a window, holds a canary in a cage. The chained legs are shown horizontally whereas the ballerina's points are shot about four times larger and vertically.

The method of the montage of attractions is the comparison of subjects for thematic effect. I shall refer to the original version of the montage resolution in the finale of my film *Strike*: the mass shooting, where I employed the associational comparison with a slaughterhouse. I did this, on the one hand, to avoid overacting among the extras from the labor exchange "in the business of dying" but mainly to excise from such a serious scene the falseness that the screen will not tolerate but that is unavoidable in even the most brilliant death scene and, on the other hand, to extract the maximum effect of bloody horror. The shooting is shown only in "establishing" long and medium shots of 1,800 workers falling over a precipice, the crowd fleeing, gunfire, and so on, and all the close-ups are provided by a demonstration of the real horrors of the slaughterhouse, where cattle are slaughtered and skinned. One version of the montage was composed roughly as follows:

1. The head of a bull. The butcher's knife takes aim and moves upward beyond the frame.
2. Close-up. The hand holding the knife strikes downward below the frame.
3. Long shot: 1,500 people roll down a slope. (Profile shot.)
4. Fifty people get up off the ground, their arms outstretched.
5. The face of a soldier taking aim.
6. Medium shot. Gunfire.

7. The bull's body (the head is outside the frame) jerks and rolls over.
8. Close-up. The bull's legs convulse. A hoof beats in a pool of blood.
9. Close-up. The bolts of the rifles.
10. The bull's head is tied with rope to a bench.
11. A thousand people rush past.
12. A line of soldiers emerges from behind a clump of bushes.
13. Close-up. The bull's head as it dies beneath unseen blows (the eyes glaze over).
14. Gunfire, in longer shot, seen from behind the soldiers' backs.
15. Medium shot. The bull's legs are bound together "according to Jewish custom" (the method of slaughtering cattle lying down).
16. Closer shot. People falling over a precipice.
17. The bull's throat is cut. Blood gushes out.
18. Medium close-up. People rise into the frame with their arms outstretched.
19. The butcher advances toward the (panning) camera holding the blood-stained rope.
20. The crowd rushes to a fence, breaks it down but is met by an ambush (two or three shots).
21. Arms fall into the frame.
22. The head of the bull is severed from the trunk.
23. Gunfire.
24. The crowd rolls down the precipice into the water.
25. Gunfire.
26. Close-up. Teeth are knocked out by the shooting.
27. The soldiers' feet move away.
28. Blood flows into the water, coloring it.
29. Close-up. Blood gushes from the bull's throat.
30. Hands pour blood from a basin into a bucket.
31. Dissolve from a platform with buckets of blood on it—in motion toward a processing plant.
32. The dead bull's tongue is pulled through the slit throat (one of the devices used in a slaughterhouse, probably so that the teeth will not do any damage during the convulsions).
33. The soldiers' feet move away. (Longer shot.)
34. The head is skinned.
35. One thousand eight hundred dead bodies at the foot of the precipice.
36. Two dead skinned bulls' heads.
37. A human hand in a pool of blood.
38. Close-up. Filling the whole screen. The dead bull's eye.
    Final title.

The downfall of the majority of Russian films derives from the fact that the people who make them do not know how to construct attractional schemas consciously but only rarely and in fumbling fashion hit on successful combinations. The American detective film and, to an even greater extent, the American comedy film (the method in its pure form) provide inexhaustible material for the study of these methods (admittedly on a purely formal level, ignoring content). Griffith's films, if we had seen them and not just known them from descriptions, would teach us a lot about this kind of montage, albeit with a social purpose that is hostile to us. It is not, however, necessary to transplant America, although in all fields the study of methods does at first proceed through imitation. It is necessary to train ourselves in the skill of selecting attractions from our own raw material.

Thus we are gradually coming to the most critical problem of the day: the script. The first thing to remember is that there is, or rather should be, no cinema other than agit-cinema. The method of agitation through spectacle consists in the creation of a new chain of conditioned reflexes by associating selected phenomena with the unconditioned reflexes they produce (through the appropriate methods). (If you want to arouse sympathy for the hero, you surround him with kittens, which unfailingly enjoy universal sympathy: not one of our films has yet failed to show White officers juxtaposed to disgusting drinking bouts, etc.) Bearing this basic situation in mind we should handle the question of played films with great care: they wield such enormous influence that we cannot ignore them. I think that the campaign against the very notion of such films has been caused by the really low level of scripts as well as the technique of the performers. I return to the latter in greater detail later. As far as the former is concerned, our approach allows us to conceive of arranging something other than "little stories" and "little romances" with a "little intrigue," kinds of film that on the whole (and not without reason) frighten people away. An example of this sort of arrangement may be provided by the project that I put forward for the treatment of historical-revolutionary material and that was accepted after long debates with the supporters of "Rightist" real-life films who dream of filming the life of some underground conspirator or notorious agent provocateur, or an imaginary story based on real-life materials. (Incidentally, these materials are completely ignored by the "wistful" men of cinema and left at the disposal of right-wing directors who abuse them: namely, *Andrei Kozhukhov, Stepan Khalturin,* and *The Palace and the Fortress*!)

The most important consideration in my approach to this theme was to give an account of and depict the technique of the underground and to provide an outline of its production methods in individual characteristic examples. How they sewed boots—how they prepared for the October Revolution. Our audience, trained to take an interest in production, is not the least interested in, and *should not be* interested in, the emotions of an actor made up as Beideman or in the tears of his bride. It is interested in the prison regime at the Peter and Paul Fortress and this is to be presented not through the personal sufferings of the hero but through the direct exposition of its methods.

It is not the life of Malinovsky the agent provocateur that interests us but the varieties and types (what are the characteristics of a particular type) and what makes an agent provocateur, not the presence of someone in a deportation prison but the prison itself, the conditions there, the mores in their numerous variants. In a word, the presentation of every element of underground work as phenomena that are represented in the greatest possible number of varieties and examples. The conditions in which proofs were corrected, the underground printing press, and so on, in the form of sequences characterizing particular moments and not joined into a seamless plot centered on an underground printing press but edited with a view to the thorough exposure, for example, of the underground printing press as one of the facts of underground work. The emphasis is on the most interesting montage tasks. Without "staging" this is quite unthinkable but in a quite different context! There is an example of the montage (e.g., in the episode of the "flight") of pure adventure material preserving all its attractional quality in the orientation toward historical familiarization. The theme of a strike was chosen first of all for the transition to constructions of this kind: in terms of its saturation with the mass it is most suited to the intermediate form between a film whose purpose is a purely emotional revolutionary effect conditioned by the plot and the new way of understanding its construction. For a number of reasons, dictated mainly by the material itself, it has to adhere more closely in its form to the first of these.

As far as the question of the necessity or otherwise of a script or of free montage of arbitrarily filmed material is concerned, we have to remember that a script, whether plot-based or not, is, in our view, a prescription (or a list) of montage sequences and combinations by means of which the author intends to subject the audience to a definite series of shocks, a "prescription" that summarizes the general projected emotional effect on the audience and the pressure that will inevitably be exerted on the audience's psyche. More often than not, given our scriptwriters' utterly feeble approach to the construction of a script, this task falls in its entirety to the director. The transposition of the theme into a chain of attractions with a previously determined end effect is the definition we have given of a director's work. The presence or absence of a written script is by no means all that important. I think that, when it is a matter of operating on the audience through material that is not closely plot-based, a general scheme of reference that leads to the desired results is enough, together with a free selection of montage material based on it (the absence of such a scheme, would not lead to the organization of the material but to hopeless impressionism around a possibly attractional theme). But, if it is carried out by means of a complex plot construction, then obviously a detailed script is necessary. Both kinds of film have the same citizenship rights because in the final analysis we are going above all to see in *Nathan the Wise* the amazing work of the cavalry, its jumping past the camera, exactly as we see it in Vertov's work at the Red Stadium.

Incidentally I shall touch here on one purely directorial moment in our work. When, in the process of constructing, shooting, and molding the montage elements, we are selecting the filmed fragments, we must fully recall the characteristics of cinema's effect that we stated initially and that establish the montage approach as the essential, meaningful, and sole possible language of cinema, completely analogous to the role of the word in spoken material. In the selection and presentation of this material the decisive factor should be the immediacy and economy of the resources expended in the cause of associative effect.

The first practical indication that derives from this is the selection of an angle of vision for every element, conditioned exclusively by the accuracy and force of impact of the necessary presentation of this element. If the montage elements are strung together consecutively this will lead to a constant movement of the angle of vision in relation to the material being demonstrated (in itself one of the most absorbing purely cinematic possibilities).

Strictly speaking, the montage elision of one fragment into another is inadmissible: each element can most profitably be shown from just one angle and part of the film fact that proceeds from, let us say, an inserted close-up, already requires a new angle that is different from the fragment that preceded the close-up. Thus, where a tightly expounded fact is concerned, the work of the film director, as distinct from the theater director, requires, in addition to a mastery of production (planning and acting), a repertoire of montage-calculated angles for the camera to capture these elements. I almost managed to achieve this kind of montage in the fight scene in *Strike*, where the repetition of sequences was almost completely avoided.

These considerations play a decisive role in the selection of camera angles and the arrangement of the lights. No plot "justification" for the selection of the angle of vision or the light sources is necessary. (Apart, that is, from a case where the task involves a particularly persistent emphasis on reality. For instance, *contre-jour* lighting is by no means "justified" in American interior shots.)

On a par with the method of staging a scene and taking it with a camera there exists what I should call the futurist method of exposition, based on the pure montage of associations and on the separate depiction of a fact: for example, the impression of that fight may be represented through the montage of the separate elements that are not joined by any logical sequence in the staging of the scene. The accumulation of the details of conflicting objects, blows, fighting methods, facial expressions, and so on produces just as great an impression as the detailed investigation by the camera of all the phases in a logically unfolding process of struggle: I contrast both kinds of montage, done separately, in the scene of the shooting. (I do not, for example, use the chain: the gun is cocked— the shot fired—the bullet strikes—the victim falls, but: the fall—the shot—the cocking—the raising of the wounded, etc.)

If we move on to the persistently posed question of the demonstration of real life as such, we must point out that this particular instance of demonstration is covered by our general position on the montage of attractions: but the assertion that the essence of cinema lies only in the demonstration of real life must be called into question. It is, I think, a matter of transposing the characteristics of a "1922–1925 attraction" (which was, as is always the case, a response to social aspirations— in this instance, the orientation toward "construction" as the raw material for these aspirations and toward a "presentation" that advertised this construction, e.g., an important event like the Agricultural Exhibition) to the entire nature of cinema as a whole. The canonization of this material and of this approach as the only acceptable ones deprives cinema of its flexibility in relation to its broadly social tasks and, by deflecting the center of gravity of public attention to other spheres (which is already noticeable), it leaves only a single aesthetic "love for real life" (to what absurd lengths the game of love for machines has been taken, despite the example of a very highly respected Soviet whodunit in which the cartridge-producing and dual-printing presses of the short film began to work for a mechanical conglomeration when the military chemical factory is set in motion!). Or we shall have to effect a revolution in the principles of cinema when it will be a matter of a simple shift of attractions.

This is by no means a matter of trailing under the cover of "agit-tasks" elements that are formally unacceptable to, and uncharacteristic of, cinema in the same way as an incalculable amount of pulp literature, hackwork, and unscrupulous behavior in theater is justified as agitational. I maintain my conviction that the future undoubtedly lies with the plot-less, actor-less form of exposition but this future will dawn only with the advent of the conditions of social organization that provide the opportunity for the general development and the comprehensive mastering of their nature and the application of all their energy in action, and the human race will not lack satisfaction through fictive energetic deeds, provided for it by all types of spectacle, distinguished only by the methods by which they are summoned forth. That time is still a long way off but, I repeat, we must not ignore the enormous effectiveness of the work of the model actor (*naturshchik*) on the audience. I submit that the campaign against the model actor is caused by the negative effect of the lack of system and principle in the organization of his work.

This "play" is either a semi-narcotic experience with no account of time or space (and really only a little off the place where the camera is standing), or a stereometric spread in three-dimensional space of the body and the extremities of the model actor in different directions, remotely recalling some forms of human action (and perceived by the audience thus: "Aha, apparently he's getting angry") or consecutive local contractions of facial muscles quite independent of one another and their systems as a whole, which are considered as mime. Both lead to a superb division of space in the shot and the surface of the screen that follow strict rhythmic schemas, with no single "daubing" or unfixed place. But, a rhythmic schema is arbitrary, it is established according to the whim or feeling of the director and not according to periods dictated by the mechanical conditions of the course of a particular motor process; the disposition of the extremities (which is precisely not "movement") is produced outside any mutual mechanical interaction such as the unified motor system of a single organism.

The audience in this kind of presentation is deprived of the emotional effect of perception, which is replaced by guesswork as to what is happening. Because emotional perception is achieved through the motor reproduction of the movements of the actor by the perceiver, this kind of reproduction can only be caused by movement that adheres to the methods that it normally adheres to in nature. Because of the confirmation of the correctness of this method of influence and perception I agree in this matter even with Lipps,[4] who cites as proof of the correctness of his investigations into the cognition of the alter ego the statement that (citing Bekhterev) "the emotional understanding of the alter ego through the imitation of the other leads only to a tendency to experience one's own emotion of the same kind but not to a conviction that the alter ego exists."

Leaving aside the last statement, which hardly concerns us, we have a very valuable confirmation of the correctness of our approach to construction, to an "effective construction" (in the particular instance of film), according to which it is not the facts being demonstrated that are important but the combinations of the emotional reactions of the audience. It is then possible to envisage in both theory and practice a construction, with no linking plot logic, which provokes a chain of the necessary unconditioned reflexes that are, at the editor's will, associated with (compared with) predetermined phenomena and by this means to create the chain of new conditioned reflexes that these phenomena constitute. This signifies a realization of the orientation toward thematic effect, that is, a fulfillment of the agitational purpose.[5]

The circle of effective arts is closed by the open essence of the agitational spectacle and a union with the primary sources is established: I think that the celebrated dances in animal skins of the primitive savages "whence theater derived" are a very reasonable institution of the ancient sorcerers directed much less toward the realization of figurative tendencies ("for what purpose?") than toward the very precise training of the hunting and fighting instincts of the primitive audience. The refinement of imitative skill is by no means a matter of satisfying those same figurative tendencies but of counting on the maximum emotional effect on the audience. This fundamental orientation toward the role of the audience was later forfeited in a purely formal refinement of methods and it is only now being revived to meet the concrete requirements of the day. This pure method of training the reflexes through performance effect deserves the careful consideration of people organizing educational films and theaters that quite unconsciously cram children with an entirely unjustified repertoire.

We move on to analyze a particular, but very important, affective factor: the work of the model actor. Without repeating in brief the observations I have already made as to what that work is and what it should be, we set out our system of work, endeavoring somehow to organize this branch of our labor (reforging someone else's psyche is no less difficult and considerable a task than forging iron and the term "playing" is by no means appropriate).

The Basic Premise

1. The value lies not in the figurativeness of the actions of the model actor, but in the degree of his motor and associatively infectious capabilities vis-à-vis the audience (i.e., the whole process of the actor's movement is organized with the aim of facilitating the imitative capacities of the audience).
2. Hence the first direction concerns the *selection* of versions presented to the audience: a reliance on invention, that is, on the *combination* of the movement, required by the purpose, from the versions that are most characteristic of real circumstances (and consequently automatically imitated by the audience) and simplest in form. The development and complication of motivations in the matter of "delays" (as literature treats them). Cinema makes very frequent use, apart from delays, of montage methods and this method too. I can cite an example of a moment that is constructed cinematically in this way from my theater production of *Can You Hear Me, Moscow?*, when the agent provocateur is handed an empty envelope that purports to contain evidence of his provocations. (There will be no reference in this section to the film I am working on in so far as the film as a whole is not orientated in its construction toward this group of actions whereas the work of the model actor is a matter of investigating the methods of "free work.") Here the detexturization (*rasfakturennost'* of the elements taken from the simplest versions of the movement of handing the envelope over and attempting to take it so excites the emotion of the audience with its delay that the "break" (the transition to the murder) makes the same impression as a bomb exploding. (In a film treat-

ment you would add a montage section following the same rhythmic module.)
3. The refinement of this version of movement: the ascertainment of the purely mechanical schema of its normal course in real life.
4. Breakdown of movement into its pseudo-primitive primary component elements for the audience—a system of shocks, rises, falls, spins, pirouettes, and so on—for the director to convey to the performer the precise arrangement of the motor version and to train these inherently neutral expressive (not in terms of plot but in terms of production) motor units.
5. Assembly (montage) and coordination into a temporal schema of these neutral elements of the movements in a combination that produces action.
6. Obfuscation of the schema in the realization of the difference in execution that exists between the play of a virtuoso with his own individual reordering of rhythm (*pereritmovka*) and the play of a pupil metrically tapping out the musical notation. (The completion of the minor details in fixing the version also enters into this obfuscation.)

The realization of the movement does not proceed in a superficially imitative and figurative manner vis-à-vis a real action (murder, drunkenness, chopping wood, etc.) but results in an organic representation that emerges through the appropriate mechanical schema and a real achievement of the motor process of the phenomena being depicted.

The norms of organicism (the laws of organic process and mechanical interaction) for motor processes have been established partly by French and German theoreticians of movement (investigating kinetics in order to establish motor primitives) and partly by me (kinetics in its application to complex expressive movements—and the dynamics of both: see below) in my laboratory work at the Proletkult Theatre.

Briefly, they lead to the following: the basic raw material—and the actor's real work lies in overcoming its resistance—is the actor's body; its resistances to motor intentions comprise its weight and its ability to conserve motor inertia.

The methods for overcoming these resistances dictated by their very nature are based on the following premises.

The basic premise was stated by G. B. Duchenne in *Physiology of Motion* as early as 1885: "l'action musculaire isolée n'est pas dans la nature," that is, a particular muscular action with no connection with the muscular system as a whole is not characteristic of nature and is found only in the pathological phenomena of cramps, hysterics, and convulsions.

Furthermore, the consequences of Rudolph Bode's[6] premise, the results of long years of practical research, are:

1. The principle of totality (*tselokupnost'*)[7] according to which the body as a whole participates in the execution of every movement.

2. The principle of a center of gravity. Because of the inorganic nature of the process of directing effort to individual muscles, only the center of gravity of the entire system can serve as the sole permissible point of application. (Hence it follows that the movements of the extremities are not independent but the mere mechanical result of the movement of the body as a whole.)
3. The principle of emancipation, that is, given general work selection, the periodic positioning—by means of the appropriate muscular relaxation (*Entspannung*)—of an extremity, of the extremities, or of the body as a whole, becomes the positioning of the purely mechanical actions of the forces of gravity and inertia.

These premises were expounded without being applied to any special kind of movement and, principally, to the norms of physical education. Nonetheless, even the first attempts to normalize the working movements of a worker at a lathe (at that time this was mainly with a view to protecting him against occupational physical distortions of the body and the spine) led to the application of those same principles, as is clear from the motor schemas and descriptions appended to the work of Hueppe, who (in 1899) first raised the question of the physical organization of labor.

In the application of these principles to the movement being demonstrated the emphasis is on the utmost expressiveness as the bearer of the influence: I have studied this further. By expressive movement I understand movement that discloses the realization of a particular realizable motor intention in the process of being realized, that is, the appropriate arrangement of the body and the extremities at any particular moment for the motor execution of the appropriate element necessary for the purpose of the movement. Expressive movements fall into three groups:

1. A set of rational directions in the direct execution of common motor intentions (all aspects of an appropriately constructed movement—of a boxer, a hammerman, etc.—and also reflex movements that have at some time been automated into conscious purposes—the leap of a tiger, etc.)
2. A set of instances with varying purpose with two or more motivations for their realization when several purposes that resolve particular motivations build up in the body.
3. The most interesting case in terms of its motor formation is the case of a psychologically expressive movement that represents a motor exposure of the conflict of motivations: an instinctively emotional desire that retards the conscious volitional principle.

It is realized in the motor conflict between the desires of the body as a whole (which respond to the tendency of instinct and represent material for the exposure of reflex movement) and the retarding role of the consciously preserved inertia[8] of the extremities (corresponding to the role of the conscious volitional retardation that is realized through the extremities).

This mechanical schema, first elaborated by me, for expressive movement finds confirmation in a series of observations by Klages[9] and the premises put forward by Nothnagel. We value the former's statements that only the affect can serve as the cause of organic motor manifestation and not the volitional impulse whose fate it usually is to act merely as a brake on and a betrayer of intentions. The latter has stated that the actual means of communicating cerebral stimulation through the facial muscles (he is writing about mime) are achieved by quite different methods, depending on whether the movement is determined by the surface of the face or as a result of affective stimulation. The latter methods involve a specific part of the brain (the so-called *Sehhügel*), the former do not. As confirmation Nothnagel cites some very interesting cases of paralysis. Given the appropriate affects, the paralyzed part of the face of certain patients was able to cry and laugh whereas the patient was incapable of the smallest movement of the lips or eyes consciously (freely) in the absence of affective prerequisites. Or the inverse instance when, in cases of very powerful emotional shock, a paralyzed face preserved a stony immobility whereas the patient was able at will to produce any muscular contractions in his face (knit his brows, move his mouth, and so on).[10]

It would be a great error to perceive our statement as advocating in the model actor's work the affective condition that was long ago condemned in theater and is absolutely unthinkable in cinema, given the peculiarities of its production. It is here a matter of assessing the mechanical interactions that constantly occur within us but that flow from us in cases where a similar process has to be consciously realized in front of an audience or a camera.[11] We must also bear in mind that both series of movements that are coming into conflict are equally consciously constructed and the effect of the affective movement is achieved by the artificial mechanical setting in motion of the body as a whole and must in no way result from the emotional state of the performer. The biodynamic method of translating artificially induced movement to the conditions of the organic flow of the process of movement through a dynamic and powerful deployment of the so-called denying movement (understood even by schools of movement that included it in their system merely in its spatial sense[12]) is an attitude expressed by theoreticians of theater as long ago as the seventeenth century[13] and due to inertia. I shall here only remind you of the particular kind of certain neutrally affective "working conditions" that also facilitates this translation. A detailed exposition of these questions, which are less important to cinema than to theater, would lead us into too much technical detail.

We should do better to concentrate on selecting a particular example of this kind of expressive movement. A particularly clear example is the baring of teeth: in our view this is not a parting of the lips but a pushing on the part of the head which, as the "leading" part of the body, is striving to break through the inert restraints of the surface of the face. The motor process is quite analogous to a particular psychological situation: in the final analysis the baring of the teeth is a gesture toward an opponent, constrained by consciousness for one reason or another. Thus, according to the stated premises, "psychological expression" also leads to unique dual gymnastics in reproducing the conflict between the motor tendencies of the body as a whole and the extremities. In the process of this "struggle" distortions arise on the surface of the face and in the centrifugal spatial trajectories of the extremities and of the interrelationships of the joints just as there will also be countless shades of expression subjected to strict calculation and conscious construction given an adequate command of this system of dual motor process. (It is very interesting that even the apparently "intellectual" parts of the body are involved in the realization of the delaying role of the intellect, that is, those parts that have been emancipated with the cultivation of the individual from "unskilled" labor in the motor servicing of the body—moving and feeding it—the hands, that we have stopped walking on, and the face, that has ceased to be a snout gulping down food—a kind of "class struggle" in its own way!)

The material that I analyzed and selected in these principles of movement is for the time being a base schema that will begin to come to life only when real forces are set in motion, and a rhythmic scale that is appropriate to the particular expressive manifestation cannot be established until that moment. (It is unnecessary to say anything about the need for a rhythmic formula in general: it is quite obvious that the same sequence of movements, with the addition of different combinations of duration, will produce quite different expressive effects.) The principal distinction of this approach will be the establishment of temporal values, selected in a far from arbitrary way, for any elements in whatever combination, and they will represent the result of the processes of distribution of power loads for shocks, and the intensity of muscular responses; the forces of centrifugal inertia on the extremities; the neutralization of the inertias of preceding elements of the movements, the conditions that arise in connection with the general position of the body in space, and so on, in the process of realizing the expressive objective.

Thus, a precise organic rhythmic schema is taking shape that corresponds to the intensity of the course of the process and itself changes in changing conditions and in the common character of the precise resolution of the objective: it is individual to each performer and corresponds to his physical characteristics (the weight and size of his extremities, his muscular state, etc.). In this context we note that in the rhythmic construction of the process of movement its degree of arbitrariness is extremely limited. In rhythmic movement we are a long way from being able to behave as we please: the actual biomechanical structure of the working organ inevitably conducts our movement toward a regular function that breaks down into the sum of simply and strictly motivated harmonic components. The role of random innervation in this process amounts to a spasmodic disturbing intervention in the organically progressing motor process and the possibility of automating this process (which represents the ultimate aim in the realization of its conviction and is achieved by training in rehearsal) is in these circumstances excluded.[14]

On the other hand, to fit temporal segments artificially to a desired expressive schema is much less economical and presents enormous difficulties. I might even go as far as to say that it is impossible because of the fact that I verified this in my production of *Gas Masks.* When a man suffocates in the hatch where a pipe is being mended the intervals between beats increase and their force abates. From the sound throughout the auditorium you could detect unmistakably each time the combination of the performer's beats occurred at a break in the movement and the artificial selection of the intervals between, and the intensity of, the beats and when they were part of an uninterrupted process, achieving the necessary effect by overcoming in the longer term the inertia of preceding movements through introducing successively weaker new shocks in the repeated blows. A visually similar phenomenon would strike us even more powerfully.

An example of the ideal form of the verbal-rhythmic effect of movement (constructed on the basis of matching a sound schema as we match the schema of an expressive objective) is provided by the performer in a jazz band: his command of movement consists in an amazing use of the process of neutralizing the inertia of a large-scale movement into a series of pantomime and percussive movements, and in their combination with small-scale new elements of movement. If this process is replaced by a process of newly emerging innervations of certain limbs (if the jazz-player is not a good dancer), without regard for the rhythmic oscillations of the body as a whole, his exaggerated movements, ceasing to fit into an organic schema, would have the effect of pathological grimaces (precisely because of the inorganic character of their origin).

Even this one example should be enough to confirm the rule of the preservation of inertia, the rule that determines how convincing a motor process is by preserving the motor inertia of what becomes a single action. As an example of this use of inertia I shall cite the clowns in Fatty Arbuckle's film group. They employ this method in such a way that they unfailingly lend to each complex of complicated movement, liquidated in the conditions of one scene or another, a completely unfounded ending of pure movement. Given their skill this is always a brilliant little trick. In mechanical terms it is this device that releases the accumulating reserve of inertia that permeates a whole complex of movement.

I shall not get involved in the details of their methodology. I merely point out that the basic requirement of a model actor for this kind of work is the healthy organic rhythm of his normal physical functions, without which it is impossible for him either to master this system or to perceive it via a rhythmically precise screen, despite the fact that in theater success (i.e., emotional infectiousness) can be greater in the light of the nervous imbalance that accompanies, or rather conditions, this characteristic. (This has been tested on two of my actors: it was curiously impossible to find two or three "unsoiled" in a row, whatever the tempo of their filmed movement, because the nervous foundation of their rhythm was so uneven.)

The question of fixation, which is so decisive for the screen, emerges here as the natural result since, whatever the outcome of the conflict depicted, that [conflict] passes through a moment of equalization, that is, a state of rest. If the disproportion of forces is too great there can be neither fixation nor expressive movement for it becomes either simply an act or a simple state of rest, depending on which tendency is dominant.

Thus we can realize a montage (assembly) of movements that are purely organic in themselves. I should call them the elements of the working movement of the model actors themselves, and the arrangement assembled in this way involves the audience to the maximum degree in imitation and, through the emotional effect of this, in the corresponding ideological treatment. In addition as a whole it produces (although it is possible to construct them without this) the visual effect of the emotion apparently experienced. We see that the methods of processing the audience are no different in the mechanics of their realization from other forms of work movement and they produce the same real, primarily physical work on their material—the audience.

In this approach to the work of the model actor there is no longer any question of the "shame" of acting (an association with the concept of acting that has taken root because of the really shameful methods of experiential schools of acting). There will be no difference in the perception via the screen of a cobbler sewing boots or a terrorist throwing a bomb (staged) because, proceeding from the identical material bases of their work, both of them first and foremost process the audience through their actions: one plays (not directly of course but through appropriate presentation by the director) on pride in work well done (more precisely, on illusory co-construction) while the other plays on the feeling of class hatred (more precisely, the illusory realization of it). In both cases this constitutes the basis of the emotional effect.

I think moreover that this kind of movement, apart from its direct effectiveness that I have verified in theater in both its tragic and its comic aspects, will be the most photogenic in so far as one can define photogenic by paraphrasing Schopenhauer's good old definition of the beautiful. An idea expressed in its completeness is photogenic; that is, an object is photogenic when it corresponds most closely to the idea that it embodies.[15] (A car is more photogenic than a cart because its whole structure corresponds more closely to its purpose of transportation, and so on.)

That the objects and costumes of previous periods are not photogenic[16] can, I think, be explained by the way that they were made: for example, costumes were not produced by a search for normal clothing or by the forms of special clothing suitable for various kinds of production, that is, for forms that corresponded most closely to the purpose they embodied, the "idea," but were determined by purely fortuitous motivation like, let us say, the fashion for red and yellow combinations, the so-called cardinal sur la paille, named in honor of Cardinal de Rohan who was imprisoned in the Bastille in connection with the affair of the Queen's necklace. Or lace headdresses à la Fontanges, connected with the saucy episode between Louis XIV and Mlle de Fontanges who lost her lace pantaloons and saved the situation by hurriedly adding them to her already elaborate hair-do. The approach that makes for photogenic costume, that is, the search for functional forms in costume, is characteristic only of recent times (noted apparently for the first time by the Japanese General Staff) so that only contemporary costumes are photogenic. Working clothes furnish the richest raw material (e.g., a diving suit).

In this particular instance movements are revealed that most logically and organically correspond to the phases of the flow of a certain action. Apart from theoretical probability, a practical indication that it is precisely this kind of movement that is most photogenic is provided by the photogenic quality of animals, whose movements are structured in strict accordance with these laws and do not infringe them by the intervention of the rational principle in their automatic nature (Bode). Labor processes, which also flow in accordance with these stated laws, have similarly been shown to be photogenic.

There remains to add to the system we have elaborated only one more circumstance that formally is more critical for cinema than for theater. For cinema the "organization of the surface" (the screen) presents an even more serious problem, indissolubly linked to the organization of the space encompassed by the frame and—and this is specific to cinema—by the fluctuation of this surface and the constant contrast between the surfaces thus organized in movement (the montage succession of shots). I think that, as far as establishing the necessary (in the sense of a correctly constructed superstructure to movement) consequent (deriving from this characteristic of cinema) spatial correctives is concerned, there is little to add to Kuleshov's "axial system" that seemed to illuminate this problem so thoroughly. Its one fundamental error lies in the fact that those who elaborated it regard it as the basic approach to movement in general, which leads to its alienation from the mechanical and dynamic foundations of movements. In Kuleshov's view we do not have a smooth process of movement but an alternation of unconnected "positions" (poses). The motor results of this lead to grimace instead of mime, and movement over and above the energetic purpose of material work, and the model actors, by their appearance as mechanical dolls, undermine our trust in the extraordinarily valuable methods of spatial organization of the material on the screen. In this instance only one thing can serve as the criterion for a production: it is the director's personal taste for overturning the rhythmic schemas of quiet scenes and [creating] chaos in the motor organization of fights and other energetically saturated places, requiring that organization be subjugated to the schemas of force and mechanics. It is only once this has been done that they can be subjected to some kind of external molding. Inevitably this kind of approach must, and does, lead to stylization.

The attractional approach to the construction of all elements, from the film as a whole to the slightest movement of the performer, is not an affirmation of personal taste or of the search for a polished style for Soviet cinema, but an assertion of the method of approach to the montage of effects that are useful to our class and of the precise recognition of the utilitarian goals of cinema in the Soviet Republic.

NOTES

1. A direct animal audience action through a motor imitative act toward a live character like oneself, as distinct from a pale shadow on a screen. These methods of theatrical effect have been tested in my production of *Can You Hear Me, Moscow?*

2. In time (in sequence) clearly: here it plays not merely the role of an unfortunate technical condition but of a condition that is necessary for the thorough inculcation of the associations.

3. And a large number of bank premises are shown first.

4. Lipps, *Das Wissen vom fremden 'Ich'* (The Consciousness of the Alien Ego).

5. We must still bear in mind that in a spectacle of dramatic effect the audience is from the very first placed in a non-neutral attitude situation and sympathizes with one party, identifying itself with that party's actions, while opposing itself to the other party, reacting from the very first through a feeling of direct opposition to its actions. The hero's anger provokes your own personal anger against his enemies; the villain's anger makes you jeer. The law of effect remains essentially the same.

6. R. Bode, *Ausdrucksgymnastik* (The Gymnastics of Expression) (Munich, 1921).

7. *Totalität* in Sergei Tretyakov's Russian translation.

8. A state of tranquility or of the preservation of the preceding movement of the object.

9. Klages, *Ausdrucksbewegung und Gestaltungskraft* (Expressive Movement and Formative Power) (Leipzig, 1923).

10. I am quoting from Krukenberg, *Vom Gesichtsausdruck des Menschen* (Human Facial Expression) (Stuttgart, 1923).

11. The majority of movements are reflex and automatic and it was Darwin who pointed out the difficulties involved in reproducing these kinds of movements. One example is the difficulty involved in reproducing a "premeditated" swallow. it is interesting to note the immediate departure from the laws of movement that occurs when they are con-

sciously reproduced: whereas if the hands of an actor (which, according to the general laws, are part of his body as a whole) are in real life always engaged in motor movement, on stage "they do not know what to do" because this law is being broken.

12. Denial in this sense is a small preparatory movement in the reverse direction to the movement being executed that serves to increase the amplitude of the movement and underline more strongly the beginning of the movement not as a starting point but as an extreme point of denial that is no longer static but is a turning point in the direction of the movement.

13. See Vsevolod N. Vsevolodskii-Gerngross, *Istoriya teatral'nogo obrazovaniya v Rossii* (The History of Theatrical Training in Russia), vol. 2 (St. Petersburg, 1913).

14. See the collection of essays by the Central Labour Institute in their application to work movement.

15. This definition fully conforms to Delluc's observation that photogenic faces are those which first and foremost possess "character," which, for a face, is the same as what we are saying about movement.

The "character" of a face is the most frequent imitation, that is, of the motivations (Klagcs).

16. As noted, for instance, by Delluc in *Veshch'*, no. 3.

Eisenstein and Soviet Cinema

Sergei Eisenstein's commitment to and energy for writing theoretical treatises continued from his days as a young theater director in the early 1920s until literally the end of his life. In fact, he was drafting a statement on color aesthetics in early 1948 when he suffered the heart attack that took his life. He proved a tireless writer throughout those years. He often worked through the night on manuscript drafts, even while he was putting in full days on film productions. He also turned the spare moments of his workday into opportunities to tinker with essays or to jot down new ideas. And he somehow managed to save virtually every scrap of paper to which he ever committed a theoretical proposition, as well as many on which he merely doodled. The Eisenstein papers eventually formed the largest single collection in Moscow's enormous Central State Archives of Literature and Art.[1]

The product of these work habits was an extraordinarily vast and complicated theoretical output. One cannot even speak of a definitive Eisenstein corpus. Much of the writing remained in the form of unfinished drafts and variants at the time of Eisenstein's death. Posthumous publication has substantially extended the corpus, and researchers continue to locate and publish previously unknown manuscript material. Thus, unlike, say, Siegfried Kracauer, whose film theory is identified largely with a coherent magnum opus, Eisenstein's ideas have to be culled from scores of essays, book manuscripts, and fragments.

More important, Eisenstein's film theory was never simply a fixed set of tenets. The ideas evolved throughout the course of his adult life. He added new theoretical propositions with each passing year, and at many points in his career, he revisited and revised opinions he had previously espoused. The theory evolved over roughly a quarter century as Eisenstein's career developed. Rather than simply committing to paper certain settled doctrines about cinema, Eisenstein explored new propositions in response to the most recent turns in his professional life. As he anticipated taking on fresh creative problems with each subsequent film, he aired those creative issues theoretically. And just as often, inspirations experienced during filming encouraged him to amend his extant theory.

Eisenstein's theory thus developed historically, and it did so in response to his creative experiences. The synergism of film theory and practical filmmaking is the hallmark of Eisenstein's career. As David Bordwell has argued, Eisenstein drew from Aristotle's principle of *techne,* the unity of theory and practice in art (*Cinema,* 35–36). In Eisenstein's case, this principle applied to the craft of filmmaking, which craft could be enhanced through theoretical inquiry and realized in the production process. The shape of Eisenstein's professional career, and the range of his creative endeavors in the course of that career, account in no small measure for his theoretical legacy.

This all suggests that Eisenstein's theory can profitably be discussed diachronically as something that developed over time. I thus propose to trace the historical evolution of his ideas in the context of his professional activities. This involves looking not only at his relevant filmmaking projects; such issues as his work in the theater and his activities as a teacher of aspiring filmmakers at Moscow's State Film Institute also figure in my discussion.[2]

A rough sketch of Eisenstein's professional life is thus in order to provide some background.[3] Eisenstein entered cinema after a brief but influential career in theater. He worked as a stage designer and director in avant-garde theater productions in 1922–1924. His earliest film productions, *Strike* (1925) and *Battleship Potemkin* (1926), bore the traces of that background. By the late 1920s, Eisenstein refined his theory around the possibilities of an aesthetic more specific to cinema, and those ideas were illustrated in his last two silent films, *October* (1928) and *Old and New* (1929; also known as *The General Line*).

Eisenstein traveled in the West from 1929 through early 1932, trying unsuccessfully to develop several film projects. During that interval Stalinist controls were imposed on all Soviet artistic practice. When Eisenstein returned to the Soviet Union, he had to adjust to the officially mandated artistic style of Soviet socialist realism. In making the adjustment, Eisenstein taught full-time at the State Film Institute (1932–1935), and he used his class lessons to develop new theoretical propositions. His revised aesthetic was evident in his first successfully completed project of the sound era, *Alexander Nevsky* (1938). That film also reflected his renewed interest in theatrical traditions, especially opera. He sustained that interest by staging a production of Richard Wagner's *The Valkyre* at the Bolshoi Theater in 1940. Operatic forms were then to influence his planned film trilogy *Ivan the Terrible* (1944–1946), two parts of which he completed before his death in 1948.

As this overview may suggest, the major shift Eisenstein had to make in his career development was between the 1920s and the 1930s–1940s. The transition is marked by Eisenstein's return from the West, when he had to recast his theory in response to the advent of sound cinema and the Stalinist doctrine of socialist realism. Even within those two general periods, however, Eisenstein subjected his ideas to more specific alterations. My chronological account also takes note of the theoretical revisions within each major phase of Eisenstein's film career. I give particular attention to the essay selected for publication in this volume, "The Montage of Film Attractions" (1924). It represents Eisenstein's first fully developed theoretical statement on cinema and an appropriate starting point for a survey of his theoretical projects. From that starting point, we can trace the development of his theory.

One constant in Eisenstein's theory is the prominence of the term "montage." The idea that artistic effects are achieved through the combination of ingredients dominates every phase of Eisenstein's writing. Nevertheless, how those combinations might be best constructed—that is, how montage effects might be realized—changed over time with the rest of the theory. The way that Eisenstein defined and redefined the term offers insight into his theoretical progression and provides a marker to help trace his theoretical course.

The 1920s

Eisenstein's first writings on cinema bear the traces of aesthetic notions he developed in the theater. Eisenstein's early stagework was marked by highly eccentric devices designed to elicit sharp responses from spectators. This was entirely in keeping with the belief that art in the new Soviet system had to have social utility, that it should reshape the consciousness of audiences as part of a larger mission to reeducate the Soviet population. Eisenstein held along with his theater mentor Vsevolod Meyerhold that arid, lifeless propaganda would be useless in such an effort. The theatrical event had to contain emotionally charged devices to galvanize audiences. Eisenstein looked to the circus as the theatrical spectacle that best achieved such effects. The stunts and death-defying turns of circus acts could be counted on to generate palpable responses from those in attendance. In his own stage productions, especially *The Wiseman* (1923), Eisenstein incorporated circus devices such as acrobatics and daredevil feats into the performance.[4]

Such devices he labeled "attractions," alluding to circus or fairground attractions. But he gave the term a specific application when writing on theater in 1923; an attraction involves "any aggressive moment in theater, i.e. an element . . . that subjects the audience to emotional or psychological influence" (*Selected*, 1:34). An acrobatic maneuver that draws a gasp from the audience would constitute such a device, since its effect is measurable. The theater production as a whole, Eisenstein asserted, should be calculated not so much to tell a story as to provide a vehicle for such effects. The whole should not be a tight narrative but a "montage of attractions," a rough assemblage of devices that influence spectators in predictable ways.

In advancing such formulations, Eisenstein emphatically rejected mimetic art. The artist's task, he held, is not to reproduce empirical reality on stage in the manner of, say, Chekovian theater. The stage apparatus should not re-create the reality that already exists but should construct an experience not previously available—hence the literal application of the term "montage" as something constructed, something built up from parts. The director would render the theatrical event expressive by making it far more emotionally powerful than visual reality. The theatrical spectacle, with its array of impressive attractions, would not reflect reality but would change it by affecting audiences. Indeed, the true material of theater, Eisenstein opined, was not the play but the audience, since the "molding of the audience in a desired direction (or mood) is the task of every utilitarian theater" (*Selected*, 1:34).

Eisenstein composed "The Montage of Film Attractions" while he was working on his first feature film *Strike*, and it marks his transition from a theatrical to a film aesthetic. The essay carries over the central concept of the attraction, and suggests how the term can be applied to film. The attraction remains any device that promises "to exercise a definite effect on the attention and emotions of the audience" (*Selected*, 1:40), but the filmmaker must work through different means than the theater director in achieving desired effects. The physical proximity of actors and audience members provides immediate expressive possibilities in live stage events. Theater audiences are in the presence of theatrical attractions. Thus, Eisenstein chose to excite audience members in *The Wiseman* by having an actor perform stunts on a tightrope directly over their heads. Film, Eisenstein concedes, must rely on photographic representation rather than the power of the immediate experience. Cinema compensates, however, by extending the possibilities for montage combinations. Film allows the director to juxtapose images as montage ingredients, and the director may draw from a vast array of images to achieve desired effects. The filmmaker is not limited to the material that can be brought onto a single stage apparatus, as in theater.

This encouraged Eisenstein to speak of the "montage of film attractions" as containing the possibility for elaborate associations. Particular images can stimulate powerful psychological associations in spectators, and in combinations with other image associations, these can provoke spectators in a manner predetermined by the filmmaker. In an assertion owing much to the research in reflex psychology conducted by the Soviet scientists Ivan Pavlov and Vladimir Bekhterev, Eisenstein declared that spectators would respond "reflexively" to images containing such powerful associations. Eisenstein spoke of creating "a new chain of conditioned reflexes" through montage associations (*Selected*, 1:45).

The prime example of this strategy appears in *Strike*, when the slaughter of a bull is cross-cut with the execution of striking workers. (Eisenstein was editing that important sequence while writing "The Montage of Film Attractions," and he cites the example in the essay [*Selected*, 1:43–44].) The sequence involves more than an exercise in analogy (bull's slaughter = workers' slaughter). The bull's death throes are shown in graphic detail. These bloody images drawn from reality generate powerful emotions in viewers. The emotions carry over to the depicted deaths of the workers through the montage association, and they provoke revulsion and outrage. That effect thus results from a sustained attraction, the insertion of the bull into the film's story of repression against workers.

In developing that attraction, Eisenstein went outside the diegesis; that is, the bull's image came from outside the logical fictional world of the film, the fictional terrain inhabited by the film's characters. The bull is not a part of that diegesis, but rather provided the source of a powerful association. That Eisenstein would include such nondiegetic components in a film narrative is justified theoretically in "The Montage of Film Attractions." Since the primary function of the film's narrative is to supply attractions that produce emotional effects, the film's script need not have a tight, cohesive story. Rather it should offer "a prescription (or a list) of montage sequences and combinations by which the author intends to subject the audience to a definite series of shocks" (*Selected*, 1:46). Thus, *Strike*'s narrative involves a set of chapters rather than a linear plot and a mass ensemble of characters rather than a central protagonist. The film provides a vehicle for a whole collection of devices designed to serve as attractions, including camera tricks (the superimposition of the three workers over the still image of the flywheel), animation (the Cyrillic intertitle "HO" ["but"] that begins to move), and acrobatics (workers athletically scaling the factory works).

His actors' acrobatic moves, in particular, hearken back to tactics Eisenstein used in his theaterwork, and he addressed that energetic acting style in his notion of "expressive movement." He defined the term as any gesture of the actor's body that produces an emotional response from spectators. He advocated that an actor learn how to channel a burst of energy throughout his or her entire body, from the torso to the extremities in some cases. The gesture was not to be mimetic; it would not imitate the actions of real people in real life. Rather, it would be expressive—a powerful, affective moment for spectators. One finds such an expressive movement in *Strike* when the spy emerges through the tangle of ropes by thrusting his chest forward and seeming to burst into the open. Thus, an expressive gesture provides one kind of attraction. Eisenstein even spoke of the "*attractionness* of movements" in this context (Eisenstein and Tretyakov, 34). The actor's body could be used as a device to generate premeditated effects along with the other devices at the filmmaker's command.

The combination of attractions—a planned "montage of attractions"—provides the substance of a film's narrative, substituting for the smooth, linear stories of mainstream commercial cinema. The core of Eisenstein's early theory was the measurable power of the individual effect, not the coherence of the film as a whole. Such an aesthetic tolerates the eclectic array of devices evident in *Strike,* the film most clearly identified with Eisenstein's celebration of cinema's capacity for raw emotional charges. His subsequent silent films would pull him toward a more refined aesthetic.

He acknowledged this refinement. In 1926, he noted that *"Strike* is a treatise; *Potemkin* is a hymn" (*Selected,* 1:69). The power of the later film was calculated to be a fuller emotional process rather than a series of discrete attractions. *Potemkin'*s narrative design demonstrates that view. Rather than a broad array of devices, *Potemkin* involves a more narrow, linear narrative. It is divided into five dramatic acts rather than rhetorical chapters like *Strike.* Each subsequent act expands on dramatic material from the previous act. The narrative as a whole shows a regular pattern of moving from the specific to the general: from a rebellion against spoiled meat to a ship's mutiny; from a ship's crew to an entire city through the unity with Odessa's residents; from a single ship to the revolt of an entire fleet. The greater narrative unity of *Potemkin* allowed Eisenstein to offer more sustained emotional effects and ideological guidance to his audience.

In making this move, Eisenstein revised his views of montage. By the late 1920s, he had edged away from the idea that montage simply produced shock effects. Montage would still affect spectators emotionally, but in subtler ways. This move was based on a more sophisticated model of human psychology. Instead of the direct reflexological notion that a given stimulus generates a single, predictable response, Eisenstein began to talk of a three-part relationship involving perception, emotion, and cognition. An external phenomenon produces stimuli that impinge on human perceptual machinery; the human subject's perceptual process leads to an emotional response; ultimately that emotional state yields a higher-order intellectual understanding of the phenomenon.

This refinement encouraged Eisenstein to explore the intellectual dimensions of montage, since he now posited a progression from emotional response to intellectual comprehension. Montage combinations in a film might now include ingredients that produced an intellectual as well as emotional engagement on the part of the spectator. Eisenstein soon began to speak of montage as being analogous to language since he now believed that it could involve higher-order processing. He asserted in 1926 that his "understanding of cinema is now entering [a] 'literary period.' The phase of approximation to the symbolism of *language*" (*Selected*, 1:80). Certain ingredients in the montage combination could have the status of signs, and their combinations could ultimately convey ideas in the manner of language. A film should still be tendentious, and it should still move spectators emotionally. But it could also support complex intellectual arguments that enhance the spectator's understanding of the world.

His work on *October* helped bring him to this view. The film was commissioned to celebrate the tenth anniversary of the Bolshevik Revolution. But Eisenstein hoped that spectators would do more than relive the excitement of those events. He wanted them to come away from the film with an understanding of the historical process of political revolution. He sought to develop in the film's form something comparable to the historical analysis that Marx provided in his essays. This would involve a film style that evoked the logic of language. "In some reels," Eisenstein confirmed, "*October* is trying to take the next step, trying to seek out *speech* that in its construction will wholly correspond to . . . vocabulary" (*Selected*, 1:104).

This ambition is most salient in the famous "God and Country" sequence of *October*, which provides something amounting to a brief essay on religion and nationalism. It begins after a narrative passage in which the Bolsheviks are threatened by a counterrevolutionary force motivated by the slogan "For God and Country." Eisenstein moves from this diegetic situation to a nondiegetic passage in which he shows icon after icon associated with religion or nationalism. The montage of the sequence links one icon with another in rapid succession and ultimately mocks whatever reverence might be associated with them. What emerges from the passage is an intellectual argument against religion and nationalism, positing that they are, finally, empty concepts. It might be useful to compare this nondiegetic passage with the nondiegetic bull's slaughter in *Strike*. Whereas the montage of the bull's slaughter simply carried one compelling emotion (revulsion) over to the execution of the workers, the montage in the "God and Country" sequence engages the viewer in a complex intellectual activity. The spectator must trace out an elaborate set of associations and arrive at a logical conclusion about the emptiness of religion and nationalism.

Eisenstein duly labeled this new form of montage "intellectual montage" in recognition of the degree to which it dealt with ideas. He even began to speculate about the possibility of eliminating story material entirely and making an entire film in the form of a nonfiction essay. He hoped to create such a cinematic essay when he made preliminary plans in 1928 for a film version of Marx's *Capital*. The project was to deal with historical issues that had to be analyzed rhetorically rather than simply depicted in this planned "film treatise" (Eisenstein, "Notes for a

Film," 119). Thus, for example, Marx's notion of dialectic would be built into the form of the film rather than simply alluded to in a narrative: "To show the *method* of dialectics. [. . .] Dialectical analysis of historical events. Dialectics in scientific problems. Dialectics of class struggle" ("Notes for a Film," 125). Eisenstein was finally unable to proceed with this ambitious project, but the very ambitiousness of the enterprise made him expand his ideas about montage.

By the end of the 1920s, those ideas had, in fact, developed to the point where Eisenstein elaborated a full montage typology. He described five montage types in a 1929 essay, "The Fourth Dimension in Cinema" (*Selected*, 1:186–94). *Metric montage* he defined as montage based entirely on the length of each shot. A filmmaker might simply organize a passage around a certain editing tempo by altering the lengths of shots mathematically (e.g., long, short, long, short, etc.). *Rhythmic montage* involves a strategy in which the lengths of shots are determined by the contents of the images. A filmmaker might, for example, measure the speed of movements within shots against the pacing of the editing, as Eisenstein sought to do with the montage of the soldiers' boots descending the steps in the "Odessa Steps" sequence of *Potemkin. Tonal montage* tries to exploit the dominant qualities within the images of the shots. Eisenstein felt that images could evoke a dominant tone and that such tonal values could guide the montage strategy. The fog and mist of the "mourning" sequence in *Potemkin* evoke an "emotional resonance" that Eisenstein duplicates in the slow, deliberate editing of the passage.

Eisenstein's next category proves more abstract. *Overtonal montage* was to take advantage of what Eisenstein perceived as the overtones of filmic images. A shot might contain more than just the main narrative information or the principal tone of the image. It might also contain subtler details that should not be ignored simply because they are not part of the shot's visual dominant. A graphic detail such as a gentle gust of wind or a play of light on a surface might coexist in a shot with the main narrative material on the screen. A filmmaker could edit so as to explore the possible associations among such subtler details. Conventional narrative cinema, Eisenstein held, simply involves a montage that traces the narrative dominant from shot to shot while ignoring overtonal possibilities. A richer film form is possible through montage which develops such subtle, sensuous details. Finally, *intellectual montage* offers the most sophisticated possibility, in Eisenstein's estimation. This involves the more rigorously logical form of montage that Eisenstein had explored in *October* and *Capital* and that we have already encountered.

Eisenstein employed this full list of montage strategies in his last silent film *Old and New.* In particular, however, he used that project to explore the possibilities of overtonal montage since he had already had opportunities to exploit the four other varieties in either *Potemkin* or *October.* Certain scenes in *Old and New* are edited in such a way as to trace the possible relationships among several graphic overtones. A prime example is the religious procession in which peasants pray for relief from a drought. The dominant issue of the episode is the increasing passion of the processioners. But Eisenstein's editing also finds relations among several overtones that are present in variants in shot after shot. The heat, dust, dry wind, panting sheep, and the like, provide an array of overtones associated with sterility. Eisenstein's overtonal editing develops this subtheme of sterility and works to undermine the processioners' passion. Thus Eisenstein links several related motifs through such overtonal editing, providing counterpoint to the scene's narrative dominant.

Clearly Eisenstein's view of montage evolved substantially from film to film throughout the 1920s, from harsh shock effects to quasi-musical strategies involving motific combinations. Never satisfied simply to repeat a formula, Eisenstein was prepared to modify his working definition of montage with each new creative challenge. He would face substantial challenges after 1930, when the conditions of Soviet filmmaking fundamentally changed.

The 1930s–1940s

The 1930s began auspiciously for Eisenstein when he traveled to the West to explore the new possibilities of sound cinema and to take advantage of an opportunity to work in Hollywood. The sojourn ended in crushing disappointment, however, when Eisenstein's film proposals for the Paramount studio were turned down and when his subsequent effort to make an independent film in Mexico collapsed. Eisenstein was summoned back to Moscow in 1932 to find that the Soviet film industry had been fully reorganized in his absence. It had begun making the transition to sound cinema. More important, it was now consolidated under tight government supervision and subjected to rigid new ideological controls.[5] The Stalinist cultural bureaucracy was developing aesthetic guidelines for an officially sanctioned artistic style to be known as socialist realism. The new artistic regime would reject the avant-garde styles of the 1920s in favor of conventional story forms and accessible styles. Soviet filmmakers who had espoused elaborate montage devices—notably Eisenstein, but also such colleagues as Vsevolod Pudovkin and Alexander Dovzhenko—had to adjust to the new system. This would not be easy for Eisenstein; he would often run up against state censors and harsh official criticism in his later career.[6] Nevertheless, Eisenstein's sense of commitment to the craft of filmmaking would encourage him to develop new ideas in response to his altered circumstances. That commitment would sustain him even within the confines of Stalinism.

When Eisenstein returned to Moscow, he took a position at the State Film Institute, teaching classes in film direction. He would teach full-time through 1935 and would offer courses and lectures periodically throughout his later life. He did not consider this move into the classroom a detour from his creative contributions to Soviet cinema. He had long been interested in training younger artists, and he found affinities between teaching and artistic creation.[7] Throughout his career, he saw his film theory as having a pedagogical function; its prescriptions were designed to guide other filmmakers.

The filmmaking courses he taught in the 1930s provided him with an excellent film theory laboratory, giving him the chance to rethink his 1920s aesthetic and to try out new ideas on his students. In fact, his class notes were to form the basis for several theoretical manuscripts and publications.[8] More important, his theory of film began to resemble the pedagogical principles he employed in his classes. This was no accident. Filmmaking would continue to have a social mission in the Soviet Union; it would still be thought of as a form of mass education. A film theory that borrowed from pedagogy would seem to be consistent with such an educational role. A film might literally provide a learning experience if its form duplicated proven teaching strategies.

Eisenstein's favorite classroom tactic was to require his class to deal with a vexing creative problem. Then, in an extended Socratic exchange with the students, he would interrogate them on possible creative strategies until they arrived at a satisfactory conclusion. He typically asked them to stage a given scene for the camera and then to elaborate a staging and editing plan. He always challenged the class to find a central, key ingredient to the scene around which all of the scene's details would be worked out. In a famous example, he told his class to film the pawnbroker's murder from *Crime and Punishment* in only one shot with a stationary camera. The strategic key emerged by placing the camera at a window that would figure importantly in the scene, and then organizing character movements in relation to that location (Nizhny, 93–139).

Each creative problem, he advised his students, contained a controlling, core idea from which would derive the many details needed to complete the scene. The core ingredient he called the "image" (*obraz* in Russian; sometimes translated as "form" or "figure"). It was to be the core concept of the scene. The process of organizing the details to articulate that image he called "representation" (*izobrazhenie*; sometimes translated as "depiction"). An artist must conceive a scene around a central image, the main theme he or she wants to convey to an audience. The artist must then must develop that image through the process of representation, by formulating and planning the countless minute ingredients of staging and filming.

Eisenstein saw this image/representation relationship as being central to the artistic experience as a whole. A spectator watching a finished scene is presented with all of the representational details resulting from the filmmaker's efforts. If the filmmaker has organized them properly, the spectator finally becomes aware of the image, the scene's main point. A filmmaker can still impart an ideological message through the image, while giving it expressive force through creative representation. "I know," Eisenstein asserted in an essay growing out of his class exercises, "that in the presence of these two elements—the representation of the particular case and the generalizing image which emerges from it—resides the inexorable and consuming power of artistic composition" (*Izbrannye*, 2:349).

Eisenstein advocated that the filmmaker begin with an intended message (image) and work at rendering it in expressive artistic form (representation). The spectator, on the other hand, begins with the scene's details (representation) and works back to the filmmaker's original intention (image). The process, Eisenstein suggested, thus becomes something of a partnership between filmmaker and spectator. Each participates in some way in the creative process; each helps make the work meaningful. Moreover, that partnership between artist and spectator suggests the relationship between teacher and student in one of Eisenstein's classes. The artist's representation draws the spectator to the image just as Eisenstein challenged his students to identify the core conception of a scene in one of his exercises.

The idea that the artist should serve as educator had an intellectual pedigree in Russia going back at least to Tolstoy, but it seemed to hold out particular possibilities in the emerging age of socialist realism. Soviet officials were rightly concerned that many of the stylized, avantgarde films of the 1920s had alienated spectators.[9] Socialist realism was to employ strategies that would engage spectators more comfortably. Eisenstein felt that he could contribute to socialist realism through a film aesthetic based on his pedagogical experience. A film form that derived from the classroom dynamic might assure that spectators would literally learn while watching movies. In his early career, Eisenstein might have proposed a frontal assault on the spectator's senses; under the system of socialist realism, he would draw the spectator into an edifying experience.

Montage would still offer the central strategy for Eisenstein's new ambition. But he now defined it as the process of organizing representational details around the central theme conveyed in a scene's image. Myriad graphic (and sound) details had to be arranged systematically through montage, Eisenstein began to advocate. Associated motifs would form the main montage ingredients, and montage would involve the organization of representational details to develop a scene's central image. The relationship among those montage ingredients would be one of organic unity, a substantial change from the view of montage as energizing conflict that Eisenstein had promoted earlier in his career.

Eisenstein noted that this pattern of associational montage was isomorphic with certain human cognitive processes identified by psychologists, linguists, and anthropologists. He took particular note of Lucien Levy-Bruhl's notion of sensuous thought and Lev Vygotsky's theory of inner speech. Adopting freely from these researchers, Eisenstein came to the view that preverbal thought involved certain predictable patterns. Verbalizable concepts emerge only after the human mind has processed many associated mental fragments. "Inner speech is precisely at the stage of image-sensual structure," Eisenstein asserted in 1935, "not yet having attained that logical formation with which speech clothes itself before stepping out into the open" (*Film Form*, 130).

Eisenstein liked to invoke examples of this process from everyday experience. A particular concept that one retains is actually the accumulation of numerous associated impressions, Eisenstein noted. One may retain an image of the concept "five o'clock." It is more than the hands on the clock depicting that time. It involves the accumulation of all the memory fragments from one's experience associated with that time: "It may be supper, or the end of the working day, or the rush hour on the metro, or the book shops closing, or the special light in those pretwilight hours which is so characteristic of that time of day" (*Selected*, 2:300). One arrives at the general idea of "five o'clock" by organizing and processing these related impressions.

Artists use similar practices regularly, Eisenstein asserted, and in doing so they practice montage. He noted, for example, that Maupassant's *Bel-Ami* contains a scene in which a character hopes to meet his love at midnight to elope but suffers a crushing disappointment when she does not appear (*Selected*, 2:303–4). Maupassant gave expressive power to the concept of midnight in the scene by describing the tolling of several clocks, not just one. He thus created a literary montage of the various tolling clocks, and the accumulation of the visual and sound fragments in the passage produces the larger, enriched image of midnight. Through such montage techniques, artists find a form that duplicates the human mental process of inner speech, and the expressive power of the artwork is enhanced by that duplication.

The Maupassant example may have been especially useful to Eisenstein since it involved both visual and sound associations. Eisenstein was expanding his definition of film montage to take into account audio as well as visual information as he adapted his theory to the age of sound cinema. Sound would provide a second layer of possible montage fragments to be associated with visual motifs in Eisenstein's new aesthetic. Music, sound effects, and speech could offer independent sources for the coordinated motific fragments used to form an artistic image. Eisenstein advocated coordinating the sound and visual tracks of a film in what he called "vertical montage," invoking the vertical, harmonic coordination of a musical score. Simultaneous sound and visual details could be vertically coordinated like the harmonic "interaction between [*sic*] the various elements of the orchestra in every given bar" (*Selected*, 2:330).

These new ideas of organic and vertical montage underpinned Eisenstein's work on *Alexander Nevsky*, his first successfully completed sound film. In fact, he worked closely with the brilliant composer Sergei Prokofiev on the film score and on strategies of audiovisual coordination. The most celebrated example of this coordination takes place in the beginning of the "Battle on the Ice" sequence in the film when Russian defenders await the charge of the Teutonic knights. (Eisenstein describes the scene in detail in his 1940 essay "Vertical Montage" [*Selected*, 2:379–97].) The first twelve shots of the scene contain graphic configurations that exactly correspond to the "shapes" of the music, at least as those shapes might be represented on a conductor's score. An ascending scale of notes is matched to a diagonal line of clouds, for example; a slow musical phrase with a single note repeated four times is rendered on screen as a horizontal line; and so on. Eisenstein even believed that spectators' eyes would scan the shapes on screen in a rhythm and movement governed by the music.

Eisenstein's example makes literal a set of metaphors about musical "shape" and musical "graphics," and he proposes somewhat arbitrarily that all viewers will scan his images in a certain way. Nevertheless, the whole sequence has clearly been organized around precise plans about audiovisual synchronization. The two tracks work together to supply a set of motifs that produce what Eisenstein identified as an intended image of "anxious expectation" as the audience awaits the eventual climactic clash of the armies (*Selected*, 2:397–99). It thus provides not only an example of vertical montage. It also suggests the possibilities of an expressive representation of a central image. The planned image of the scene, the feeling of anxiety, is the stronger for the fact that it is elaborated through both visual and audio motifs.

The *Nevsky* production renewed Eisenstein's interest in theater, particularly opera. Prokofiev's elaborate *Nevsky* score, with its extensive use of a chorus, for example, suggests that Eisenstein and Prokofiev had conventions of opera in mind in *Nevsky*. Eisenstein soon had the chance to examine the possibilities of musical drama when he was commissioned by the Bolshoi Theater in 1940 to mount a production of Wagner's *The Valkyrie*.

What most attracted Eisenstein to Wagner "were his opinions on synthetic spectacle" and his operas' "internal unity of sound and sight" (*Film Essays*, 85). Eisenstein saw in Wagner an artist in another medium who mastered the dramatic possibilities of coordinating motifs from various sources into a synthetic drama, a theatrical version of vertical montage. Wagner's aesthetic doctrine of the *Gesamtkunstwerk*, the total artwork, proved especially germane. The doctrine held that all the ingredients of the theatrical spectacle had to work toward a unified dramatic effect: orchestral scoring, voice, sets, costuming, lighting, and so on had be coordinated to achieve dramatic synthesis. Also, according to Eisenstein, Wagner along with such artists as the composer Alexander Scriabin effectively exploited the phenomenon of synesthesia, the fusion of sensory data from different senses. Sound, image, smell, and touch may interact and overlap in the sensory process. Wagner's effort to build dramatic effects from the synthesis of sound, staging, lighting, and so on provide overlapping channels of sensory data for the spectator, thus enriching the spectator's sensory experience. In acknowledging Wagner, Eisenstein noted that cinema had even greater potential for synesthesia and for the totalizing experience of the *Gesamtkunstwerk* than the musical stage. Not only could film draw from both sound and mise-en-scène; film also enjoyed possibilities for additional coordinated devices from such areas as editing, camera movement, lens selections, color film, and the like.

Eisenstein's *Ivan the Terrible* was to provide a fully integrated dramatic experience in the manner of Wagner. Not only was the scale of the production to be Wagnerian, an epic dealing with nothing less than the unification of Russia under Tsar Ivan's ruthless rule; Eisenstein also planned each scene so that it would involve the synthesis of representational details from an array of audiovisual sources. Following through on his views about inner speech and the image/representation dynamic, Eisenstein organized individual scenes around a given motif that appeared in several variants. Those variants might emerge from any of several sources: music, sound effects, costuming, figure movement, and so on. The montage drew these variants together into a unified experience that conveyed the scene's image.

This strategy is evident in the episode in which Ivan oversees the Russian army's siege of Kazan in Part I.[10] The core of the sequence is the enhanced sense of power of the title character as he faces his first challenge from an enemy of Russia. Eisenstein finds a particular motif to suggest this power: energy radiating out from a single source in the manner of rays. Eisenstein's montage links various objects that offer versions of this design: the spokes of a wheel, the sun crest on Ivan's armor, the bomb fuses, and even the fan-like cloud formation that appears behind Ivan. That motif of radiating energy carries over to the sound track (trumpets blast, bombs detonate, cannons fire). Finally, it is picked up in Ivan's behavior at the scene's end when he flings his arms wide in celebration of his victory. This final gesture gives particularly graphic form to the idea of power extending from the person of the tsar and is thus a fitting culmination. Eisenstein takes an abstraction—political power—and represents it through many small, concrete details in the scene, all of which grow logically out of the dramatic situation. Their accumulated effect is to guide the spectator toward a comprehension of that larger image in a manner reminiscent of inner speech.

Eisenstein's later theory was thus calculated to effect subtle, pre-conscious manipulations of the film spectator through a montage strategy posited on the phenomenon of inner speech. He did not abandon, however, the important ingredient of spectator emotion. As we have seen, he first posited emotion as the source of film's power in the 1920s. He absorbed the issue of emotion into the expressive qualities of the image/representation dynamic in the 1930s. At the end of his career, however, he returned to a purer definition of emotion in art. He advocated that the work should produce a powerful, sustained emotional experience, in the manner of Wagner. In his last extended theoretical project, *Nonindifferent Nature*, he took up the issue of emotional power by invoking the principles of pathos and ecstasy.

An emotionally powerful artwork manifests what he called pathos, a controlling emotional strain. Such an emotional force should overwhelm the spectator, forcing him or her to lose any ability to resist the work's planned effects. If the work's pathos does truly overpower the spectator's critical faculties, it will take the spectator to the condition of ecstasy, literally "out of stasis" and, more figuratively, out of one's normal state (*Nature*, 27). In a well-crafted film scene, the spectator can be completely absorbed into the dramatic event by her or his emotions, losing any sense of critical distance from the drama.

Several of the scenes in *Ivan the Terrible* are calculated to produce such an overpowering emotional effect. Anyone watching the "Dance of the Oprichniks" passage in Part II, for example, is likely to be caught up in the raw energy of the dance. Eisenstein achieves this through the episode's frenzied rhythm, which results from the complementary tempos of the music, choreography, and editing. Each works off the other without duplicating it (see Thompson, 243–47). The editing does not show dance steps in full, for example, but instead breaks up the steps into fragments; the tempo of the cuts plays off musical rhythms. Shifting color values—Eisenstein was able to shoot the scene in color on captured German film stock—play across the screen, providing additional stimuli. In an elaborate exercise in vertical montage, Eisenstein weaves together several different lines—music, choreography, editing, color—to produce the scene's dynamic force. The successful film scene, Eisenstein would maintain, thus works on the spectator through a calculated emotional strain (provoking ecstasy) as well as through a unified motific strain (evoking inner speech).

In appealing to the issue of emotion in his late theory, Eisenstein returned to the premise of his earliest work in "The Montage of Film Attraction," that of using film techniques to control the responses of spectators. Despite the many twists and turns of his twenty-five-year career—and the resulting amendments to his theory—he never lost sight of that issue. He remained convinced that film enjoyed a special capacity to affect spectators and thus to have persuasive force. Through such power, film could ultimately educate a mass audience. Eisenstein's theoretical program was to identify the persuasive possibilities available to filmmakers. His filmmaking practice put those possibilities to the test.

Subsequent generations of filmmakers have likewise put Eisenstein's ideas to the test. Eisenstein's historical legacy includes an array of major directors who have adopted elements of his theory. Eisenstein's views on the didactic possibilities of cinema have been taken up time and again by politically committed directors in the years since his death. Leftist fimmakers outside the Soviet Union, for example, embraced Eisenstein's ideas as soon as they became available in translation. From the Workers' Film and Photo Leagues of the 1930s through the Third World revolutionary cinema of the 1960s and 1970s, Eisenstein provided a model for directors who looked to cinema to promote social change.

The formal aspects of Eisensteinian montage appealed to artists seeking alternatives to mainstream narrative film. The avant-garde cinema of Bruce Conner and Stan Brakhage, for example, adapted montage principles to films that interrogated the very nature of cinema. Such European modernists as Jean-Luc Godard and Alain Resnais acknowledged the importance of montage theory to their experiments in cinematic form. Indeed, the generation of "political modernists" that included Godard, Alexander Kluge, and Dusan Makavejev found in Eisenstein both an effective didacticist and a source of formal principles that challenged classical cinema's formulas. Those directors who sought to mount rich spectacles involving elaborate staging and lush scoring—Luchino Visconti and Sergio Leone provide two notable examples—looked to Eisenstein's late theory, with its emphasis on the emotional saturation of spectacle productions.

Even while Eisenstein's cinema was being invoked as an alternative to commercial cinema, mainstream commercial filmmakers borrowed freely from his methods. From the ubiquitous "montage sequences" in studio-era Hollywood films to the replaying of Eisensteinian scenes in modern American films—the bull's slaughter in Francis Coppola's *Apocalypse Now,* the baby carriage in Brian DePalma's *The Untouchables*—Hollywood has self-consciously cited Eisenstein and the montage aesthetic.

Such appropriations suggest the varied nature of Eisenstein's theoretical corpus. It evolved sufficiently in the course of his career that modern filmmakers could select from an extensive array of possible cinema prescriptions. Directors of various persuasions could find something in Eisenstein's diverse writings to enhance their craft. The considerable breadth of his theory accounts in no small measure for its continuing influence.

NOTES

1. A fascinating insight into Eisenstein's working methods is available in Leyda and Voynov. This useful volume not only provides an overview of Eisenstein's life and career, but also contains many primary materials. Several drafts, sketches, manuscript fragments,

and the like are reproduced in the text. In looking over such entries, one can sense how often seemingly casual jottings figured into Eisenstein's enormous creative output. One can begin to appreciate the complicated nature of the corpus.

2. This procedure does not mean that there are not other ways of understanding Eisenstein's writings. Other scholars, for example, have effectively analyzed the theory by appealing primarily to Eisenstein's political commitments, emphasizing his contributions to Marxist aesthetics. His associations with various artistic communities can also provide illustrative background, since he drew on such aesthetic schools as Russian constructivism, formalism, and symbolism. For examples of alternative ways to frame Eisenstein's work, see Goodwin, Bordwell (*Cinema*), and selections in Taylor and Christie (*Rediscovered*).

3. For biographical background, see Barna, Seton, and Leyda and Voynov. See also Bordwell, *Cinema*, ch. 1. Eisenstein's rather eccentric and freewheeling effort at autobiography is also available in English (Eisenstein, *Memories*), although it is more useful as an insight into Eisenstein's thoughts on his own experiences than it is as a source for the actual chronology of his life.

4. On this episode in Eisenstein's career, see Gerould and Gordon. The former provides a particularly useful account of Eisenstein's important production of *The Wiseman*.

5. This interval in Eisenstein's career is well covered in the English-language literature. On Eisenstein's efforts to work in Hollywood at Paramount, see Montague. On his frustrating effort to make an independent film in Mexico, see Geduld and Gottesman. On changes in the Soviet film industry in the 1930s, see Kenez, chs. 5–8.

6. Eisenstein had several planned projects rejected by the state cinema bureaucracy, and two of his films were banned outright. *Bezhin Meadow* (1937) was banned by film industry officials during final production, and Eisenstein was never able to complete the picture. *Ivan the Terrible*, Part II, was banned upon its completion in 1946 by order of the Party. Eisenstein's account of Tsar Ivan's powerful reign was widely perceived as having historical parallels with the Stalin regime. A 1946 Party decree on cinema asserted that Part II failed to emphasize Ivan's strength but represented him as weak and indecisive, in the manner of Hamlet. That finding justified banning the film entirely since the Party leadership did not want Stalin associated with such a figure. The film was finally released during the post-Stalin cultural "thaw" of the 1950s.

7. Eisenstein acquired teaching experience prior to taking the full-time position at the Film Institute in 1932. He ran many acting and directing workshops during his days as a theater director, and he taught a seminar in film direction at the Film Institute in 1928.

8. Eisenstein hoped to publish a set of book-length treatises on filmmaking to be called *Direction* (*Rezhissura*), which was never published in full during his lifetime. Part of that project forms the core of the English-language volume *Selected Works*, vol. 2. The best primary source in English on his teaching is Nizhny, which contains transcriptions of various Eisenstein lesson plans. For a secondary source on this episode in Eisenstein's career, see Kepley. Full transcripts of several of Eisenstein's class lessons are included in the six-volume Russian-language collection of Eisenstein writings, mainly in volume 4 of the collection (Eisenstein, *Izbrannye*).

9. See, e.g., Youngblood and Kenez. This criticism was directed at certain of Eisenstein's early films as well. Party officials attacked *October*, for example, for allegedly being too difficult for average viewers to understand. Eisenstein's exercise in intellectual cinema drew particular criticism from officials, who portrayed such passages as too experimental for a mass form like cinema. See, e.g., documents in Taylor and Christie, *Factory*, 216–32.

10. The scene has been cogently analyzed by both Bordwell ("Shift," 43) and Thompson (149–52). My use of the example is indebted to their discussions.

WORKS CITED

Barna, Yon. *Eisenstein*. Trans. Lee Hunter. Bloomington: Indiana University Press, 1973.

Bordwell, David. *The Cinema of Eisenstein*. Cambridge, Mass.: Harvard University Press, 1993.

———. "Eisenstein's Epistemological Shift." *Screen* 15, no. 4 (1975): 29–46.

Eisenstein, Sergei. *Film Essays and a Lecture.* Ed. Jay Leyda. Princeton, N.J.: Princeton University Press, 1982.

———. *Film Form: Essays in Film Theory.* Ed. and trans. Jay Leyda. New York: Harcourt, 1949.

———. *Immoral Memories: An Autobiography.* Trans. Herbert Marshall. Boston: Houghton Mifflin, 1983.

———. *Izbrannye proizvedeniia v shesti tomakh.* 6 vols. Ed. S. I Iutkevich et al. Moscow: Iskusstvo, 1964–1969.

———. *Nonindifferent Nature.* Trans. Herbert Marshall. Cambridge: Cambridge University Press, 1987.

———. "Notes for a Film of *Capital.* " Trans. Maciej Sliwowski, Jay Leyda, and Annette Michelson. *October* 2 (1976): 3–26.

———. *Selected Works,* vol. 1, *Writings, 1922–34.* Ed. and trans. Richard Taylor. London: BFI, 1988.

———. *Selected Works,* vol. 2, *Towards a Theory of Montage.* Ed. and trans. Michael Glenny and Richard Taylor. London: BFI, 1991.

Eisenstein, Sergei, and Sergei Tretyakov. "Expressive Movement." Trans. Alma H. Law. *Millennium Film Journal* 3 (1979): 30–38.

Geduld, Harry, and Ron Gottesman, eds. *Sergei Eisenstein and Upton Sinclair: The Making and Unmaking of "Que Viva Mexico!"* Bloomington: Indiana University Press, 1970.

Gerould, Daniel. "Eisenstein's *Wiseman.* " *The Drama Review* 18, no. 1 (1974): 71–76.

Goodwin, James. *Eisenstein, Cinema, and History.* Urbana: University of Illinois Press, 1993.

Gordon, Mel. "Eisenstein's Later Work at Proletcult." *The Drama Review* 22, no. 3 (1978): 107–12.

Kenez, Peter. *Cinema and Soviet Society, 1917–1953.* Cambridge: Cambridge University Press, 1992.

Kepley, Vance, Jr. "Eisenstein as Pedagogue." *Quarterly Review of Film and Video* 14, no. 4 (1993): 1–16.

Leyda, Jay, and Zina Voynov. *Eisenstein at Work.* New York: Pantheon, 1982.

Montagu, Ivor. *With Eisenstein in Hollywood.* New York: International Publishers, 1967.

Nizhny, Vladimir. *Lessons with Eisenstein.* Ed. and trans. Ivor Montagu and Jay Leyda. New York: Hill and Wang, 1962.

Seton, Marie. *Sergei M. Eisenstein: A Biography.* London: Dobson, 1952.

Taylor, Richard, and Ian Christie, eds. *Eisenstein Rediscovered.* London and New York: Routledge, 1993.

———, eds. *The Film Factory: Russian and Soviet Cinema in Documents, 1896–1939.* Cambridge, Mass.: Harvard University Press, 1988.

Thompson, Kristin. *Eisenstein's "Ivan the Terrible": A Neoformalist Analysis.* Princeton, N.J.: Princeton University Press, 1981.

Youngblood, Denise. *Movies for the Masses: Popular Cinema and Soviet Society in the 1920s.* Cambridge: Cambridge University Press, 1992.

ANNOTATED BIBLIOGRAPHY

Primary

Eisenstein, Sergei. *Beyond the Stars: The Memoirs of Sergei Eisenstein.* Ed. Richard Taylor. Trans. William Powell. London: BFI, 1995.

A careful translation of the autobiographical notes and drafts Eisenstein prepared near the end of his life. More valuable as a source for Eisenstein's reflections on his own experience than as a record of his career.

———. *Film Essays and a Lecture.* Ed. Jay Leyda. Princeton, N.J.: Princeton University Press, 1982.

A miscellaneous collection of Eisenstein's writings and statements from 1926 through 1946. Also contains an excellent bibliography.

————. *Film Form: Essays in Film Theory.* Ed. and trans. Jay Leyda. New York: Harcourt, 1949.

A valuable collection of Eisenstein's writings from the late 1920s and 1930s.

————. *The Film Sense.* Ed. and trans. Jay Leyda. New York: Harcourt, 1942.

The best source for Eisenstein's montage theory in the 1930s. Includes his views on sound and color.

————. *Immoral Memories: An Autobiography.* Trans. Herbert Marshall. Boston: Houghton Mifflin, 1983.

First English-language translation of the autobiography. Surpassed by the Taylor and Powell edition listed above.

————. *Nonindifferent Nature.* Trans. Herbert Marshall. Cambridge: Cambridge University Press, 1987.

Eisenstein's last major theoretical project. Contains his ideas on ecstasy and pathos.

————. *Selected Works,* vol. 1, *Writings, 1922–34.* Ed. and trans. Richard Taylor: London, BFI, 1988.

A new translation of the most significant early essays. Overlaps with some of the materials in the Leyda editions listed above. The translations in this volume and in volume 2 of the set (listed below) surpass the Leyda translations in accuracy and precision.

————. *Selected Works,* vol. 2, *Towards a Theory of Montage.* Ed. and trans. Michael Glenny and Richard Taylor. London: BFI, 1991.

Covers Eisenstein's 1930s theory. A new edition of material included in *The Film Sense.*

Secondary

Barna, Yon. *Eisenstein.* Trans. Lee Hunter. Bloomington: Indiana University Press, 1973.

A short but useful biography of Eisenstein. Stresses his creative influences.

Bordwell, David. *The Cinema of Eisenstein.* Cambridge, Mass.: Harvard University Press, 1993.

The best-sustained analysis in English of Eisenstein's film theory and practice. A good place to begin the serious study of Eisenstein's work.

Goodwin, James. *Eisenstein, Cinema, and History.* Urbana: University of Illinois Press, 1993.

Discussion of Eisenstein's work in the context of Marxist theories of history.

Seton, Marie. *Sergei M. Eisenstein: A Biography.* London: Dobson, 1952.

The first full account of Eisenstein's life and career to appear in English. The author was a close associate and admirer of Eisenstein, and the text betrays that adulation.

Bazin

André Bazin

The Evolution
of the Language of Cinema

By 1928, the silent film had reached its artistic peak. The despair of its elite as they witnessed the dismantling of this ideal city, while it may not have been justified, is at least understandable. As they followed their chosen aesthetic path it seemed to them that the cinema had developed into an art most perfectly accommodated to the "exquisite embarrassment" of silence and that the realism that sound would bring could only mean a surrender to chaos.

In point of fact, now that sound has given proof that it came not to destroy but to fulfill the Old Testament of the cinema, we may most properly ask if the technical revolution created by the sound track was in any sense an aesthetic revolution. In other words, did the years from 1928 to 1930 actually witness the birth of a new cinema? Certainly, as regards editing, history does not actually show as wide a breach as might be expected between the silent and the sound film. On the contrary there is discernible evidence of a close relationship between certain directors of 1925 and 1935 and especially of the 1940s through the 1950s. Compare, for example, Erich von Stroheim and Jean Renoir or Orson Welles, or again Carl Theodore Dreyer and Robert Bresson. These more or less clear-cut affinities demonstrate first of all that the gap separating the 1920s and the 1930s can be bridged, and second, that certain cinematic values actually carry over from the silent to the sound film and, above all, that it is less a matter of setting silence over against sound than of contrasting certain families of styles, certain basically different concepts of cinematographic expression.

Aware as I am that the limitations imposed on this essay restrict me to a simplified and to that extent enfeebled presentation of my argument, and holding it to be less an objective statement than a working hypothesis, I distinguish, in the cinema between 1920 and 1940, between two broad and opposing trends: those directors who put their faith in the

From *What is Cinema?* by André Bazin, ed. and trans. Hugh Gray, 2 vols. (Berkeley and Los Angeles: University of California Press, 1967), 1:23–40. Copyright © by the Regents of the University of California.

image and those who put their faith in reality. By "image" I here mean, very broadly speaking, everything that the representation on the screen adds to the object there represented. This is a complex inheritance, but it can be reduced essentially to two categories: those that relate to the plastics of the image and those that relate to the resources of montage, which, after all, is simply the ordering of images in time.

Under the heading "plastics" must be included the style of the sets, of the makeup, and, up to a point, even of the performance, to which we naturally add the lighting and, finally, the framing of the shot that gives us its composition. As regards montage, derived initially as we all know from the masterpieces of Griffith, we have the statement of Malraux in his *Psychologie du cinéma* that it was montage that gave birth to film as an art, setting it apart from mere animated photography, in short, creating a language.

The use of montage can be "invisible," and this was generally the case in the prewar classics of the American screen. Scenes were broken down just for one purpose, namely, to analyze an episode according to the material or dramatic logic of the scene. It is this logic that conceals the fact of the analysis, the mind of the spectator quite naturally accepting the viewpoints of the director, which are justified by the geography of the action or the shifting emphasis of dramatic interest.

But the neutral quality of this "invisible" editing fails to make use of the full potential of montage. On the other hand these potentialities are clearly evident from the three processes generally known as parallel montage, accelerated montage, and montage by attraction. In creating parallel montage, Griffith succeeded in conveying a sense of the simultaneity of two actions taking place at a geographical distance by means of alternating shots from each. In *La Roue*, Abel Gance created the illusion of the steadily increasing speed of a locomotive without actually using any images of speed (indeed the wheel could have been turning on one spot) simply by a multiplicity of shots of ever-decreasing length.

Finally there is montage by attraction, the creation of S. M. Eisenstein; it is not as easily described as the others, but may be roughly defined as the reenforcing of the meaning of one image by association with another image not necessarily part of the same episode—for example, the fireworks display in *The General Line* following the image of the bull. In this extreme form, montage by attraction was rarely used even by its creator but one may consider as very near to it in principle the more commonly used ellipsis, comparison, or metaphor, examples of which are the throwing of stockings onto a chair at the foot of a bed or the milk overflowing in H. G. Clouzot's *Quai des orfèvres*. There are of course a variety of possible combinations of these three processes.

Whatever these may be, one can say that they share that trait in common which constitutes the very definition of montage, namely, the creation of a sense or meaning not objectively contained in the images themselves but derived exclusively from their juxtaposition. The well-known experiment of Kuleshov with the shot of Mozhukhin, in which a smile was seen to change its significance according to the image that preceded it, sums up perfectly the properties of montage.

Montage as used by Kuleshov, Eisenstein, or Gance did not show us the event; it alluded to it. Undoubtedly they derived at least the greater part of the constituent elements from the reality they were describing, but the final significance of the film was found to reside in the ordering of those elements much more than in their objective content. The substance of the narrative, whatever the realism of the individual image, is born essentially from these relationships—Mozhukhin plus dead child equals pity—that is to say, an abstract result, none of the concrete elements of which are to be found in the premises; maidens plus apple trees in bloom equals hope. The combinations are infinite. But the only thing they have in common is the fact that they suggest an idea by means of a metaphor or by an association of ideas. Thus between the scenario properly so-called, the ultimate object of the recital, and the image pure and simple, there is a relay station, a sort of aesthetic "transformer." The meaning is not in the image; it is in the shadow of the image projected by montage onto the field of consciousness of the spectator.

Let us sum up. Through the contents of the image and the resources of montage, the cinema has at its disposal a whole arsenal of means whereby to impose its interpretation of an event on the spectator. By the end of the silent film we can consider this arsenal to have been full. On the one side the Soviet cinema carried to its ultimate consequences the theory and practice of montage while the German school did every kind of violence to the plastics of the image by way of sets and lighting. Other cinemas count too besides the Russian and German, but whether in France or Sweden or the United States, it does not appear that the language of cinema was at a loss for ways of saying what it wanted to say.

If the art of cinema consists in everything that plastics and montage can add to a given reality, the silent film was an art on its own. Sound could only play at best a subordinate and supplementary role: a counterpoint to the visual image. But this possible enhancement—at best only a minor one—is likely not to weigh much in comparison with the additional bargain-rate reality introduced at the same time by sound.

Thus far we have put forward the view that expressionism of montage and image constitute the essence of cinema. And it is precisely on this generally accepted notion that directors from silent days, such as Erich von Stroheim, F. W. Murnau, and Robert Flaherty, have by implication cast a doubt. In their films, montage plays no part, unless it be the negative one of inevitable elimination where reality superabounds. The camera cannot see everything at once, but it makes sure not to lose any part of what it chooses to see. What matters to Flaherty, confronted with

Nanook hunting the seal, is the relation between Nanook and the animal—the actual length of the waiting period. Montage could suggest the time involved. Flaherty, however, confines himself to showing the actual waiting period; the length of the hunt is the very substance of the image, its true object. Thus in the film this episode requires one setup. Will anyone deny that it is thereby much more moving than a montage by attraction?

Murnau is interested not so much in time as in the reality of dramatic space. Montage plays no more of a decisive part in *Nosferatu* than in *Sunrise.* One might be inclined to think that the plastics of his image are expressionistic. But this would be a superficial view. The composition of his image is in no sense pictorial. It adds nothing to the reality; it does not deform it; it forces it to reveal its structural depth, to bring out the preexisting relations which become constitutive of the drama. For example, in *Tabu,* the arrival of a ship from left screen gives an immediate sense of destiny at work so that Murnau has no need to cheat in any way on the uncompromising realism of a film whose settings are completely natural.

But it is most of all von Stroheim who rejects photographic expressionism and the tricks of montage. In his films reality lays itself bare like a suspect confessing under the relentless examination of the commissioner of police. He has one simple rule for direction. Take a close look at the world, keep on doing so, and in the end it will lay bare for you all its cruelty and its ugliness. One could easily imagine as a matter of fact a film by von Stroheim composed of a single shot as long-lasting and as close-up as you like. These three directors do not exhaust the possibilities. We would undoubtedly find scattered among the works of others elements of nonexpressionistic cinema in which montage plays no part—even including Griffith. But these examples suffice to reveal, at the very heart of the silent film, a cinematographic art the very opposite of that which has been identified as *cinéma par excellence,* a language the semantic and syntactical unit of which is in no sense the Shot; in which the image is evaluated not according to what it adds to reality but what it reveals of it. In the latter art the silence of the screen was a drawback, that is to say, it deprived reality of one of its elements. *Greed,* like Dreyer's *Jeanne d'Arc,* is already virtually a talking film. The moment that you cease to maintain that montage and the plastic composition of the image are the very essence of the language of cinema, sound is no longer the aesthetic crevasse dividing two radically different aspects of the seventh art. The cinema that is believed to have died of the sound track is in no sense *"the* cinema." The real dividing line is elsewhere. It was operative in the past and continues to be through thirty-five years of the history of the language of the film.

Having challenged the aesthetic unity of the silent film and divided it off into two opposing tendencies, now let us take a look at the history of the past twenty years.[1]

From 1930 to 1940, there seems to have grown up in the world, originating largely in the United States, a common form of cinematic language. It was the triumph in Hollywood, during that time, of five or six major kinds of film that gave it its overwhelming superiority: (1) American comedy (*Mr. Smith Goes to Washington*, 1936); (2) the burlesque film (The Marx Brothers); (3) the dance and vaudeville film (Fred Astaire and Ginger Rogers and the Ziegfield Follies); (4) the crime and gangster film (*Scarface, I Am a Fugitive from a Chain Gang, The Informer*); (5) psychological and social dramas (*Back Street, Jezebel*); (6) horror or fantasy films (*Dr. Jekyll and Mr. Hyde, The Invisible Man, Frankenstein*); (7) the western (*Stagecoach*, 1939). During that time the French cinema undoubtedly ranked next. Its superiority was gradually manifested by way of a trend toward what might be roughly called stark somber realism, or poetic realism, in which four names stand out: Jacques Feyder, Jean Renoir, Marcel Carné, and Julien Duvivier. My intention not being to draw up a list of prize-winners, there is little use in dwelling on the Soviet, British, German, or Italian films for which these years were less significant than the ten that were to follow. In any case, American and French production sufficiently clearly indicates that the sound film, prior to World War II, had reached a well-balanced stage of maturity.

First as to content. Major varieties with clearly defined rules capable of pleasing a worldwide public, as well as a cultured elite, provided it was not inherently hostile to the cinema.

Second as to form: well-defined styles of photography and editing perfectly adapted to their subject matter; a complete harmony of image and sound. In seeing again today such films as *Jezebel* by William Wyler, *Stagecoach* by John Ford, or *Le Jour se lève* by Marcel Carné, one has the feeling that in them an art has found its perfect balance, its ideal form of expression, and reciprocally one admires them for dramatic and moral themes to which the cinema, while it may not have created them, has given a grandeur, an artistic effectiveness, that they would not otherwise have had. In short, here are all the characteristics of the ripeness of a classical art.

I am quite aware that one can justifiably argue that the originality of the postwar cinema as compared with that of 1938 derives from the growth of certain national schools, in particular the dazzling display of the Italian cinema and of a native English cinema freed from the influence of Hollywood. From this one might conclude that the really important phenomenon of the years 1940–1950 is the introduction of new blood, of hitherto unexplored themes. That is to say, the real revolution took place more on the level of subject matter than of style. Is not neorealism primarily a kind of humanism and only secondarily a style of filmmaking? Then as to the style itself, is it not essentially a form of self-effacement before reality?

Our intention is certainly not to preach the glory of form over content. Art for art's sake is just as heretical in cinema as elsewhere, and probably more so. On the other hand, a new subject matter demands new form and as good a way as any toward understanding what a film is trying to say to us is to know how it is saying it.

Thus by 1938 or 1939 the talking film, particularly in France and in the United States, had reached a level of classical perfection as a result, on the one hand, of the maturing of different kinds of drama developed in part over the past ten years[2] and in part inherited from the silent film, and, on the other, of the stabilization of technical progress. The 1930s were the years, at once, of sound and of panchromatic film. Undoubtedly studio equipment had continued to improve but only in matters of detail, none of them opening up new, radical possibilities for direction. The only changes in this situation since 1940 have been in photography, thanks to the increased sensitivity of the film stock. Panchromatic stock turned visual values upside down; ultrasensitive emulsions have made a modification in their structure possible. Free to shoot in the studio with a much smaller aperture, the operator could, when necessary, eliminate the soft-focus background once considered essential. Still there are a number of examples of the prior use of deep focus, for example, in the work of Jean Renoir. This had always been possible on exteriors, and given a measure of skill, even in the studios. Anyone could do it who really wanted to. So that it is less a question basically of a technical problem, the solution of which has admittedly been made easier, than of a search after a style—a point to which we will come back. In short, with panchromatic stock in common use, with an understanding of the potentials of the microphone, and with the crane as standard studio equipment, one can really say that since 1930 all the technical requirements for the art of cinema have been available.

Since the determining technical factors were practically eliminated, we must look elsewhere for the signs and principles of the evolution of film language, that is to say by challenging the subject matter and as a consequence the styles necessary for its expression.

By 1939, the cinema had arrived at what geographers call the equilibrium-profile of a river. By this is meant that ideal mathematical curve that results from the requisite amount of erosion. Having reached this equilibrium-profile, the river flows effortlessly from its source to its mouth without further deepening of its bed. But if any geological movement occurs that raises the erosion level and modifies the height of the source, the water sets to work again, seeps into the surrounding land, goes deeper, burrowing and digging. Sometimes when it is a chalk bed, a new pattern is dug across the plain, almost invisible but found to be complex and winding, if one follows the flow of the water.

The Evolution of Editing since the Advent of Sound

In 1938, there was an almost universal standard pattern of editing. If, somewhat conventionally, we call the kind of silent films based on the plastics of the image and the artifices of montage "expressionist" or "symbolistic," we can describe the new form of storytelling "analytic" and "dramatic." Let us suppose, by way of reviewing one of the elements of the experiment of Kuleshov, that we have a table covered with food and a hungry tramp. One can imagine that in 1936 it would have been edited as follows:

1. Full shot of the actor and the table.
2. Camera moves forward into a close-up of a face expressing a mixture of amazement and longing.
3. Series of close-ups of food.
4. Back to full shot of person who starts slowly toward the camera.
5. Camera pulls slowly back to a three-quarter shot of the actor seizing a chicken wing.

Whatever variants one could think of for this scene, they would all have certain points in common:

1. The verisimilitude of space in which the position of the actor is always determined, even when a close-up eliminates the decor.
2. The purpose and the effects of the cutting are exclusively dramatic or psychological.

In other words, if the scene were played on a stage and seen from a seat in the orchestra, it would have the same meaning; the episode would continue to exist objectively. The changes of point of view provided by the camera would add nothing. They would present the reality a little more forcefully, first by allowing a better view and then by putting the emphasis where it belongs.

It is true that the stage director like the film director has at his disposal a margin within which he is free to vary the interpretation of the action, but it is only a margin and allows for no modification of the inner logic of the event. Now, by way of contrast, let us take the montage of the stone lions in *The End of St. Petersburg*. By skillful juxtaposition a group of sculptured lions are made to look like a single lion getting to its feet, a symbol of the aroused masses. This clever device would be unthinkable in any film after 1932. As late as 1935, Fritz Lang, in *Fury*, followed a series of shots of women scandalmongering with shots of clucking chickens in a farmyard. This relic of associative montage came as a shock even at the time, and today seems entirely out of keeping with the rest of the film. However decisive the art of Marcel Carné, for example, in our estimate of the respective values of *Quai des Brumes* or of *Le Jour se lève* his editing remains on the level of the reality he is analyzing. There is only one proper way of looking at it. That is why we are witnessing the almost complete disappearance of optical effects such as superimpositions, and even, especially in the United States, of the close-up, the too violent impact of which would make the audience conscious of the cutting. In the typical American comedy the director returns as often as he can to a shot of the characters from the knees up, which is said to be best suited to catch the spontaneous attention of the viewer—the natural point of balance of his mental adjustment.

Actually this use of montage originated with the silent movies. This is more or less the part it plays in Griffith's films, for example, in *Broken Blossoms*, because with *Intolerance* he had already introduced that synthetic concept of montage which the Soviet cinema was to carry to its ultimate conclusion and which is to be found again, although less exclusively, at the end of the silent era. It is understandable, as a matter of fact, that the sound image, far less flexible than the visual image, would carry montage in the direction of realism, increasingly eliminating both plastic expressionism and the symbolic relation between images.

Thus, around 1938, films were edited, almost without exception, according to the same principle. The story was unfolded in a series of set-ups numbering as a rule about six hundred. The characteristic procedure was by shot-reverse-shot, that is to say, in a dialogue scene, the camera followed the order of the text, alternating the character shown with each speech.

It was this fashion of editing, so admirably suitable for the best films made between 1930 and 1939, that was challenged by the shot in depth introduced by Orson Welles and William Wyler. The influence of *Citizen Kane* cannot be overestimated. Thanks to the depth of field, whole scenes are covered in one take, the camera remaining motionless. Dramatic effects for which we had formerly relied on montage were created out of the movements of the actors within a fixed framework. Of course Welles did not invent the in-depth shot any more than Griffith invented the close-up. All the pioneers used it and for a very good reason. Soft focus only appeared with montage. It was not only a technical must consequent upon the use of images in juxtaposition; it was a logical consequence of montage, its plastic equivalent. If at a given moment in the action the director, as in the scene imagined above, goes to a close-up of a bowl of fruit, it follows naturally that he also isolates it in space through the focusing of the lens. The soft focus of the background confirms therefore the effect of montage, that is to say, while it is of the essence of the storytelling, it is only an accessory of the style of the photography. Jean Renoir had already clearly understood this, as we see from a statement he made in 1938 just after *La Bête humaine* and *La Grande illusion* and just prior to *La Règle du jeu*: "The more I learn about my trade the more I incline to direction in depth relative to the screen. The better it works, the less I use the kind of setup that shows two actors facing the camera, like two well-behaved subjects posing for a still portrait." The truth of the matter is, that if you are looking for the precursor of Orson Welles, it is not Louis Lumière or Zecca, but Jean Renoir. In his films, the search after composition in depth is, in effect, a partial replacement of montage by frequent panning shots and entrances. It is based on a respect for the continuity of dramatic space and, of course, of its duration.

To anybody with eyes in his head, it is quite evident that the one-shot sequences used by Welles in *The Magnificent Ambersons* are in no sense the purely passive recording of an action shot within the same framing. On the contrary, his refusal to break up the action, to analyze the dramatic field in time, is a positive action, the results of which are far superior to anything that could be achieved by the classical "cut."

All you need to do is compare two frames shot in depth, one from 1910, the other from a film by Wyler or Welles, to understand just by looking at the image, even apart from the context of the film, how different their functions are. The framing in the 1910 film is intended, for all intents and purposes, as a substitute for the missing fourth wall of the theatrical stage, or at least in exterior shots, for the best vantage point to view the action, whereas in the second case the setting, the lighting, and the camera angles give an entirely different reading. Between them, director and cameraman have converted the screen into a dramatic checkerboard, planned down to the last detail. The clearest if not the most original examples of this are to be found in *The Little Foxes* where the mise-en-scène takes on the severity of a working drawing. (Welles's pictures are more difficult to analyze because of his baroque excesses.) Objects and characters are related in such a fashion that it is impossible for the spectator to miss the significance of the scene. To get the same results by way of montage would have necessitated a detailed succession of shots.

What we are saying then is that the sequence of shots "in depth" of the contemporary director does not exclude the use of montage—how could he, without reverting to a primitive babbling?—he makes it an integral part of his "plastic." The storytelling of Welles or Wyler is no less explicit than John Ford's, but theirs has the advantage over his that it does not sacrifice the specific effects that can be derived from unity of image in space and time. Whether an episode is analyzed bit by bit or presented in its physical entirety cannot surely remain a matter of indifference, at least in a work with some pretensions to style. It would obviously be absurd to deny that montage has added considerably to the progress of film language, but this has happened at the cost of other values, no less definitely cinematic.

This is why depth of field is not just a stock in trade of the cameraman like the use of a series of filters or of such-and-such a style of lighting; it is a capital gain in the field of direction—a dialectical step forward in the history of film language.

Nor is it just a formal step forward. Well used, shooting in depth is not just a more economical, a simpler, and at the same time a more subtle way of getting the most out of a scene. In addition to affecting the structure of film language, it also affects the relationships of the minds of the spectators to the image, and in consequence it influences the interpretation of the spectacle.

It would lie outside the scope of this essay to analyze the psychological modalities of these relations, as also their aesthetic consequences, but it might be enough here to note, in general terms, the following:

1. Depth of focus brings the spectator into a relation with the image closer to that which he enjoys with reality. Therefore it is correct to say that, independently of the contents of the image, its structure is more realistic.
2. It implies, consequently, both a more active mental attitude on the part of the spectator and a more positive contribution on his part to the action in progress. While analytical montage only calls for him to follow his guide, to let his attention follow along smoothly with that of the director who will choose what he should see, here he is called upon to exercise at least a minimum of personal choice. It is from his attention and his will that the meaning of the image in part derives.
3. From the two preceding propositions, which belong to the realm of psychology, there follows a third, which may be described as metaphysical. In analyzing reality, montage presupposes of its very nature the unity of meaning of the dramatic event. Some other form of analysis is undoubtedly possible, but then it would be another film. In short, montage by its very nature rules out ambiguity of expression. Kuleshov's experiment proves this *per absurdum* in giving on each occasion a precise meaning to the expression on a face, the ambiguity of which alone makes the three successively exclusive expressions possible.

On the other hand, depth of focus reintroduced ambiguity into the structure of the image if not of necessity—Wyler's films are never ambiguous—at least as a possibility. Hence it is no exaggeration to say that *Citizen Kane* is unthinkable shot in any other way but in depth. The uncertainty in which we find ourselves as to the spiritual key or the interpretation we should put on the film is built into the very design of the image.

It is not that Welles denies himself any recourse whatsoever to the expressionistic procedures of montage, but just that their use from time to time in between one-shot sequences in depth gives them a new meaning. Formerly montage was the very stuff of cinema, the texture of the scenario. In *Citizen Kane* a series of superimpositions is contrasted with a scene presented in a single take, constituting another and deliberately abstract mode of storytelling. Accelerated montage played tricks with time and space while that of Welles, on the other hand, is not trying to deceive us; it offers us a contrast, condensing time, and hence is the equivalent of the French imperfect or the English frequentative tense. Like accelerated montage and montage of attractions these superimpositions, which the talking film had not used for ten years, rediscovered a possible use related to temporal realism in a film without montage.

If we have dwelt at some length on Orson Welles it is because the date of his appearance in the filmic firmament (1941) marks more or less the beginning of a new period and also because his case is the most spectacular and, by virtue of his very excesses, the most significant.

Yet *Citizen Kane* is part of a general movement, of a vast stirring of the geological bed of cinema, confirming that everywhere up to a point there had been a revolution in the language of the screen.

I could show the same to be true, although by different methods, of the Italian cinema. In Roberto Rossellini's *Paisà* and *Allemania Anno Zero* and Vittorio De Sica's *Ladri de Biciclette*, Italian neorealism contrasts with previous forms of film realism in its stripping away of all expressionism and in particular in the total absence of the effects of montage. As in the films of Welles and in spite of conflicts of style, neorealism tends to give back to the cinema a sense of the ambiguity of reality. The preoccupation of Rossellini when dealing with the face of the child in *Allemania Anno Zero* is the exact opposite of that of Kuleshov with the close-up of Mozhukhin. Rossellini is concerned to preserve its mystery. We should not be misled by the fact that the evolution of neorealism is not manifest, as in the United States, in any form of revolution in editing. They are both aiming at the same results by different methods. The means used by Rossellini and De Sica are less spectacular, but they are no less determined to do away with montage and to transfer to the screen the continuum of reality. The dream of Zavattini is just to make a ninety-minute film of the life of a man to whom nothing ever happens. The most "aesthetic" of the neorealists, Luchino Visconti, gives just as clear a picture as Welles of the basic aim of his directorial art in *La Terra Trema*, a film almost entirely composed of one-shot sequences, thus clearly showing his concern to cover the entire action in interminable deep-focus panning shots.

However, we cannot pass in review all the films that have shared in this revolution in film language since 1940. Now is the moment to attempt a synthesis of our reflections on the subject.

It seems to us that the decade from 1940 to 1950 marks a decisive step forward in the development of the language of the film. If we have appeared since 1930 to have lost sight of the trend of the silent film, as illustrated particularly by von Stroheim, F. W. Murnau, Robert Flaherty, and Dreyer, it is for a purpose. It is not that this trend seems to us to have been halted by the talking film. On the contrary, we believe that it represented the richest vein of the so-called silent film and, precisely because it was not aesthetically tied to montage, but was indeed the only tendency that looked to the realism of sound as a natural development. On the other hand it is a fact that the talking film between 1930 and 1940 owes it virtually nothing save for the glorious and retrospectively prophetic exception of Jean Renoir. He alone in his searchings as a director prior to *La Règle du jeu* forced himself to look back beyond the resources provided by montage and so uncovered the secret of a film form that would permit everything to be said without chopping the world up into little fragments, that would reveal the hidden meanings in people and things without disturbing the unity natural to them.

It is not a question of thereby belittling the films of 1930 to 1940, a criticism that would not stand up in the face of the number of masterpieces; it is simply an attempt to establish the notion of a dialectic progress, the highest expression of which was found in the films of the 1940s. Undoubtedly, the talkie sounded the knell of a certain aesthetic of the language of film, but only wherever it had turned its back on its vocations in the service of realism. The sound film nevertheless did preserve the essentials of montage, namely, discontinuous description and the dramatic analysis of action. What it turned its back on was metaphor and symbol in exchange for the illusion of objective presentation. The expressionism of montage has virtually disappeared, but the relative realism of the kind of cutting that flourished around 1937 implied a congenital limitation that escaped us so long as it was perfectly suited to its subject matter. Thus American comedy reached its peak within the framework of a form of editing in which the realism of the time played no part. Dependent on logic for its effects, like vaudeville and plays on words, entirely conventional in its moral and sociological content, American comedy had everything to gain, in strict line-by-line progression, from the rhythmic resources of classical editing.

Undoubtedly it is primarily with the von Stroheim–Murnau trend—almost totally eclipsed from 1930 to 1940—that the cinema has more or less consciously linked up once more over the past ten years.[3] But it has no intention of limiting itself simply to keeping this trend alive. It draws from it the secret of the regeneration of realism in storytelling and thus of becoming capable once more of bringing together real time, in which things exist, along with the duration of the action, for which classical editing had insidiously substituted mental and abstract time. On the other hand, so far from wiping out once and for all the conquests of montage, this reborn realism gives them a body of reference and a meaning. It is only an increased realism of the image that can support the abstraction of montage. The stylistic repertory of a director such as Hitchcock, for example, ranged from the power inherent in the basic document as such, to superimpositions, to large close-ups. But the close-ups of Hitchcock are not the same as those of C. B. de Mille in *The Cheat* (1915). They are just one type of figure, among others, of his style. In other words, in the silent days, montage evoked what the director wanted to say; in the editing of 1938, it described it. Today we can say that at last the director writes in film. The image—its plastic composition and the way it is set in time, because it is founded on a much higher degree of realism—has at its disposal more means of manipulating reality and of modifying it from within. The filmmaker is no longer the competitor of the painter and the playwright; he is, at last, the equal of the novelist.

NOTES

First appearing in vol. 1 of Qu'est-ce que le cinéma? (Ontologie et langage), (pp. 131–148) this essay is a composite that Bazin made of 3 articles: the first was written for the anniversary volume, *Vingt ans de cinéma à Venise* (1952); the second, entitled, "Le découpage et son Evolution," appeared in n° 93 (July 1955) of *L'Age Nouveau*; and the third appeared in issue no. 1 (1950) of *Cahiers du Cinéma*.

1. The reference to the past twenty years in this essay means generally 1934–54.
2. The reference to the past ten years in this essay means generally 1944–54.
3. See note 2.

Dudley Andrew

André Bazin's "Evolution"

for Angelo Bertocci

The Variable Tasks of Film Theory

"What is cinema?" André Bazin asked in ever-varying ways throughout his brief but concentrated career. It was a question he never expected to answer fully, a question demanding inquiry into technology, the arts, literature, and culture, demanding as well the close scrutiny of films from the full history of cinema across all its modes and genres. In Bazin's hands this question prompted what many consider to be the most brilliant, subtle, and consequential body of writing the cinema engendered in its first century. It was a question that sustained and excited him right up to the moment of his death from leukemia in November 1958. He was forty years old.

Just weeks after his death the December issue of *Cahiers du Cinéma* (no. 91) carried the following appraisals side by side: "La 'Somme' d'André Bazin" by Eric Rohmer and "A Work in Progress" by Georges Sadoul. Crystallized in these titles is the tension that has governed and confounded analysis of Bazin ever since. Rohmer's title invokes St. Thomas Aquinas's *Summa Theologica,* suggesting a magisterial command of a diverse set of questions, organized hierarchically and answered from first principles. Sadoul's, on the other hand, employing an English phrase Bazin himself liked to use, maintains that Bazin ought best be deemed a historian or critic who had little patience with overviews of cinema, but who sought and found value in particular occasions, some of which permitted him to accumulate what he had learned about a phenomenon still in the throes of its early development.

Rohmer appeals to the logical organization that Bazin imposed on the four volumes of *Qu'est-ce que le cinéma?* (all but the first of which were published posthumously).[1] Volume 1 treats cinema's internal aspects—ontology and language in that order—that might be deemed essential to its definition. Ontology addresses the kind of "being" a photographed image is (based on its physical properties and on the physiology and psychology of those looking at it), while language involves the potential for meaning and communication that this new kind of image bears with it or has been asked to serve across the brief history of its existence. Volume 2 approaches the problem from the outside, triangulating the situation of cinema among the other arts as a surveyor might. Volume 3 then turns to patently contextual issues and is subtitled "Cinema and Sociology." Bazin reserved volume 4 as a case study of neorealism, the most important development in sound cinema, and a development that ratified his own treatment of the medium. Here an exemplary contemporary phenomenon could be accounted for by means of the principles developed in the earlier volumes.

Rohmer implies that Bazin did not impose this order hastily atop his essays while searching for the main threads of his thought on his deathbed. Rather he carried this lucid design with him throughout his career, so that it was the design that inspired and animated his hundreds of reviews on apparently throwaway films and his scores of essays on random topics (Rohmer, 95). Nothing is random or thrown away when attached to a master project, and indeed in Bazin's case we can peer behind the most seemingly ephemeral piece in a daily newspaper to discover with him some aesthetic law or trend exposed to full view. "These pieces, all of which were inspired by specific events, were part of the development of a methodical outline that is now becoming apparent. And there is no doubt that they are part of an *outline* established beforehand and not of an argument assembled after the fact" (Rohmer, 95). In short, Rohmer's Bazin is a man whose sense of the cinema preexisted his writing, a man so confident of his position and of the art he loved that he could patiently write of the films that passed through Paris year after year, knowing that in the end his views which apparently followed the natural flow of history would cohere with definite theoretical force.

Rohmer goes further than this, insisting not just on the architecture and logic of Bazin's writings, but on the specific axiom that guarantees the stability of that logic. And he finds it in the title and content of the lead essay of *What Is Cinema?*—the essay on "The Ontology of the Photographic Image" (Bazin 1967): "Each article, but also the whole work, has the rigor of a real mathematical proof. It is true that all of Bazin's work is centered on one idea, the affirmation of cinematic 'objectivity,' but it does so in the same way that geometry centers on the properties of the straight line" (Rohmer, 95).

This "strong" Bazin that Rohmer emphasizes so as to raise his friend above the standard journalism that passed for film studies at the time (but also to anchor his own rigidly realist precepts) is the Bazin who would come under furious attack after 1968, an era that either refused the key idea of "cinematic objectivity" or proclaimed there were many geometric systems beyond that of Euclid (Harvey, 106–8). By defining Bazin's position so clearly, by making his "summa" stand out as a timeless position, Rohmer set his friend up for later theorists, "protestants," we might call them, who bristled at the very idea of a "summa" and who rejected the implications of such a far-reaching theology of the movies.

Although Rohmer insists on Bazin's logic, he praises him for not striving to rewrite Aristotle's *Poetics* for the cinema the way so many aestheticians vainly sought to do in the first era of film studies. Rohmer notes that, following Sartre and Malraux, Bazin was concerned with the "*metaphysical* dimension . . . or if one prefers, the *phenomenological* approach" of an art form that was in full evolution (Rohmer, 97). The term "evolution," on which Rohmer concludes, aligns his Bazin more closely with Sadoul's who, incredulous of systems, never wanted his writing to be more than "work in progress," never entertained a hope of coming to any final or essential formulation about cinema, a phenomenon that he believed to be in permanent evolution, like all things human. A devoted amateur student of botany and zoology, Bazin knew how life scientists track the delicate issue of the identity of species across time and place. (Darwin had had his effect in the humanities too). Bazin, formed during his school years (but in opposition to what was taught in school) by Henri Bergson's philosophy of "creative evolution" and by a proselytizing proponent of Teilhard de Chardin's shockingly new evolutionary theology, shared a discourse of "becoming" that one could read in journals across the disciplines after World War II (Andrew, 19–25; 65–68).

And so how shall we describe Bazin's manner of thinking about the cinema? Rohmer thought of him according to several models: the mathematician working deductively, the life scientist working inductively, the metaphysician, and the phenomenologist. Sadoul adds to this list by providing a pointed epigraph from Jean Renoir: "When they come to write the history of French Art . . . a place of honor will be made for André Bazin, himself an historian" (Sadoul, 46). Meanwhile, Bazin referred to himself as a film critic, never a theorist. Let us not debate the justness of one or the other characterization, for no matter the model, we can applaud Bazin for the rigor and aptness of his output; more important, we can recognize that it was in his calculated mixture of the inductive and deductive, of the phenomenological and the historical, that his writing achieves an unusual resilience and fertility. Here Rohmer was on target to remind us of those explicit debts to Sartre and Malraux.

Although this variety of ways that he can be read subjects any particular account of Bazin to dangerous distortion, let us for convenience initially examine Bazin in theory—with his putative "summa"—and then consider Bazin in history—Bazin as historian—whose work resists summation and, tied to his own era and its particular issues, would ever be self-consciously "in progress." My own sympathy for Bazin[2] results from several factors that it is only fair to state at the outset: a general, though not utter, agreement with his precepts; a distinct preference for the kind of cinema he helped usher in; a moral enthusiasm for the politics of culture he practiced; a fascination with the French cultural ambiance that made his work timely and consequential; a pride that cinema (and essays about cinema) could assume the preeminent status they attained in his era and the period that followed his death; a pleasure in the ingenuity of his essays and the amazing range and brilliance of his style and figures; and—finally, crucially—a ratification of a kind of film scholarship that gives first place to one's instinct for seeing possibilities in films and for identifying films with just such possibilities, an instinct to trust films that initiate and guide whatever it is we might valuably say with, through, or even against them. Before being anything else, Bazin was a superb viewer of movies; his readers may or may not be convinced of his ideas and goals, but anyone who engages with his essays becomes a better, deeper, more articulate viewer. This would surely have gratified him.

Bazin in Theory: The Logic of the "Summa"

Let us begin with Rohmer's observation that, when given the chance in the last year of his life to collect the most important of his writings, Bazin selected a few dozen from well over two thousand pieces and unhesitatingly established the table of contents for *Qu'est-ce que le cinéma?* In a preface he notes the importance of certain short and unassuming essays, comparing them to small pieces in architecture that function as wedges or shims, without which the edifice would crumble into isolated rocks. Some more massive essays, on the other hand, can be seen over time to be dispensable or replaceable (Bazin 1981, 7–8). The cornerstone, the little eight-page essay he chose to situate at the beginning of all his writing, was also the first important piece he ever penned, "The Ontology of the Photographic Image" (Bazin 1967, 9–16). Here he forcefully laid out the axioms that would subtend an entire career of criticism, a career that ingeniously and joyfully explored theorems and corollaries of a demonstrable geometry based on those axioms. And yet, "The Ontology of the Photographic Image" behaves strangely as a foundational essay for any film theory. First of all, it primarily concerns photography and scarcely mentions cinema, bringing it in as an afterthought in a final, startling sentence ("On the other hand, of course, cinema is also a language"); second, the essay's memorable opening seems to deflect inquiry away from ontology to ontology's nemesis: "If the plastic arts were put under psychoanalysis, the practice of embalming the dead might turn out to be a fundamental factor in their creation" (9).

Apparently, to understand "what is cinema" one must understand not the ontology so much as the psychology at play behind both the social function and the personal experience of visual images; moreover, one must understand this psychology to be historically variable, responding to changes in theology, politics, and culture. At one time, for instance in ancient Egypt, human beings evidently believed in the ontological identity of model and image, but no one in our Western culture believes this anymore. Images today are thought to serve symbolic and aesthetic functions, not magical ones; they signify what is important to culture and they do so in styles that lay out values visually. Nevertheless, even sophisticated or decadent cultures have been fascinated by something beyond style, by the possibility of duplicating appearances: "If the history of the plastic arts is less a matter of their aesthetic than of their psychology then it will be seen to be essentially the story of resemblance, or, if you will, of realism" (10).

That history's "most important event" is clearly the invention of photography in the nineteenth century, for a crucial change in the support of images (which might be construed to be "ontological" because material) forced a reconfiguration of the ever-variable "balance between the symbolic and realism" (10), the names that traditionally mark the limits of the functions and experiences offered by images. These oppositions between aesthetics and psychology, and between the symbolic and realism, distinguish photography as a medium from painting; they also distinguish the two great traditions that Bazin uses to organize his understanding of the evolution of the cinema. "I will distinguish . . . between two broad and opposing trends: those directors who put their faith in the image and those who put their faith in reality" (24).

Bazin is often inappropriately accused of being a proponent of a realist style, but realism to him is not primarily an aesthetic or stylistic category. It is an impulse, a goal, a function. He couldn't be more explicit in insisting that "the quarrel over realism in art stems from a misunderstanding . . . between the aesthetic and psychological" (12). Neorealism, he asserts, has nothing in common with the sort of aesthetic realism championed by Zola, and it has nothing to do with "likeness." As he points out, for a long time after the birth of photography, oil paint remained superior in producing likenesses. "A very faithful drawing may actually tell us more about the model but . . . it will never have the irrational power of the photograph to bear away our faith. . . . Hence the charm of family albums. Those grey or sepia shadows, phantomlike and almost undecipherable, are no longer traditional family portraits but rather the disturbing presence of lives halted at a set moment in their duration, freed from their destiny." It comes down to this: "No matter how fuzzy, distorted, or discolored, no matter how lacking in documentary value the [photographic] image may be, it shares, by virtue of the very process of its becoming, the being of the model of which it is the reproduction" (14). The way an image comes into being, then, utterly alters the way we take it in, and in this psychological rather than aesthetic sense photography "satisfied our appetite for illusion by a mechanical reproduction in the making of which man plays no part" (12).

Effectively the photograph brings back the fetish character of the image that it lost in Western culture years ago; by virtue of the indexicality of the photograph, guaranteed by the impression of light on emulsion, the object photographed is felt to be present in the photo. Bazin's marvelous litany of analogies now flows easily: the photograph as fingerprint, as death mask, as the veil of Veronica, and so forth. We accept or even venerate these not because they look like the originals, but because their origin stems from direct contact with the objects they call up. Bazin never returned to photography as a subject, but treated it as part of the DNA of cinema. This may explain the absence in his writing of any consideration of animated cartoons, an image mode that shares cinema's exhibition technology but that in his day depended not on the photographic index but on human talent and imagination in its production.

Animation is a pertinent distinguishing mode, for in our day it has been taken out of the hands of humans and given over to computer algorithms. Thus animation serves cultural functions both more traditional than cinema (the hand of the cartoonist distorting or imitating nature)[3] and more futuristic than cinema (the rotoscoping and digitalizing that replaces photography or manipulates it as in the increasingly sophisticated use of morphing that will surely dominate twenty-first century entertainment images). As the century winds down, so too does the force of the indexical image. Régis Debray's *Vie et mort de l'image* claims that the digital video image has made good on some of the implications Bazin prematurely located in the photograph. If the latter gained an advantage over painting from the "absence of man" (Bazin 1967, 13), the video image must be its apotheosis. Inhuman, cold in their technical perfection, digital images not only ignore the artist; they ignore all reality beyond the televisual. The cinema had certainly demoted the artist in favor of the world which it serves as a decal; but in comparison the video world seems utterly self-contained, autoreferential, and immediate (Debray, 413). Its viewers live with it in their living rooms; TV has become their reality. The film spectator, on the other hand, watches movies in a dark theater that promotes meditation on the reflected images carrying us to a world we believe to be both present and elsewhere. The videosphere has changed all that. Courts no longer accept photographic evidence as they once did; audiences no longer have an implicit faith that the images they consume derive from their referents. Digitalization allows for the indefinite manipulation of the image, including the photographic image, until its indexical function is obliterated. No longer do we pass from the image to the referent that was in some sense responsible for it. Images in the videosphere have no need of a source.

What might Bazin have said of this new step in the evolution of image culture? He would surely have addressed it as a step likely to demote the cinema as the medium of our time. Would he have seen it as a regression to idolatry, as Debray does, where the video image is prized for itself and its instant effect rather than as a double of an absent world existing somewhere outside the theater (Debray, 414)? Bazin was primed to deal with such issues. His film theory begins as an anthropology of shifting image cultures, indebted no doubt to the influential ideas of Malraux and parallel, to some extent, with the slightly earlier notions Walter Benjamin had proposed concerning photography's relation to the arts.[4]

And yet unlike Debray, Benjamin, Marshall McLuhan, and others who speculate long-range on the media, Bazin refused what he felt was the temptation of a simple materialism whereby shifts in technology automatically initiate alterations in the thought and behavior of a culture. In Bazin's view, technology affects culture only after being itself triggered by something first, by the "cultural will," I would term it. His detractors in the 1970s pronounced Bazin's views "idealist" (a word he himself employed on one crucial occasion),[5] since they seem to posit an independent life of the spirit that affects material changes, including the invention of specific technologies. And indeed he was interested in asking why photography came to be invented only in the nineteenth century when so many of its principles had been available to previous eras (Bazin 1967, 17–19). Bazin entertains the idea that culture must itself be cultivated by the arts in specific ways until the taste for something like photography becomes overwhelming enough to promote and reward inventive tinkerers. The historical research of Peter Galassi and Jacques Aumont on the pre-photographic realism in paintings of the eighteenth and early nineteenth centuries, not to mention the growing cultural history of the period emphasizing the expansion of popular needs and tastes, journalism, and so forth, all sustain Bazin's desire to complicate the formula of change.

These abstract speculations about the shifting function of images under the pressure of new technologies and cultural needs resulted in some of Bazin's most important essays on the specificity of cinema in relation to the other arts. Volume 2 of *Qu'est-ce que le cinéma?* consists of the two-part "Theater and Cinema," together with discussions of cinematic adaptations from novels and of the relation of cinema to painting. In all these cases he treats cinema as an addition to cultural production that neither threatens nor dilutes prized masterpieces in other media; in its most interesting moments cinema makes use of culture as it does of phenomena in nature, photographing plays or novels or paintings as it might animals or social rituals. The hybrids that result from this encounter between the aesthetics of a novel and the photographic properties of cinema, as in *Le Journal d'un curé de campagne* (Bresson, 1950), for instance, can be taken as new readings of the original or as new objects altogether, obeying quite rigorous internal laws (Bazin 1967, 142). What in all cases Bazin tried to counter was the pervasive belief that good cinema must turn whatever material it treats into something "cinematic," as though the cinema had already been identified as having properties specific to particular qualities of images (expanse, speed, picturesqueness, and so forth). The only property cinema need adhere to, in his view, is the photographic property of indexicality that puts us in touch with the original. In the case of making a movie using paintings as his material, Alain Resnais filmed Van Gogh's oeuvre "as freely as in any ordinary documentary . . . [with] a realism once removed, following upon the abstraction that is the painting" (Bazin 1967, 166–67). "Filmed theater," to take another example, need not be a term of opprobrium, since Cocteau proved that the stagy films of his plays amplified the dramatic effects he had conceived for the theater (Bazin 1967, 112). Via the cinema, twentieth-century audiences can rediscover classic and modern plays, whereas via the theater, the cinema discovers new capabilities and a prowess it hadn't been aware of previously.

The photographic axioms at the heart of cinema situate the medium at a certain phase within the "destiny of culture" (as Malraux would have it), differentiating it from the Renaissance phase before it (the era of oil painting) and the postmodern phase we have entered (the era of the digital image) (Debray 292). Within this period of the photographic, however, Bazin was far less inclined than most other theorists to identify any a priori aspects of the cinema. The photographic axioms provide cinema with only a quasi-identity, whose essence, scarcely describable in itself, adapts to historical circumstances. Bazin, the amateur botanist, sought to establish the specific shape and power of films or, more pertinently, genres, by examining the specific historical terrain upon which they grow. Genres can be understood as the successful adaptations of cinema to the cultural and cinematic conditions operating in a given moment or period. Bazin wrote brilliantly on the western, for example, tracking its continuities and changes through mutations in society, in cinematic fashion, and in the genre itself which, after a time, can take on its own identity as a kind of organism that grows to maturity and eventually decays (Bazin 1971). Bazin appreciated decadent as well as youthful and classic westerns; in fact, it was the entire process of generic and cultural evolution that he appreciated. When he criticized a film, he cared mainly to point not to its "intrinsic worth" (which most likely he had no belief in) but to its timeliness or inappropriateness. Aside from the photographic axiom, he maintained no timeless standards that all films must measure up to.

This doesn't mean that a film may do as it pleases. In fact every film can be measured by the regulations tied to the project to which it implicitly belongs. In one of his most clever essays, "The Virtues and Limitations of Montage," Bazin applied the characteristics he identified in "The Evolution of the Language of Cinema" to the minor genre of the children's film. In this case, the genre was not treated as an evolving organism but as a constant human impulse: people of all eras and cultures entertain children with fabulous tales. Bazin reasoned that in the cinema certain laws—or, more precisely, certain limits—of montage promote or defeat the effect of "the marvelous" aimed at by the genre. One cannot, for the sake of eloquence or convenience, cut into the space of the marvelous without turning it into mere cinematic spectacle. While watching a conjurer work, the spectator at a live magic show stares without blinking in an effort to note the moment when reality is tricked; were a filmmaker to shoot the trick from multiple angles, editing it for the best view, who would believe in the magic (Bazin 1967, 51)?

Films of magic and fairy tales are two subgenres of the marvelous where rules of editing derive from a relation between psychological and aesthetic factors. Rules governing other genres follow. Some, like restrictions of shot changes in slapstick comedy, seem relatively stable across time; others—for instance, the prohibition against reconstructed events in newsreels—are less permanent. At certain times in film history audiences were convinced by reconstructions, either because they were gullible or because reconstructions served an intermediate function between reportage and fictionalized history. Today's docu-dramas that show up on television within months of the sensational issues they represent are a contemporary example of this mixed form.

Even were we to discover all the laws of cinema that govern its more timeless generic functions, however, we would scarcely have answered the driving question, "what is cinema?" Moreover, we would have characterized cinema only insofar as it takes up cultural functions (fairy tales, physical comedy) that preexisted it. When it comes to understanding what cinema has added to cultural history, Bazin is certain that only local laws prevail and that, whatever cinema is, it evolves in contact with shifting cultural needs and situations. Cinema's stable photographic axiom together with the few corollaries demanded by stable genres interact in myriad ways in history, and they do so in an evolutionary manner.

The bulk of Bazin's reviews and essays tacitly trace this interaction that he called "the evolution of the language of cinema." They accumulate evidence from current and older films that can help us see the development not of cinema as an abstract potential, but of the multiple species of films that have flourished and survived. The thickest branch on this evolutionary tree has grown in the United States, from the proscenium framing of the earliest films and even of slapstick, to the narrative space pioneered by Griffith, to the invisible, psychologically motivated editing of the classical Hollywood style. European alternatives pushed the silent film to a level of great graphic eloquence either through what Bazin termed deformation of "the plastics of the image" in the case of German Expressionism or through the kind of muscular montage by which the Soviets ripped images out of their spatial and temporal continuity to develop strings of association producing metaphors and other figures that permit discursive complexity (Bazin 1967, 26).

The era during which Bazin wrote, from the outset of World War II up to the New Wave, saw an important evolution away from what he described as the efficient representation of clever scenarios and toward the carving of stories out of a deeper, thicker, more complex space. There were precedents for the primacy of space in silent masterpieces by Flaherty, Murnau, and von Stroheim. Virtually submerged during the 1930s—except for the luminous Jean Renoir—this strain suddenly burst again into bloom with *Citizen Kane* and then in Italy with neorealism (Bazin 1967, 37). Using his intuitions about the variable ratio of space to script, Bazin traced the Darwinian struggle for survival of many species of film, often isolating conflicting impulses in a single movie.

The richness of Bazin's conception of cinema stems from the interpenetration of style and matter that he so ingeniously observed and even more ingeniously described in the hundreds of films he treated. Because of the photographic axiom, cinema—more than the other arts—adjusts itself to, and is altered by, the projects it is asked to take up. When the Second World War brought new material to represent, the cinema responded with an enlarged set of codes (particularly governing the documentary) and with new technologies of representation. When a trend developed after 1945 to adapt first-person novels (in American film noir, as in *La Symphonie pastorale* [1946], *Le Silence de la mer* [1947], and of course *Le Journal d'un curé de compagne* [1950]), sound and image relations needed to be radically readjusted to deliver subjectivity, reflection, and perception in new ways. Bazin became the leading theorist of these postwar developments, elaborating Alexandre Astruc's famous 1948 plea for "la caméra-stylo," that is, for an approach to cinema that would be as supple as a writer's approach to his or her projects. Bazin's "Evolution of the Language of Cinema" concludes by suggesting that the new realist impulse in cinema has made the filmmaker the "equal of the novelist" (40) in that the ability to carve stories out of complex space invites the spectator to view the world in a new way, inflected—but not utterly dominated—by the consciousness of the artist through which it is filtered. Space is thus respected, as is the artist's vision of things. As for the spectator, the complexity of the world represented and of the vision of it that the filmmaker holds out produces a shimmering perception of reality that is properly "ambiguous" and full of "mystery" and revelation. Cinema reveals to the anxious and alert spectator a world alive with possibilities, where perception results in care and where aesthetics finds its fulfillment in morality.

Bazin was led to such far-reaching conclusions about the power of cinema by trailing those postwar films that so excited him. How appropriate, then (and how "logical," Rohmer would say), that Bazin's "summa" should conclude with his vivid "Defense of Rossellini" (Bazin

1971, 93). Especially in the Ingrid Bergman films (*Stromboli* [1950], *Europa 51* [1952], and unforgettably *Viaggio in Italia* [1953]) Rossellini's phenomenological description of postwar Europe challenged the cinema, the spectator, and Western culture in a manner that was absolutely modern, on the cutting edge of aesthetics, philosophy, and religion. Rossellini became Bazin's most powerful and elegant "demonstration" of cinema's fundamental axioms and of its transcendent consequences.

Bazin in History

When one speculates on the cultural significance of film theorists, Sergei Eisenstein remains Bazin's only competitor. The journal Bazin cofounded and over which he maintained a moral authority well after his death, *Cahiers du Cinéma*, shaped more than one generation of filmmakers, scholars, and viewers. It was Bazin who brought Truffaut and Godard in contact with Rossellini and Renoir. It was on the shoulders of Bazin and the kind of filmmaking he championed that the New Wave developed first in France as a vibrant new aesthetic, and then, more politically, in many places around the world. The auteur policy, often credited to him, has dominated film studies even if it has come under serious scrutiny, and even if he himself questioned its priority (Graham, 135ff.). For anyone concerned with the question the title of his collected works asks, Bazin has been quite simply unavoidable.

He has also, by that fact, been controversial. During his lifetime, heated arguments cropped up at *Ecran Français*, the leftist weekly he contributed to until it shifted to a trenchantly Stalinist position when the Marshall Plan polarized Europe. The value of American filmmakers like Hitchcock and Welles was at stake, as was the value of refined analysis of mise-en-scène. Bazin left the journal just before publishing his most controversial piece, "The Myth of Stalin in the Soviet Cinema."[6] A daring essay in any case, early in 1950 it begged for a fight; yet the arguments he attracted were purely political, and no one questioned the aesthetic principles that had led him to deliver his judgment against recent Soviet filmmaking. This political tenor would color debates surrounding Bazin after his death and after the startling rise to fame of his New Wave progeny. *Positif*, the rival journal to *Cahiers du Cinéma*, ridiculed key Bazinian concepts—especially "ambiguity" and "revelation"—since these had become touchstones in the often vapid auteurist criticism practiced by Bazin's followers (Graham, 52ff.). Bazin's Catholicism was blamed for the frequently adolescent concerns and the social apathy of Truffaut, Chabrol, and even the early Godard,[7] a curious charge since he practiced as well as held progressive political beliefs (Andrew, 82–95) and cautioned

his followers to be wary of the rugged individualism implicit in their auteurist creed.

More theoretical objections, however, have been harder for
Bazinians to shake. Reviewing *What Is Cinema?* in 1968, Annette
Michelson questioned Bazin's aesthetic, rather than political, parochial-
ism.[8] Semiotics (which had come into fashion in the ten years since he
died) would have shown Bazin that his obsession with realism accounts
for but half the capability of any language form. Here she took up a line of
thought Jean Mitry had initiated in 1963, and she would be followed by
Peter Wollen and others, all of whom questioned Bazin's refusal to truly
acknowledge the linguistic, constructed aspect of cinema.[9] At best Bazin
theorized the metonymic pole of the cinematic sign system, refusing to
countenance the metaphoric pole. Hence his penchant for realist films
and his disdain for such abstractions as could be created through montage. Noël Carroll would return to this theme in 1989 in the most sustained attack on Bazin's theory, an attack waged not under the banner of
semiotics, a "science" that today seems hopelessly incapable of coming
to terms with cinema, but under that of aesthetics.[10]

All these quarrels—whether political, semiotic, or aesthetic—reject Bazin's insistence on the prelinguistic substratum of cinema's photographic base. Where his opponents define cinema as they would any other
art or medium of communication (though recognizing it as the most significant one operating in the twentieth century), Bazin holds that cinema
really is something new, drawing its peculiar power from its intermediate
status between ontology and language, between being and meaning. Its
automatic capture of audiovisual moments[11] affects all films that use the
photographic process, whether they take advantage of it or not, and this
includes educational and children's fare, home movies, art films, and the
full range of fictional genres. Insisting that cinema's power lies in the extremes of life and death (the spontaneous animation of filmed events on
the one hand and the mummy complex on the other),[12] Bazin could only
scandalize Mitry, Carroll, and anyone for whom cinema is to be fully explained as a cultural phenomenon. Individual movies, in a view that has
been characterized as "naive" or "extreme," mediate this indigestible
core of experience that motion photography automatically accesses. His
criticism aims to bring out this dialectic, visible in the most telling of
films, between cultural meaning (what he and many semioticians call
"language") and a perceptual and experiential plenum.

Unquestionably the most influential attack on this radical notion
in Bazin came from the self-proclaimed "radical" critics in France after
May 1968. In one sense they picked up *Positif*'s party line. No matter how
politically correct Bazin may have been in his life and beliefs, no matter
how subtle in his political acumen, he had become the figurehead whose
reputation and authority propped up New Wave criticism and New Wave
films, and these could readily be excoriated as Romantic and regressive. In

1968, this was an embarrassment to the new and militant administration of Bazin's own journal, *Cahiers*. They struck hard at him and at Eric Rohmer, whom they considered his heir. In the wake of the heady social movement of the day and under the tutelage of Louis Althusser, *Cahiers* and *Cinéthique* in France, followed by *Screen* in England, rebuked Bazin in the name of materialism; they proclaimed the death of the auteur in favor of cultural praxis; and they replaced *Cahier*'s former hierarchy of films based on aesthetic value with one based on political efficacy.[13] The concept of "ideology," a term conspicuously absent in Bazin, took them beyond the arena of mere political altercation where *Positif* had flailed at him. Ideology became the cornerstone subtending a new orthodoxy in film theory that reigned into the 1980s during the nadir of Bazin's influence.

Althusser's brand of Marxism drove Jean-Louis Baudry, Marcelyn Pleynet, Jean-Louis Comolli, Jean Narboni, and an army of other materialist film theorists to insist on the constructed (hence, negotiable) nature not just of culture, but of technology and even of perception, the zone Bazin[14] held to be potentially pristine. In the orthodoxy of the 1970s, the cinema is through and through a tool of the ruling (bourgeois) class because it "naturally" centers the passive viewer before a spectacle laid out as a visual possession. The cinema plays a major role in constructing the very subjectivity of those who watch it, preparing them to replicate the social relations that keep bourgeois culture in place. Bazin's image theory as well as his political instincts misunderstand this, coming as they do from Sartrean principles that emphasize freedom. He had no idea that a complex ideology stands between the human being as viewer and the world viewed either in nature or on the screen. Nor did he understand the material power struggle behind the invention of cinema in the nineteenth century and the perfection of "machines of the visible," as Comolli called them so as to emphasize their insidious aspect.[15] The cinema indeed evolves, but not innocently toward greater realism; rather it evolves the better to serve a cultural power elite by progressively enervating those who watch it.[16]

Sometimes one can best measure the strength of a thinker by the vehemence of the attacks he or she is subject to later on. André Bazin occasioned such a stream of virulent responses after 1968 that his thought must have weighed heavily on those needing to throw off that weight so as to undertake a kind of thinking proper to their generation. Perhaps many were jealous of his times and of the niche he had carved out for himself within those times. His opponents living in the TV age found themselves competing in noisy journals, conferences, and classrooms with other film scholars hoping to have the kind of effect on cinema that Bazin had been able to claim with such apparent ease in what was more clearly the age of cinema. Writing before the assimilation of "cinema studies" into the academy, writing before the era when one needed to marshall a methodology, writing even before the era of the extended exegesis (his 1950 *Orson Welles* stands among the first monographs on a director), Bazin grew up during the heyday of the classical Hollywood cinema and began to write at the very moment when serious alternatives to that system looked for heroic champions. He proved to be a modest champion, but behind him rode the vainglorious knights of *Cahiers du Cinéma.*

Of course not just anyone could take on the mantle of champion. It required more than intelligence and an engaging style; more too than a passion for cinema; it required a specific cultural background with an attendant agenda. This, as much as anything, his later critics targeted. Because tied to a dated discourse, Bazin—or at least his thought—can be diminished by being shown to be determined; more important, the consequences of his beliefs can be largely circumscribed by the historical situation that engendered them. Historical materialism liberates one in this way from one's inconvenient predecessors. Bazin was forcibly removed as an impediment to the post-1968 political agenda of cinema studies. Was it too much to expect those who removed him to realize that the same historical contingency governed their own efforts? Did they not know that within a decade other commentators would analyze the rhetorical context that required them to have written with such virulence?

Yet the historicity of culture—as Bazin and orthodox Marxists alike would agree—need not thereby escape the grasp of understanding. Culture follows laws that Bazin spoke of again and again as evolutionary. And if some law akin to Heisenberg's uncertainty principle obfuscates a clear vision of the cinema by any of its commentators, one need not give up the game of theory altogether. In physics as in film studies one must be sensitive to the rhetoric of inquiry and to the politics of knowledge while engaging precisely in an adventure of inquiry and knowledge.

We should not forget that while Bazin may have authored one of the first auteurist books, he also cautioned his disciples at *Cahiers* against the excesses of a "politique des auteurs" (Graham, 137ff.). Keep in mind the cultural determinants, he warned them, including genre, studio, technology, and other production and reception constraints. Film history may be most clearly, conveniently, and dramatically understood via the names of directors signing the films that mark high points and turning points, but a complex ecology sustains every film and every filmmaker. Bazin did not claim we might achieve a comprehensive view from outside the system to oppose to the value-laden apology for certain films and auteurs; rather, he argued that every critical endeavor is perforce value-laden, situated inside the system it hopes to understand and in some way promote.[17] Bazin's life philosophy, essentially hermeneutic, could be termed a project of understanding human processes that itself, in turn, contributes to those processes, since human knowledge is knowledge ever catching up with its object.

Bazin was essentially a theorist embodying the historicist assumptions of his day. Philip Rosen has tied his style of thinking precisely to the intensified time-consciousness of European intellectuals since 1850. As in phenomenology, Bazin relied on very few first principles; symptomatically his chief axiom, stemming from the mummy complex, was part of a 19th century obsession with preserving time. "To read Bazin is to constantly encounter privileged nineteenth-century discoveries and disciplines, from the evolutionary and dialectical approaches in his historical formulations, to the archeological and geological comparisons that mark both his literary and cognitive style" (Rosen, 28).

And so Bazin can be seen as part of his historical moment by being viewed as a historical thinker who took evolution as an unwavering principle. Even, indeed especially, his relation with a journal tellingly named *Les Temps Modernes* marks him as historical and historicist. This was the one journal every European intellectual had to read after World War II just to participate in the discussions of the era; and, while it propounded the existential Marxism of its illustrious founders Jean-Paul Sartre and Maurice Merleau-Ponty, it provided a certain leadership for the new humanisms that were becoming the vogue, including the progressive, evolutionary Catholicism Bazin contributed to (Andrew, 19–37). Sartre, a towering intellectual presence at the peak of his fame, flattered Bazin by clandestinely attending his ciné-club during the Occupation and later by commissioning several important articles from him for *Les Temps Modernes*. It was a heady moment for cinema, for leftist culture, and for philosophy, and Bazin must have felt that a certain notion of "becoming" was itself coming into being. He wanted desperately to contribute to the emerging current of thought by treating a medium of "becoming" (which cinema had been termed) not in an essentialist but in an evolutionary way. It was to broaden Sartre's project that he paraphrased the philosopher in proclaiming his own mission: "We must say of the cinema that its existence precedes its essence; even in his most adventurous extrapolations, it is this existence from which the critic must take his point of departure" (Bazin 1967, 71).

Such "ciné-existentialism" may have prevented Bazin from writing a grand treatise on the medium, and certainly made him the target of other critics, such as Annette Michelson, who feel his thought to be circumscribed by the concerns of his era and therefore unresponsive to other moments when cinema has been or might be called on to serve other functions. Specifically, she claims that Bazin's allergy to montage may have been proper to the era of neorealism but it ignores the incredible service of cinema to the revolutionary aesthetics of the early Soviet Union and to the generation of 1968 headed by Godard. Bazin's attitude has been called that of a critic and a historian with a theoretical bent rather than that of a theorist pure and simple. But one must admit that his belief that films precede a theory of cinema helped him avoid the pomposity of abstract aesthetic reflection on the media. It also led him to trace the cinematic impulse not just in the artistic films he saw at festivals but wherever its presence might be tangibly felt: in nineteenth-century science and popular culture, in the architecture of theaters, in low genres like the travel film, in adaptations from fiction and the stage.

Whereas most theorists rooted in the silent era (Munsterberg, Vertov, Arnheim, Lindsay, Pudovkin, and even Eisenstein) as well as serious critics of the 1920s (Gance, Epstein, Delluc) wrote of "pure cinema, "essential cinema," the "laws" of the medium, Bazin—theorist of that clumsy amalgam which is the sound film—felt it was premature to think of cinema so much in the abstract. Cinema is, after all, less than a century old. Its aesthetics are a mad mixture of aspects taken from many arts, not to mention the low entertainments of melodramatic theater, the dime novel, and the music hall. Georges Sadoul put it this way: a theory of the cinema ought to be analogous not to a theory of literature but to a theory of the printing press, and it ought to cover every sort of text produced and consumed by its machinery (Sadoul, 48). Bazin's perspective went well beyond that of art; it opened onto aspects of cinema at once more general than media aesthetics (the psychology of perception and narration) and more aware of the historically particular (the sociology of melodrama and the star system, not to mention the economics of capital investment and marketing). Within this history, Bazin attempted to observe and calculate the ecological factors that governed whatever it is that cinema is and might be.

If he has returned again to a certain prominence, it may be because intellectual fashions have again changed. The rigorous Marxism of the late 1960s and 1970s, with its call for purity of intention and effect, has been replaced by an indulgent postmodernism fascinated by cultural hybrids. Bazin, it is increasingly evident, believed the cinema to be essentially impure. He would have dwelt on the films of Hans-Jürgen Syberberg and on the imploded genres of the 1990s, like neo-noir.

Decidedly he would have been at home with the film theories of Gilles Deleuze, who in fact opens the second volume of his film theory by directly citing Bazin (Deleuze, 1). Deleuze's impressive project opposes a classical, organic "movement-image" in the prewar era to a modern, "time-image" that became possible during and after the war. This is precisely a reformulation of Bazin's prescient view of the utterly new cinema constituted by the appearance of *La Règle du jeu, Citizen Kane*, and Rossellini. Deleuze pushes beyond Bazin's dialectical sense of the evolution of cinema as new forms respond to new material, but he pushes in the same direction.

This is the direction likewise followed by the writer who can most legitimately lay claim to Bazin's heritage and reputation: Serge Daney.

Coming to love the cinema explicitly through *Cahiers du Cinéma* and Rossellini, Daney's film criticism ever urged the "morality of style." His famous slap at Gilles Pontecorvo's *Kapo*, a fictional reconstruction of the concentration camps, turned on the immorality of a single track-in that effectively aestheticized a moment of horror, making it dramatic and picturesque (Daney, 15ff.). Drawing on Alain Resnais' *Nuit et brouillard* (1955) and echoing Theodor Adorno, Daney argued that aesthetics was forever changed, perhaps destroyed, by the Holocaust. World War II may mark the onset of the modern cinema because it marks the end of a rational or classical view of civilization.

Daney left *Cahiers du Cinéma* in the 1980s and turned increasingly toward television. His many essays on the videosphere take up the kind of thinking about images in culture Bazin brought to such a level of sophistication. Daney most pertinently reminds one of Bazin in the manner by which both men were so able to track the crucial shifts of their respective image cultures (Bazin from classical to modern cinema, Daney from the era of cinema to that of television) from within, and to do so by the ingenious observation of symptoms in the details of the visual phenomena they so obviously loved to write about.[18]

In the end, Bazin's importance goes far beyond his "summa"; it goes even beyond the remarkable evolutionary vision he has provided of the cinema and of the postwar period he chronicled; it reaches furthest when it reaches a spirit like Daney's that knows how to see, to think, and to write in a reflex that the cinema somehow seems to have inspired. What is the cinema to be able to light up eyes and minds in such a way? What, indeed, is cinema?

NOTES

1. *Qu'est-ce que le cinéma?* appeared serially as "Ontologie et langage" (1958), "Le Cinéma et les autres arts" (1959), "Le Cinéma et sociologie" (1960), and "Le Neoréalisme italien" (1962). In 1981, these four volumes were consolidated into a single volume from which some articles were excised. The English translation by Hugh Gray, *What Is Cinema?* (University of California Press, 1967), is a selection of eleven essays, all but one of which come from the first two French volumes. In 1971, Gray brought out volume 2 of *What Is Cinema?* (University of California Press), translating essays from volumes 3 and 4 of the French. Bazin did not oversee the several other collections that have appeared in both French and English (on Chaplin, Renoir, *French Cinema of the Occupation and Resistance*, *Le Cinéma français de la libération à la nouvelle vague, The Cinema of Cruelty,* and the expanded edition of the Orson Welles monograph).

2. My biography, *André Bazin* (1978, 1990), aims to make palpable these various attractions by situating his ideas within a vibrant cultural climate (philosophical, artistic, political, religious).

3. Donald Crafton (1990) reminds us that the inventor of animation, Emile Cohl, had been a prominent caricaturist at the end of the nineteenth century, not unlike his predecessor Daumier.

Dudley Andrew

4. Walter Benjamin's famous "Work of Art in the Age of Mechanical Reproduction," in *Illuminations* (New York: Schocken, 1968), was written in 1936 but was not in circulation in France during Bazin's lifetime. André Malraux, on the other hand, was well known to Bazin. Bazin participated in a Malraux study group during the war. Malraux had published his brief film theory, "Esquisse d'une psychologie du cinéma," in 1940. More important, he had written articles and lectured on the evolution of art in preparation for the multivolume *Museum without Walls* that began to appear in 1947.

5. The term "idealistic" is used, in the standard English translation (Bazin 1967, 17), but his French word is *idéaliste* and is used as part of a daring antimaterialist, anti-Marxist argument (Bazin 1981, 19).

6. Bazin, "The Myth of Stalin in the Soviet Cinema," trans. with an introduction by Dudley Andrew in Bill Nichols, *Movies and Methods* (Berkeley: University of California Press, 1985), 2:29–39.

7. After the New Wave had crested, a few American critics joined in these charges. An especially strong essay came from John Hess, *Jump Cut* 1 (1971).

8. Annette Michelson in *Artforum* 6, no. 10 (1968): 66–71.

9. See section 48 of the first volume of Mitry's *Esthétique et psychologie du cinéma* (Paris: Editions Universitaires, 1963). Peter Wollen's remarks on Bazin can be found in the chapters "*Citizen Kane*" and "'Ontology' and 'Materialism' in Film Theory," in his *Readings and Writings: Semiotic Counter-strategies* (London: Verso, 1982).

10. Noël Carroll, *Philosophical Problems in Classical Film Theory* (Princeton, N.J.: Princeton University Press, 1989). Carroll separates the undeniable value of Bazin's critical and historical observations from the more disputable anthropological and aesthetic ones. Bazin's tendency to see cinema in evolution, rather than in essence, may protect him and his views from distortion by his friends (Rohmer) and his later detractors (Carroll). My brief overview here, meant to present and bring coherence to Bazin's stunning but disorderly array of ideas, allows no space to develop and dispute the considered contestations of Carroll and others.

11. The nature of the "automatic" is addressed by Noël Carroll (*Philosophical Problems*) and David Brubaker, "André Bazin on Automatically Made Images," *Journal of Aesthetics and Art Criticism* 51, no. 1 (Winter 1993). In a different key, Stanley Cavell takes up "automaticity" in *The World Viewed* (Cambridge, Mass.: Harvard University Press, 1971). Unfortunately, the complexity of the debate involving all these writers makes it impossible to treat them here.

12. See especially his essay, "Mort tout les après-midis," in *Qu'est-ce que le cinéma*, *I*, where he talks of the objectivity of cinema confronting the pure subjectivity of the moment of death.

13. For an extended discussion of this period, see Sylvia Harvey, *May '68 and Film Culture* (London: BFI, 1984) and *Cahiers du Cinéma 1968–1972*, ed. Nick Browne (Cambridge, Mass.: Harvard University Press, 1992).

14. The tone and much of the substance of this view can be found in sections of Christopher Williams's *Realism in the Cinema* (London: BFI, 1978).

15. Jean-Louis Comolli, "Machines of the Visible," in *The Cinematic Apparatus*, ed. Teresa De Lauretis and Stephen Heath (New York: St. Martin's, 1981).

16. Even this heated rhetoric betrays continuity between Bazin and the editors of the radicalized *Cahiers du Cinéma*. Like Bazin, Comolli wants cinema to reveal the hidden nature of the visible, though for him this nature consists of invisible social relations. Like Bazin, Comolli and Narboni maintain the priority of complex films and of complex readings of them. The most famous piece of *Cahiers* criticism of that period, on John Ford's *Young Mr. Lincoln*, is reminiscent of one of Bazin's venturesome readings of key movies.

17. Here Bazin seems most at odds with Noël Carroll, who insists that every serious theory must stand outside its object and describe all its possibilities.

18. It is worth pointing out that in turning toward television, Davey still continued the *Cahiers* tradition, since the original subtitle of that journal ("Revue du cinéma et du

télécinéma"] reflected an interest in television too. By issue no. 49 (July 1955), *Cahiers* dropped television from its mantle, becoming simply a "Revue mensuelle du cinéma." Throughout the 1950s, Bazin wrote a great many essays on TV, and contributed often to a journal such as *Radio-Cinéma-Télévision.*

WORKS CITED

Andrew, Dudley. *André Bazin.* New York: Columbia University Press, 1990 [1978].
Aumont, Jacques. *L'Oeil interminable.* Paris: Seguier, 1989.
Bazin, André. *Orson Welles.* Trans. Jonathan Rosenbaum. Venice, Calif.: Acrobat, 1991.
———. *Qu'est-ce que le cinéma?* Paris: Cerf, 1981.
———. "The Stalin Myth in the Soviet Cinema." In *Movies and Methods.* Ed. Bill Nichols. Berkeley: University of California Press, 1985 2:29–39.
———. *What Is Cinema, I?* Berkeley: University of California Press, 1967.
———. *What Is Cinema, II?* Berkeley: University of California Press, 1971.
Cahiers du Cinéma, 1950s. Ed. Jim Hillier. Cambridge, Mass.: Harvard University Press, 1990.
Cahiers du Cinéma, 1969–1972. Ed. Nick Browne. Cambridge, Mass.: Harvard University Press, 1990.
Carroll, Noël. *Philosophical Problems of Classical Film Theory.* Princeton, N.J.: Princeton University Press, 1988.
Crafton, Donald. *Emile Cohl, Caricature, and Film.* Princeton, N.J.: Princeton University Press, 1990.
Daney, Serge. *Persévérence.* Paris: P.O.L., 1994.
Debray, Régis. *Vie et mort de l'image.* Paris: Gallimard, 1992.
Deleuze, Gilles. *Cinema 2: The Time-Image.* Minneapolis: University of Minnesota Press, 1989.
Galassi, Peter. *Before Photography: Painting and the Invention of Photography.* New York: Museum of Modern Art, 1981.
Graham, Peter, ed. *The New Wave.* Garden City, N.Y.: Doubleday, 1968.
Harvey, Sylvia. *May '68 and Film Culture.* London: British Film Institute, 1978.
Rohmer, Eric. "La 'Somme' d'André Bazin." *Cahiers du Cinéma,* no. 91, December 1958. Translated in idem, *A Taste for Beauty.* New York: Cambridge University Press, 1989. (Page references are to the English edition.)
Rosen, Philip. "History of Image, Image of History: Subject and Ontology in Bazin." *Wide Angle 9,* no. 4 (Winter 1987).
Sadoul, Georges. "A Work in Progress." *Cahiers du Cinéma,* no. 91, December 1958.

Compiled by Sally Shafto

SELECT BIBLIOGRAPHY OF WRITINGS
BY ANDRÉ BAZIN AND WRITINGS ON ANDRÉ BAZIN

The first bibliography includes only Bazin's monographs and edited volumes, and therefore represents but a modest portion of his prodigious output between 1943 and his death in 1958. His more than two thousand articles appeared in such publications as *L'Ecran Français, Le Parisien Libéré, Radio-Cinéma-Télévision, L'Observateur,* and, of course, *Cahiers du Cinéma.* The entries are organized in the order in which they first appeared, occasionally including a later French edition in brackets if there were textual changes (see the Welles entry). When an English translation exists, it has been cited with the French original. Unless otherwise noted, Bazin is the sole author.

Much of Bazin's writing appeared posthumously, and it is worth recalling that his coming-into-print coincides with the entry of film studies into the university curriculum.

The prediction made in one of his earliest articles that Ph.D. dissertations on the cinema would one day be written has certainly come true (qtd. Andrew 1978, xiv). To date there have been ten dissertations addressing his ideas on cinema. It has been said that Bazin was not a synoptic thinker, and he has often been faulted for precisely this reason. Dudley Andrew suggests that he was a sociable thinker: one whose profound engagement not just with films but also with people kept him from sequestering himself to write theory from on high (Andrew 1976, 135). Perhaps, too, the precariousness of his livelihood kept him on the move, firing off article after article. Likewise the acute reality of his physical condition and the certainty of its outcome may have made him seek out human companionship. If the title of his project series (*Qu'est-ce que le cinéma?*), on the one hand, intimates a desire to provide a primer, revealing Bazin's pedagogic mission, then the subtitle of volume 1 ("Ontologie et langage"), on the other hand, suggests an ambition to situate cinema within philosophical discourse. Volume 1 of *Qu'est-ce que le cinéma?* appeared before Bazin's death on November 11, 1958, and while today we are accustomed to seeing the weekly reviews of Pauline Kael, Stanley Kauffmann, and Jonathan Rosenbaum subsequently published in an anthology, Bazin was one of the first critics to collect his ephemeral pieces. That the publication of his writings continued after his death we owe largely to the efforts of his adoptive son and colleague at *Cahiers*, François Truffaut. Other filmmakers besides Truffaut have paid tribute to Bazin, and if in the recent past it has seemed easy to dismiss his idealism and humanism, there still can be no doubt as to the extent of his contribution and his influence. The second bibliography attests to this truth. Film theorists—like works of art—exist in time.

Monographs and Anthologies by André Bazin

1950   Bazin, André, and Jean Cocteau. *Orson Welles*. Paris: Edition le Chavanne. 64 pp. [Bazin, André. *Orson Welles*. Préface de André S. Labarthe. Collection "7ᵉ art." Paris: Editions du Cerf, 1972. 219 pp.]

Bazin, André. *Orson Welles: A Critical View*. Foreword by François Truffaut. Profile by Jean Cocteau. Trans. from the French by Jonathan Rosenbaum. New York: Harper & Row, 1978; Los Angeles: Acrobat, 1991. 138 pp.

1953   *Vittorio de Sica*. Con una nota di Guido Aristarco. Nota biografica, filmografia e bibliografia a cura di Gianfrano Calderoni. Parma: Guanda. 78 pp.

No English translation.

1958–1962

Q'est-ce que le cinéma? vol. 1: *Ontologie et langage* (1958); vol. 2: *Le cinéma et les autres arts* (1959); vol. 3: *Cinéma et sociologie* (1961); vol. 4: *Une esthétique de la réalité: Le Néo-réalisme* (1962). Collection "7ᵉ art." Paris: Editions du Cerf.

What Is Cinema? vol. 1. Essays selected and translated by Hugh Gray. Foreword by Jean Renoir. Berkeley: University of California Press, 1967.

1971   *What Is Cinema?* vol. 2. Essay selected and translated by Hugh Gray. Foreword by François Truffaut. Berkeley: University of California Press.

Jean Renoir. Préface de François Truffaut. Paris: Editions Champ Libre.

Jean Renoir. Edited, and with an introduction by François Truffaut. Translated from the French by W. W. Halsey II and William H. Simon. Introduction by Jean Renoir. New York: Da Capo, 1992 (c. 1973).

1972   Bazin, André, and Eric Rohmer. *Charlie Chaplin*. Préface de François Truffaut. Paris: Editions du Cerf; Paris: Ramsay, 1990. 123 pp.

Essays on Chaplin. With contributions by François Truffaut, Jean Renoir, and Eric Rohmer. Edited and translated by Jean Bodon. Preface by François Truffaut. New Haven, Conn.: University of New Haven Press, 1985. 125 pp.

1975   *Le Cinéma de l'Occupation et de la Résistance.* Préface de François Truffaut. Paris: Union générale d'édition.

    French Cinema of the Occupation and Resistance: The Birth of a Critical Esthetic. Collected and with an introduction by François Truffaut. Translated by Stanley Hochman. New York: Frederick Ungar, 1981. 166 pp.

1975   *Le Cinéma de la cruauté: Eric Von Stroheim, Carl Th. Dreyer, Preston Sturges, Luis Buñuel, Alfred Hitchcock, Akira Kurosawa.* Préface de François Truffaut. Paris: Flammarion. 224 pp.

    The Cinema of Cruelty: From Buñuel to Hitchcock. Edited and with an introduction by François Truffaut. Translated by Sabine d'Estree with the assistance of Tiffany Fliss. New York: Seaver, 1982. 204 pp.

1983   *Le Cinéma français de la libération à la nouvelle vague (1945–1958).* Textes réunis et préface par Jean Narboni. Paris: Editions de L'Etoile. 255 pp.

    No English translation.

1984   Bazin, André, et al. *La Politique des auteurs: Entretiens avec Jean Renoir* [et al.]. Préface de Serge Daney. Paris: Editions Champ Libre. 331 pp.

    No English translation.

1996   *Bazin at Work: Major Essays and Reviews from the Forties and Fifties.* Translated from the French by Alain Piette and Bert Cardullo. Edited by Bert Cardullo. New York: Routledge. 252 pp.

Critical Writings on André Bazin in English

1959   Roud, Richard. "Face to Face: André Bazin." *Sight and Sound* 28, nos. 3–4 (Summer–Autumn): 176–79.

1968   Gozlan, Gérard. "In Praise of André Bazin." In *The New Wave.* Critical landmark essays selected by Peter Graham. Garden City, N.Y.: Doubleday, 57–71; trans. reprint, *Positif* 47 (1962).

1968   Michelson, Annette. "Books [Review of *What is Cinema?*]" *Artforum* 6, no. 10 (1968): 66–71.

1968   Roud, Richard. "André Bazin: His Fall and Rise." *Sight and Sound* 37, no. 2 (Spring): 94–96.

1972   Henderson, Brian. "The Structure of Bazin's Thought." *Film Quarterly* 25, no. 5 (Summer): 18–27.

1973   Andrew, Dudley. "Critics: André Bazin." *Film Comment* 9, no. 2 (March–April): 64–68.

1973–1974

    Williams, Christopher. "Bazin, on Neo-Realism." *Screen* 14, no. 5 (Winter): 61–68.

1976   Andrew, Dudley. "Realist Film Theory: André Bazin." In *The Major Film Theories: An Introduction.* London and New York: Oxford University Press, 1976, 134–78.

1978   Andrew, Dudley. *André Bazin.* Foreword by François Truffaut. Appendix, "André Bazin from 1945 to 1950: The Time of Struggles and Consecration," by Jean-Charles Tacchella. New York: Columbia University Press, 1978, 1990. 277 pp.

1979   Henderson, Brian. "Bazin Defended against His Devotees." *Film Quarterly* 32, no. 4: 26–37.

1982   Andrew, Dudley. "Cinematic Politics in Postwar France: Bazin before *Cahiers.* " *Cineaste* 12, no. 1: 12–16.

1984   Staiger, Janet. "Theorist, Yes, But What Of? Bazin and History." *Iris* 2, no. 2: 99–109.

1987   *Wide Angle* 9, no. 4 (Winter). Special issue on Bazin: J. Belton, "Bazin is Dead! Long Live Bazin!" (74–81); Pam Falkenberg, "The Text! The Text!: André Bazin's Mummy Complex, Psycho-analysis and the Cinema" (35–55); Philip Rosen, "History of Image, Image of History: Subject and Ontology in Bazin" (7–34); Jean Narboni, "André Bazin's Style" (56–60); Jean-Charles Tacchella, "André Bazin from 1945–1950: The Time of Struggles and Consecration" (61–73).

1993   Brubaker, David. "André Bazin on Automatically Made Images." *Journal of Aesthetics and Art Criticism* 51, no. 1 (Winter): 59–67.

1994   Bordwell, David. "The Power of a Research Tradition: Prospects for Progress in the Study of Film Style." *Film History* 6, no. 1 (Spring): 59–79.

Kracauer

Basic Concepts

Like the embryo in the womb, photographic film developed from distinctly separate components. Its birth came about from a combination of instantaneous photography, as used by Muybridge and Marey, with the older devices of the magic lantern and the phenakistoscope.[1] Added to this later were the contributions of other nonphotographic elements, such as editing and sound. Nevertheless photography, especially instantaneous photography, has a legitimate claim to top priority among these elements, for it undeniably is and remains the decisive factor in establishing film content. The nature of photography survives in that of film.

Originally, film was expected to bring the evolution of photography to an end—satisfying at last the age-old desire to picture things moving. This desire already accounted for major developments within the photographic medium itself. As far back as 1839, when the first daguerreotypes and talbotypes appeared, admiration mingled with disappointment about their deserted streets and blurred landscapes.[2] And in the fifties, long before the innovation of the hand camera, successful attempts were made to photograph subjects in motion.[3] The very impulses that thus led from time exposure to snapshot engendered dreams of a further extension of photography in the same direction—dreams, that is, of film. About 1860, Cook and Bonnelli, who had developed a device called a photobioscope, predicted a "complete revolution of photographic art. . . . We will see . . . landscapes," they announced, "in which the trees bow to the whims of the wind, the leaves ripple and glitter in the rays of the sun."[4]

Along with the familiar photographic leitmotif of the leaves, such kindred subjects as undulating waves, moving clouds, and changing facial expressions ranked high in early prophecies. All of them conveyed the longing for an instrument that would capture the slightest incidents of the world about us—scenes that often would involve crowds, whose incalculable movements resemble, somehow, those of waves or leaves. In a memorable statement published before the emergence of instantaneous photography, Sir John Herschel not only predicted the basic features of the film camera but assigned to it a task that it has never since disowned: "the vivid and lifelike reproduction and handing down to the latest posterity of any transaction in real life—a battle, a debate, a public solemnity, a pugilistic conflict."[5] Ducos du Hauron and other forerunners also looked forward to what we have come to label newsreels and documentaries—films devoted to the rendering of real-life events.[6] This insistence on recording went hand in hand with the expectation that motion pictures could acquaint us with normally imperceptible or otherwise induplicable movements—flashlike transformations of matter, the slow growth of plants, and so on.[7] All in all, it was taken for granted that film would continue along the lines of photography. . . .[*]

Properties of the Medium

The properties of film can be divided into basic and technical properties.

The basic properties are identical with the properties of photography. Film, in other words, is uniquely equipped to record and reveal physical reality and, hence, gravitates toward it.

Now there are different visible worlds. Take a stage performance for a painting: they too are real and can be perceived. But the only reality we are concerned with is actually existing physical reality—the transitory world we live in. (Physical reality will also be called "material reality," or "physical existence," or "actuality," or loosely just "nature." Another fitting term might be "camera-reality." Finally, the term "life" suggests itself as an alternate expression.) The other visible worlds reach into this world without, however, really forming a part of it. A theatrical play, for instance, suggests a universe of its own that would immediately crumble were it related to its real-life environment.

As a reproductive medium, film is of course justified in reproducing memorable ballets, operas, and the like. Yet even assuming that such reproductions try to do justice to the specific requirements of the screen, they basically amount to little more than "canning," and are of no interest to us here. Preservation of performances that lie outside physical reality proper is at best a sideline of a medium so particularly suited to explore that reality. This is not to deny that reproductions, say, of stage production numbers may be put to good cinematic use in certain feature films and film genres.

---

[*]Mr. Georges Sadoul, *L'Invention du cinéma*, 298, sagaciously observes that the names given the archaic film cameras offer clues to the then prevailing aspirations. Such names as vitascope, vitagraph, bioscope, and biograph were undoubtedly intended to convey the camera's affinity for "life," while terms like kinetoscope, kinetograph, and cinematograph testified to the concern with movement.

Of all the technical properties of film the most general and indispensable is editing. It serves to establish a meaningful continuity of shots and is therefore unthinkable in photography. (Photomontage is a graphic art rather than a specifically photographic genre.) Among the more special cinematic techniques are some that have been taken over from photography—the close-up, soft-focus pictures, the use of negatives, double or multiple exposure, and so on. Others, such as the lap-dissolve, slow and quick motion, the reversal of time, certain "special effects," and so forth, are for obvious reasons exclusively peculiar to film.

These scanty hints will suffice. It is not necessary to elaborate on technical matters that have been dealt with in most previous theoretical writings on film. . . .[8]

This remark on procedures implies what is fairly obvious anyway: that the basic and technical properties differ substantially from each other. As a rule the former take precedence over the latter in the sense that they are responsible for the cinematic quality of a film. Imagine a film which, in keeping with the basic properties, records interesting aspects of physical reality but does so in a technically imperfect manner; perhaps the lighting is awkward or the editing uninspired. Nevertheless such a film is more specifically a film than one that utilizes brilliantly all the cinematic devices and tricks to produce a statement disregarding camera-reality. Yet this should not lead one to underestimate the influence of the technical properties. It will be seen that in certain cases the knowing use of a variety of techniques may endow otherwise nonrealistic films with a cinematic flavor.

The Two Main Tendencies

If film grows out of photography, the realistic and formative tendencies must be operative in it also. Is it by sheer accident that the two tendencies manifested themselves side by side immediately after the rise of the medium? As if to encompass the whole range of cinematic endeavors at the outset, each went the limit in exhausting its own possibilities. Their prototypes were Lumière, a strict realist, and Méliès, who gave free rein to his artistic imagination. The films they made embody, so to speak, thesis and antithesis in a Hegelian sense.[9]

Lumière and Méliès

Lumière's films contained a true innovation, as compared with the repertoire of the zootropes or Edison's peep boxes:[10] they pictured everyday life after the manner of photographs.[11] Some of his early pictures, such as *Baby's Breakfast* (*Le Déjeuner de bébé*) or *The Card Players* (*La Partie d'écarté*), testify to the amateur photographer's delight in family idylls and genre scenes.[12] And there was *Teasing the Gardener* (*L'Arroseur arrosé*), which enjoyed immense popularity because it elicited from the flow of everyday life a proper story with a funny climax to boot. A gardener is watering flowers and, as he unsuspectingly proceeds, an impish boy steps on the hose, releasing it at the very moment when his perplexed victim examines the dried-up nozzle. Water squirts out and hits the gardener smack in the face. The denouement is true to style, with the gardener chasing and spanking the boy. This film, the germ cell and archetype of all film comedies to come, represented an imaginative attempt on the part of Lumière to develop photography into a means of storytelling.[13] Yet the story was just a real-life incident. And it was precisely its photographic veracity that made Maxim Gorki undergo a shock-like experience. "You think," he wrote about *Teasing the Gardener,* "the spray is going to hit you too, and instinctively shrink back."[14]

On the whole, Lumière seems to have realized that storytelling was none of his business; it involved problems with which he apparently did not care to cope. Whatever storytelling films he, or his company, made—some more comedies in the vein of his first one, tiny historical scenes, and so on—are not characteristic of his production.[15] The bulk of his films recorded the world about us for no other purpose than to present it. This is in any case what Mesguich, one of Lumière's "ace" cameramen, felt to be their message. At a time when the talkies were already in full swing, he epitomized the work of the master as follows: "As I see it, the Lumière Brothers had established the true domain of the cinema in the right manner. The novel, the theater, suffice for the study of the human heart. The cinema is the dynamism of life, of nature and its manifestations, of the crowd and its eddies. All that asserts itself through movement depends on it. Its lens opens on the world."[16]

Lumière's lens did open the world in this sense. Take his immortal first reels *Lunch Hour at the Lumière Factory* (*Sortie des usines Lumière*), *Arrival of a Train* (*L'Arrivée d'un train*), *La Place des Cordeliers a Lyon:*[17] their themes were public places, with throngs of people moving in diverse directions. The crowded streets captured by the stereographic photographs of the late fifties thus reappeared on the primitive screen. It was life at its least controllable and most unconscious moments, a jumble of transient, forever dissolving patterns accessible only to the camera. The much-imitated shot of the railway station, with its emphasis on the confusion of arrival and departure, effectively illustrated the fortuity of these patterns; and their fragmentary character was exemplified by the clouds of smoke that leisurely drifted upward. Significantly, Lumière used the motif of smoke on several occasions. And he seemed anxious to avoid any personal interference with the given data. Detached records, his shots resembled the imaginary shot of the grandmother that Proust contrasts with the memory image of her.

Contemporaries praised these films for the very qualities that the prophets and forerunners had singled out in their visions of the medium. It was inevitable that, in the comments on Lumière, "the ripple of leaves stirred by the wind" should be referred to enthusiastically. The Paris journalist Henri de Parville, who used the image of the trembling leaves, also identified Lumière's overall theme as "nature caught in the act."[18] Others pointed to the benefits that science would derive from Lumière's invention.[19] In America his camera-realism defeated Edison's kinetoscope with its staged subjects.[20]

Lumière's hold on the masses was ephemeral. In 1897, not more than two years after he had begun to make films, his popularity subsided. The sensation had worn off; the heyday was over. Lack of interest caused Lumière to reduce his production.[21]

Georges Méliès took over where Lumière left off, renewing and intensifying the medium's waning appeal. This is not to say that he did not occasionally follow the latter's example. In his beginnings he too treated the audience to sightseeing tours; or he dramatized, in the fashion of the period, realistically staged topical events.[22] But his main contribution to the cinema lay in substituting staged illusion for unstaged reality and contrived plots for everyday incidents.[23]

The two pioneers were aware of the radical differences in their approach. Lumière told Méliès that he considered film nothing more than a "scientific curiosity,"[24] thereby implying that his cinematograph could not possibly serve artistic purposes. In 1897, Méliès on his part published a prospectus that took issue with Lumière: "Messrs. Méliès and Reulos specialize mainly in fantastic or artistic scenes, reproductions of theatrical scenes, etc. . . . thus creating a special genre which differs entirely from the customary views supplied by the cinematograph—street scenes or scenes of everyday life."[25]

Méliès' tremendous success would seem to indicate that he catered to demands left unsatisfied by Lumière's photographic realism. Lumière appealed to the sense of observation, the curiosity about "nature caught in the act"; Méliès ignored the workings of nature out of the artist's delight in sheer fantasy. The train in *Arrival of a Train* is the real thing, whereas its counterpart in Méliès' *An Impossible Voyage* (*Voyage à travers l'impossible*) is a toy train as unreal as the scenery through which it is moving. Instead of picturing the random movements of phenomena, Méliès freely interlinked imagined events according to the requirements of his charming fairy-tale plots. Had not media very close to film offered similar gratifications? The artist-photographers preferred what they considered aesthetically attractive compositions to searching explorations of nature. And immediately before the arrival of the motion picture camera, magic lantern performances indulged in the projection of religious themes, Walter Scott novels, and Shakespearean dramas.[26]

Yet even though Méliès did not take advantage of the camera's ability to record and reveal the physical world, he increasingly created his illusions with the aid of techniques peculiar to the medium. Some he found by accident. When taking shots of the Paris Place de l'Opéra, he had to discontinue the shooting because the celluloid strip did not move as it should; the surprising result was a film in which, for no reason at all, a bus abruptly transformed itself into a hearse.[27] True, Lumière also was not disinclined to have a sequence of events unfold in reverse, but Méliès was the first to exploit cinematic devices systematically. Drawing on both photography and the stage, he innovated many techniques that were to play an enormous role in the future—among them the use of masks, multiple exposure, superimposition as a means of summoning ghosts, the lap-dissolve, and so on.[28] And through his ingenuity in using these techniques he added a touch of cinema to his playful narratives and magic tricks. Stage traps ceased to be indispensable; sleights-of-hand yielded to incredible metamorphoses that film alone was able to accomplish. Illusion produced in this climate depended on another kind of craftsmanship than the magician's. It was cinematic illusion, and as such went far beyond theatrical make-believe. Méliès' *The Haunted Castle* (*Le Manoir du diable*) "is conceivable only in the cinema and due to the cinema," says Henri Langlois, one of the best connoisseurs of the primitive era.[29]

Notwithstanding his film sense, however, Méliès still remained the theater director he had been. He used photography in a pre-photographic spirit—for the reproduction of a papier-mâchée universe inspired by stage traditions. In one of his greatest films, *A Trip to the Moon* (*Le Voyage dans la lune*), the moon harbors a grimacing man in the moon and the stars are bull's-eyes studded with the pretty faces of music hall girls. By the same token, his actors bowed to the audience, as if they performed on the stage. Much as his films differed from the theater on a technical plane, they failed to transcend its scope by incorporating genuinely cinematic subjects. This also explains why Méliès, for all his inventiveness, never thought of moving his camera;[30] the stationary camera perpetuated the spectator's relation to the stage. His ideal spectator was the traditional theatergoer, child or adult. There seems to be some truth in the observation that, as people grow older, they instinctively withdraw to the positions from which they set out to struggle and conquer. In his later years Méliès more and more turned from theatrical film to filmed theater, producing *féeries* that recalled the Paris Châtelet pageants.[31]

The Realistic Tendency

In following the realistic tendency, films go beyond photography in two respects. First, they picture movement itself, not only one or another of its phases. But what kinds of movements do they picture? In the primitive era when the camera was fixed to the ground, it was natural for filmmakers to concentrate on moving material phenomena; life on the screen was life only if it manifested itself through external, or "objective," motion. As cinematic techniques developed, films increasingly drew on camera mobility and editing devices to deliver their messages. Although their strength still lay in the rendering of movements inaccessible to other media, these movements were no longer necessarily objective. In the technically mature film "subjective" movements—movements, that is, which the spectator is invited to execute—constantly compete with objective ones. The spectator may have to identify himself with a tilting, panning, or traveling camera that insists on bringing motionless as well as moving objects to his attention.[32] Or an appropriate arrangement of shots may rush the audience through vast expanses of time or space so as to make it witness, almost simultaneously, events in different periods and places.

Nevertheless the emphasis is now as before on objective movement; the medium seems to be partial to it. As René Clair puts it: "If there is an aesthetics of the cinema . . . it can be summarized in one word: 'movement.' The external movement of the objects perceived by the eye, to which we are today adding the inner movements of the action."[33] The fact that he assigns a dominant role to external movement reflects, on a theoretical plane, a marked feature of his own earlier films—the ballet-like evolution of their characters.

Second, films may seize upon physical reality with all its manifold movements by means of an intermediary procedure that would seem to be less indispensable in photography—staging. In order to narrate an intrigue, the filmmaker is often obliged to stage not only the action but the surroundings as well. Now this recourse to staging is most certainly legitimate if the staged world is made to appear as a faithful reproduction of the real one. The important thing is that studio-built settings convey the impression of actuality, so that the spectator feels he is watching events that might have occurred in real life and have been photographed on the spot.[34]

Falling prey to an interesting misconception, Emile Vuillermoz champions, for the sake of "realism," settings that represent reality as seen by a perceptive painter. To his mind they are more real than real-life shots because they impart the essence of what such shots are showing. Yet from the cinematic point of view these allegedly realistic settings are no less stagy than would be, say, a cubist or abstract composition. Instead of staging the given raw material itself, they offer, so to speak, the gist of it. In other words, they suppress the very camera-reality that film aims at incorporating. For this reason, the sensitive moviegoer will feel disturbed by them.[35]

Strangely enough, it is entirely possible that a staged real-life event evokes a stronger illusion of reality on the screen than would the original event if it had been captured directly by the camera. The late

Ernö Metzner, who devised the settings for the studio-made mining disaster in Pabst's *Kameradschaft,* an episode with the ring of stark authenticity, insisted that candid shots of a real mining disaster would hardly have produced the same convincing effect.[36]

One may ask, on the other hand, whether reality can be staged so accurately that the camera-eye will not detect any difference between the original and the copy. Blaise Cendrars touches on this issue in a neat hypothetical experiment. He imagines two film scenes that are completely identical except for the fact that one has been shot on the Mont Blanc (the highest mountain in Europe) while the other was staged in the studio. His contention is that the former has a quality not found in the latter. There are on the mountain, says he, certain "emanations, luminous or otherwise, which have worked on the film and given it a soul."[37] Presumably large parts of our environment, natural or man-made, resist duplication.

The Formative Tendency

The filmmaker's formative faculties are offered opportunities far exceeding those offered the photographer. The reason is that film extends into dimensions that photography does not cover. These differ from each other according to area and composition. With respect to areas, filmmakers have never confined themselves to exploring only physical reality in front of the camera but, from the outset, persistently tried to penetrate the realms of history and fantasy. Remember Méliès. Even the realistic-minded Lumière yielded to the popular demand for historical scenes. As for composition, the two most general types are the story film and the non-story film. The latter can be broken down into the experimental film and the film of fact, which on its part comprises, partially or totally, such subgenres as the film on art, the newsreel, and the documentary proper.

It is easy to see that some of these dimensions are more likely than others to prompt the filmmaker to express his formative aspirations at the expense of the realistic tendency. As for areas, consider that of fantasy: movie directors have at all times rendered dreams or visions with the aid of settings that are anything but realistic. Thus in *Red Shoes* Moira Shearer dances, in a somnambulistic trance, through fantastic worlds avowedly intended to project her unconscious mind—agglomerates of landscape-like forms, near-abstract shapes, and luscious color schemes that have all the traits of stage imagery. Disengaged creativity thus drifts away from the basic concerns of the medium. Several dimensions of composition favor the same preferences. Most experimental films are not even designed to focus on physical existence; and practically all films following the lines of a theatrical story evolve narratives whose significance overshadows that of the raw material of nature used for their implementation. For the rest, the filmmaker's formative endeavors may also impinge on his realistic loyalties in dimensions which, because of their emphasis on physical reality, do not normally invite such encroachments; there are enough documentaries with real-life shots that merely serve to illustrate some self-contained oral commentary.

Clashes between the Two Tendencies

Films that combine two or more dimensions are very frequent; for instance, many a movie featuring an everyday-life incident includes a dream sequence or a documentary passage. Some such combinations may lead to overt clashes between the realistic and formative tendencies. This happens whenever a filmmaker bent on creating an imaginary universe from freely staged material also feels under an obligation to draw on camera-reality. In his *Hamlet* Laurence Olivier has the cast move about in a studio-built, conspicuously stagy Elsinore, whose labyrinthine architecture seems calculated to reflect Hamlet's unfathomable being. Shut off from our real-life environment, this bizarre structure would spread over the whole of the film were it not for a small, otherwise insignificant scene in which the real ocean outside that dream orbit is shown. But no sooner does the photographed ocean appear than the spectator experiences something like a shock. He cannot help recognizing that this little scene is an outright intrusion; that it abruptly introduces an element incompatible with the rest of the imagery. How he then reacts to it depends upon his sensibilities. Those indifferent to the peculiarities of the medium, and therefore unquestioningly accepting the staged Elsinore, are likely to resent the unexpected emergence of crude nature as a letdown, while those more sensitive to the properties of film will in a flash realize the make-believe character of the castle's mythical splendor. Another case in point is Renato Castellani's *Romeo and Juliet*. This attempt to stage Shakespeare in natural surroundings obviously rests upon the belief that camera-reality and the poetic reality of Shakespeare verse can be made to fuse into each other. Yet the dialogue as well as the intrigue establish a universe so remote from the chance world of real Verona streets and ramparts that all the scenes in which the two disparate worlds are seen merging tend to affect one as an unnatural alliance between conflicting forces.

Actually collisions of this kind are by no means the rule. Rather, there is ample evidence to suggest that the two tendencies which sway the medium may be interrelated in various other ways. Since some of these relationships between realistic and formative efforts can be assumed to be aesthetically more gratifying than the rest, the next step is to try to define them.

The Cinematic Approach

Films may claim aesthetic validity if they build from their basic properties; like photographs, that is, they must record and reveal physical reality. The possible counterargument is that media peculiarities are in
general too elusive to serve as a criterion; for obvious reasons it does not
apply to the cinematic medium either. Yet another objection suggests itself. One might argue that too exclusive an emphasis on the medium's
primary relation to physical reality tends to put film in a straitjacket.
This objection finds support in the many existing films that are completely unconcerned about the representation of nature. There is the
abstract experimental film. There is an unending succession of "photo-
plays" or theatrical films that do not picture real-life material for its own
sake but use it to build up action after the manner of the stage. And there
are the many films of fantasy that neglect the external world in freely
composed dreams or visions. The old German expressionist films went
far in this direction; one of their champions, the German art critic Her-
man G. Scheffauer, even eulogizes expressionism on the screen for its re-
moteness from photographic life.[38]

Why, then, should these genres be called less "cinematic" than
films concentrating on physical existence? The answer is of course that it
is the latter alone which afford insight and enjoyment otherwise unattainable. True, in view of all the genres that do not cultivate outer reality
and yet are here to stay, this answer sounds somewhat dogmatic. But perhaps it will be found more justifiable in the light of the following two
considerations.

First, favorable response to a genre need not depend on its ade-
quacy to the medium from which it issues. As a matter of fact, many a
genre has a hold on the audience because it caters to widespread social
and cultural demands; it is and remains popular for reasons that do not involve questions of aesthetic legitimacy. Thus the photoplay has succeeded in perpetuating itself even though most responsible critics are
agreed that it goes against the grain of film. Yet the public that feels attracted, for instance, by the screen version of *Death of a Salesman*, likes
this version for the very virtues that made the Broadway play a hit
and does not in the least care whether it has any specifically cinematic
merits.

Second, let us for the sake of argument assume that my definition
of aesthetic validity is actually one-sided; that it results from a bias for
one particular, if important, type of cinematic activities and hence is unlikely to take into account, say, the possibility of hybrid genres or the influence of the medium's nonphotographic components. But this does not
necessarily speak against the propriety of that definition. In a strategic
interest it is often more advisable to loosen up initial one-sidedness—

provided it is well founded—than to start from all too catholic premises and then try to make them specific. The latter alternative runs the risk of blurring differences between the media because it rarely leads far enough away from the generalities postulated at the outset; its danger is that it tends to entail a confusion of the arts. When Eisenstein, the theoretician, began to stress the similarities between the cinema and the traditional art media, identifying film as their ultimate fulfillment, Eisenstein, the artist, increasingly trespassed the boundaries that separate film from elaborate theatrical spectacles: think of his *Alexander Nevskey* and the operatic aspects of his *Ivan the Terrible.* [39]

In strict analogy to the term "photographic approach" the film-maker's approach is called "cinematic" if it acknowledges the basic aesthetic principle. It is evident that the cinematic approach materializes in all films that follow the realistic tendency. This implies that even films almost devoid of creative aspirations, such as newsreels, scientific or educational films, artless documentaries, and the like, are tenable propositions from an aesthetic point of view—presumably more so than films which for all their artistry pay little attention to the given outer world. But as with photographic reportage, newsreels and the like meet only the minimum requirement.

What is of the essence in film no less than photography is the intervention of the filmmaker's formative energies in all the dimensions that the medium has come to cover. He may feature his impressions of this or that segment of physical existence in documentary fashion, transfer hallucinations and mental images to the screen, indulge in the rendering of rhythmical patterns, narrate a human-interest story, and so on. All these creative efforts are in keeping with the cinematic approach as long as they benefit, in some way or other, the medium's substantive concern with our visible world. As in photography, everything depends on the "right" balance between the realistic tendency and the formative tendency; and the two tendencies are well balanced if the latter does not try to overwhelm the former but eventually follows its lead.

The Issue of Art

When calling the cinema an art medium, people usually think of films that resemble the traditional works of art in that they are free creations rather than explorations of nature. These films organize the raw material to which they resort into some self-sufficient composition instead of accepting it as an element in its own right. In other words, their underlying formative impulses are so strong that they defeat the cinematic approach with its concern for camera-reality. Among the film types customarily considered art are, for instance, the above-mentioned German expressionist films of the years after World War I; conceived in a painterly spirit, they seem to implement the formula of Hermann Warm, one of the designers of *The Cabinet of Dr. Caligari* settings, who claimed that "films must be drawings brought to life."[40] Here also belongs many an experimental film; all in all, films of this type are not only intended as autonomous wholes but frequently ignore physical reality or exploit it for purposes alien to photographic veracity. By the same token, there is an inclination to classify as works of art feature films that combine forceful artistic composition with devotion to significant subjects and values. This would apply to a number of adaptations of great stage plays and other literary works.

Yet such a usage of the term "art" in the traditional sense is misleading. It lends support to the belief that artistic qualities must be attributed precisely to films that neglect the medium's recording obligations in an attempt to rival achievements in the fields of the fine arts, the theater, or literature. In consequence, this usage tends to obscure the aesthetic value of films that are really true to the medium. If the term "art" is reserved for productions like *Hamlet* or *Death of a Salesman*, one will find it difficult indeed to appreciate properly the large amount of creativity that goes into many a documentary capturing material phenomena for their own sake. Take Ivens' *Rain* or Flaherty's *Nanook*, documentaries saturated with formative intentions: like any selective photographer, their creators have all the traits of the imaginative reader and curious explorer; and their readings and discoveries result from full absorption in the given material and significant choices. Add to this that some of the crafts needed in the cinematic process—especially editing—represent tasks with which the photographer is not confronted. And they too lay claim to the filmmaker's creative powers.

This leads straight to a terminological dilemma. Due to its fixed meaning, the concept of art does not, and cannot, cover truly "cinematic" films—films, that is, which incorporate aspects of physical reality with a view to making us experience them. And yet it is they, not the films reminiscent of traditional artworks, which are valid aesthetically. If film is an art at all, it certainly should not be confused with the established arts.* There may be some justification in loosely applying this fragile concept to such films as *Nanook*, or *Paisan*, or *Potemkin*, which are deeply steeped in camera-life. But in defining them as art, it must always be kept in mind that even the most creative filmmaker is much less independent of nature in the raw than the painter or poet; that his creativity manifests itself in letting nature in and penetrating it.

---

*Arnold Hauser belongs among the few who have seen this. In his *The Philosophy of Art History*, 363, he says: "The film is the only art that takes over considerable pieces of reality unaltered; it interprets them, of course, but the interpretation remains a photographic one." His insight notwithstanding, however, Hauser seems to be unaware of the implications of this basic fact.

NOTES

1. Sadoul, *L'Invention du cinéema*, 8, 49ff., 61–81 (about Marey). This book is a "must" for anyone interested in the complex developments that led up to Lumière. For Muybridge, see also Newhall, "Photography and the Development of Kinetic Visualization," *Journal of the Warburg and Courtauld Institutes*, 1944, vol. 7, 42–43. T. Ra., "Motion Pictures," *Encyclopedia Britannica*, 1932, vol. 15, 854–56, offers a short survey of the period.

2. Newhall, op. cit., 40.

3. Ibid.

4. Sadoul, *L'Invention du cinéma*, 38.

5. Herschel, "Instantaneous Photography," *Photographic News*, 1860, vol. 4, no. 88:13. I am indebted to Mr. Beaumont Newhall for his reference to this quote.

6. Sadoul, *L'Invention du cinéma*, 36–37, 86, 241–42.

7. It was Ducos du Hauron who, as far back as 1864, predicted these developments; see Sadoul, ibid., 37.

8. See, for instance, Balázs, *Der Geist des Films*; Arnheim, *Film*; Eisenstein, *The Film Sense* and *Film Form*; Pudovkin, *Film Technique and Film Acting*; Rotha, *The Film Till Now*; Spottiswoode, *A Grammar of the Film* and *Basic Film Techniques* (University of California Syllabus series, no. 303); Karel Reisz, *The Technique of Film Editing*, etc.

9. Caveing, "Dialectique du concept du cinéma," *Revue internationale de filmologie* (part I: July–August 1947, no. 1; part II: October 1948, nos. 3–4) applies, in a somewhat high-handed manner, the principles of Hegel's dialectics to the evolution of the cinema. The first dialectic stage, he has it, consists of Lumière's reproduction of reality and its antithesis—complete illusionism, as exemplified by Méliès (see esp. part I, 74–78). Similarly, Morin, *Le Cinéma ou l'homme imaginaire*, 58, conceives of Méliès' "absolute unreality" as the antithesis, in a Hegelian sense, of Lumière's "absolute realism." See also Sadoul, *Histoire d'un art*, 31.

10. Sadoul, *L'Invention du cinéma*, 21–22, 241, 246.

11. Langlois, "Notes sur l'histoire du cinéma," *La Revue du cinéma*, July 1948, vol. III, no. 15:3.

12. Sadoul, op. cit., 247.

13. Ibid., 249, 252, 300; and Sadoul, *Histoire d'un art*, 21.

14. Gorki, "You Don't Believe Your Eyes," *World Film News*, March 1938, 16.

15. Bessy and Duca, *Louis Lumière, inventeur*, 88. Sadoul, op. cit., 23–24.

16. Quoted by Sadoul, *L'Invention du cinéma*, 208. See also 253.

17. Ibid., 242–44, 248. Vardac, *Stage to Screen*, 166–67. Vardac emphasizes that an ever-increasing concern with realism prompted the nineteenth-century stage to make elaborate use of special devices. For instance, Steele MacKaye, a theatrical producer who died shortly before the arrival of the vitascope, invented a "curtain of light" so as to produce such effects as the fade-in, the fade-out, and the dissolve (143).

18. Sadoul, op. cit., 246.

19. Bessy and Duca, *Louis Lumière, inventeur*, 49–50. Sadoul, *Histoire d'un art*, 23.

20. Sadoul, *L'Invention du cinéma*, 222–24, 227.

21. Ibid., 332, and Sadoul, *Histoire d'un art*, 24.

22. Sadoul, *L'Invention du cinéma*, 322, 328.

23. Ibid., 332. Langlois, "Notes sur l'histoire du cinéma," *La Revue du cinéma*, July 1948, vol. III, no. 15:10.

24. Quoted by Bardèche and Brasillach, *The History of Motion Pictures*, 10.

25. Sadoul, *L'Invention du cinéma*, 332.

26. Ibid., 102, 201; esp. 205.

27. Ibid., 324–26.

28. For Méliès' technical innovations, see Sadoul, *Les Pionniers du cinéma*, 52–70.

29. Langlois, "Notes sur l'histoire du cinéma," *La Revue du cinéma*, July 1948, vol. III, no. 15:5.

30. Sadoul, op. cit., 154, 166.

31. Sadoul, *L'Invention du cinéma*, 330–31.

32. Cf. Meyerhoff, *Tonfilm und Wirklichkeit*, 13, 22.

33. Clair, *Réflexion faite*, 96; he made this statement in 1924.

34. Ibid., 150.

35. Vuillermoz, "Réalisme et expressionisme," *Cinéma* (Les cahiers du mois, 16/17), 1925, 78–79.

36. See Kracauer, *From Caligari to Hitler*, 240.

37. Berge, "Interview de Blaise Cendrars sur le cinéma," *Cinéma* (Les cahiers du mois, 16/17), 1925, 141. For the problems involved in the staging of actuality, see also Mauriae, *L'Amour du cinéma*, 36, and Obraszow, "Film und Theater," in *Von der Filmidee zum Drehbuch*, 54.

38. Scheffauer, "The Vivifying of Space," *The Freeman*, November 24 and December 1, 1920.

39. Eisenstein, *Film Form*, 181–82.

40. See Kracauer, *From Caligari to Hitler*, 68.

Kracauer's *Theory of Film*

Introduction

This essay is about Siegfried Kracauer's book *Theory of Film: The Redemption of Physical Reality*, which was published in 1960.[1] It is important to stress this from the outset because, during the course of his career, Kracauer made a number of contributions to the topic of film theory, not all of which are strictly compatible with the theses of *Theory of Film*.[2] Exploring the relations and the tensions between Kracauer's earlier writings and *Theory of Film* is a worthy task for intellectual historians,[3] but, in contrast, my purpose is to examine the argument of *Theory of Film*. That book alone provides more than enough material to engage a brief introductory essay such as this one.

Perhaps the initial thing to say to someone confronting *Theory of Film* for the first time is that it is a very difficult book to read.[4] On the face of it, Kracauer's theory has a clear structure, possibly reflecting his early training as an architect.[5] Effort appears to be lavished on drawing sharp distinctions between categories, and the argument seems to progress logically. However, the deeper one goes in the text, the more the clear categories seem to muddy. As Kracauer applies his theory to examples, caveats, qualifications, extenuating circumstances, mitigating conditions, and compensating considerations multiply so that one is never sure that one could apply Kracauer's system in a way that would coincide with Kracauer's own results. Consequently, the book, as a whole, has a very ad hoc flavor to it.[6]

For example, Kracauer argues that film has a special affinity for recording and revealing "physical existence," but then he also includes under this category "special modes of reality"—"physical reality as it appears to individuals in extreme states of mind" (58). This is at least a surprising, if not inconsistent, turn in the text, since two of the cognates that Kracauer offers for "physical existence" are "material reality" and "nature," categories typically used to draw a conceptual contrast with subjective experience. Throughout the book, unexpected elaborations of the core theory, such as this one, abound, making the reader uncertain about his or her grasp of the theory.

If such slipperiness poses problems for the reader, of course, it also poses problems for an expositor of the theory such as myself. In a short essay, it is impossible to tie up all the loose ends in Kracauer's book, particularly in terms of the apparent anomalies that crop up in his applications of the theory to examples. Thus, in what follows, I only attempt to elucidate and to criticize the central arguments of the text as they are typically understood. I do not try to reconcile all the logical tensions in the book; I doubt whether I could even if I tried. Hence, this essay may be an idealization of Kracauer's text. But I see no alternative as a way of beginning a discussion of *Theory of Film*.

The Kracauer of *Theory of Film* is standardly regarded as a realist. In fact, along with André Bazin,[7] Kracauer is taken to be one of the most paradigmatic examples of this tendency in film theory. There are, of course, differences between the two theorists. Bazin, as is well known, is deeply concerned with the realist potentials of certain cinematic techniques, such as the long-take, deep-focus shot, whereas Kracauer shows no special allegiance to any particular cinematic technique, including the sequence shot. Kracauer is more concerned with the *use* of various techniques.

However, Kracauer does echo Bazin's taste for a certain level of ambiguity ("shots not yet stripped of their multiple meanings" [69]) and for episodic narrative structures (ch. 14). And, most significantly, Kracauer's and Bazin's theories converge in the shared conviction that the most important fact about film theoretically is its putative provenance in photography.

Indeed, this conviction is one of the defining features of what I call film realists in this essay. Both Kracauer and Bazin meet this criterion, since both believe that film is essentially photographic. Film realists also believe that this supposed fact about the nature of film has normative consequences—consequences about what is and is not suitable when it comes to filmmaking. Bazin's arguments and conclusions in behalf of film realism differ from Kracauer's. Our concern is with Kracauer's position.

In a nutshell, Kracauer begins with "the assumption that film is essentially an extension of photography and therefore shares with this medium a marked affinity for the visible world around us. Films come into their own when they record and reveal physical reality" (ix). Furthermore, "since any medium is partial to the things it is uniquely equipped to render, the cinema is conceivably animated by a desire to picture transient material life, life at its most ephemeral" (ibid.). And this so-called desire, in turn, gives rise to the standards of achievement that are relevant to film: "films are true to the medium to the extent that they penetrate the world before our eyes" (ibid.). That is, films are cinematic to the extent that they realize "the desire to picture transient material life."

Kracauer calls his theory a material aesthetics because it is concerned with content, whereas, he contends, previous theories emphasized form. What content appears to mean here is something like "what is rendered." Following a theoretical persuasion popularized by people like Lessing,[8] Kracauer presumes that each medium has a certain subject matter or content that it is uniquely and best suited to represent or to render. The natural, so to speak, subject matter or content of photography, and, by extension, film comprises such things as the unstaged, the fortuitous, the indeterminate, and endlessness as these properties manifest themselves visibly in things and events. Content bereft of such properties, or things rendered in such a way that these properties are not salient, are unsuitable for film; content rendered in such a way that such properties are evident and/or emphasized are cinematic naturals. Of course, implicit in this way of thinking are certain canons of evaluation. Films are cinematic (a.k.a. good) only if they portray cinematic content and they are uncinematic (and most probably bad)[9] if they lack cinematic content or fail to foreground the relevant properties, such as indeterminacy, in the things and events they depict.

Of course, Kracauer is aware that there are more elements to film than its photographic constituents. There are, for instance, editing and set design. Kracauer refers to these other-than-photographic features of film as technical properties. And he argues that the technical properties of film should be coordinated with the photographic dimension of cinema in such a way that they support or enhance the pursuit of the natural photographic proclivities of cinema toward depicting the unstaged, the fortuitous, the indeterminate and endlessness. That is, the technical features of film should be subservient to its essential photographic purposes. Or, photography, with its natural inclinations, leads the charge; everything else is auxiliary.

Given this conception of film, a recurring question for Kracauer is how the various technical aspects of film, such as the sound track, can be deployed to support, abet, or at least not impede the purposes of the basic photographic element and its properties. This, of course, also leads Kracauer to comment on the ways in which the technical aspects of film may conflict with or even thwart the photographic potentials of cinema. Where such conflicts occur and the technical means of the cinema are used to serve their own purposes, in contradistinction to the purposes of photographic realism, Kracauer deems such usages of the technical features of film uncinematic.

Of especial interest to Kracauer is also the question of which film genres—such as the historical film, the fantasy film, the experimental film, and so on—are suitable to the photographic commitments of cinema and which are not. Indeed, the bulk of the text is turned over to adjudicating this issue genre by genre—to assessing which ones are amenable to or compatible with the purposes of film realism and which ones are not.

Most of the core of Kracauer's theory of film is set out in the first section, entitled "General Characteristics," while most of the subsequent text is spent applying the theory to the uses of various technical features and film genres.

From a theoretical point of view, Kracauer's core theory is the first order of interest, since from the viewpoint of theory it could be the case that the theory might be solid, while Kracauer's own applications of it turn out to be problematic. If this were the case, the central theses of *Theory of Film* might be sustained at the cost of minor adjustments here and there. But the million-dollar question is whether the theory that Kracauer applies is itself compelling. Thus, I concentrate my attention on the core theory comprising the following fundamental claims: that film is essentially photographic; that the photographic nature of film has normative implications for filmmaking; that these implications include commitments to certain content or to the treatment of cinematic content in certain specifiable ways; and that failure to respect these commitments, all things being equal, results in films of dubious cinematic value.

To my way of thinking, Kracauer has two different, though related, ways of laying out and defending this theory. I call the first "the medium specificity argument" and the second "the historical/cultural argument."

The Medium Specificity Argument

Kracauer explicitly limits the domain of his theory to the black-and-white, photographic film. Color films and cartoons are excluded from his purview (vii). Kracauer is frank about his reasons for these exclusions. He believes that neither color films nor cartoons are realistic. The case against cartoons is fairly obvious, though Kracauer's qualms about color films show a very period-specific prejudice. Certainly by the late sixties, the suspicion that color films were inherently unrealistic had virtually disappeared. Moreover, one might also worry whether by excluding these categories of film, for the reasons Kracauer gives, doesn't beg the question in favor of his theory from the get-go by banishing obvious counterexamples to his theory by fiat.

But for heuristic purposes, maybe it is best to begin by allowing Kracauer to stipulate the domain of his theory as he sees fit. On his view, his subject is the photographic film, understood, tendentiously, as the black-and-white film. Kracauer's stated intention is to provide insight into the intrinsic nature of the photographic film (vii). From a historical point of view, one can see why Kracauer lays emphasis on the photographic film. Film can be regarded as a development of still photography—an expansion of its technological powers—and, in addition, the films known to Kracauer were standardly made by means of photography, that is, by shooting what are called pro-filmic events. Computer-generated films were beyond Kracauer's ken historically and cartoons were excluded from his theoretical domain by stipulation. However, when Kracauer calls films *photographic,* he is not merely acknowledging a historical fact. He means to make an ontological point, namely, that films are essentially photographic.

Why is this significant? As we have already noted, film has many constituents, including not only photography but editing, set design, and so on. Kracauer asks whether one of these is more essential than all the rest, since he believes that if one is more essential, then it should play an important role in the way in which we think about film. That is, he believes that if film has an essential nature, then this will provide us with a key to how it is best used. Kracauer, of course, is not shy about which constituent of film he takes to be essential. It is the photographic component.

But one wonders whether Kracauer can provide any reasons for this decision? You might think that Kracauer would answer that his conclusion is true by definition—after all, by his own stipulation, we are talking about *photographic* film. The use of photography is the feature that serves to identify membership in the class of things under discussion. But, of course, a common identifying mark need not correspond to an essential feature. Stripes serve to mark off tigers for us, but they do not reveal the essential nature of tigers. Genetic structure does. Perhaps because he realizes that the sort of essence he is after cannot be verbally stipulated, Kracauer never tries this gambit.

Instead, Kracauer maintains that

> Like the embryo in the womb, the photographic film developed from distinctly separate components. Its birth came about from a combination of instantaneous photography, as used by Muybridge and Marey, with older devices of the magic lantern and the phenakistoscope. Added to this later were the contribution of other nonphotographic elements, such as editing and sound. Nevertheless photography, especially instantaneous photography, has a legitimate claim to top priority among these elements for it undeniably is and remains the decisive factor in establishing film content. The nature of photography survives in that of film. (27)

If we read "top priority" here as signaling the essential feature or basic property of film, then it is natural to take Kracauer to be arguing that:

1. Whatever establishes the content of a medium is its basic property.
2. Photography establishes the content of film.
3. Therefore, photography is the basic property of film.

The first premise in this argument is implicit; the second is asserted in the penultimate sentence of the quotation. To assess either premise, we need a handle on the notion of establishing the content of a medium. One must admit that this is a very obscure idea, both in terms of what comprises the content of a medium and what establishes it.[10]

With regard to the first premise, one wonders whether media in general have "established content." Part of the problem is that in many cases the content of a medium is not established once and for all. Rather, it is open to innovation. So, in principle, one might argue that it is impossible to fix the content of a medium, unless Kracauer has some special sense of "establish" about which he has not deigned to inform us.

But there is also another problem with the first premise. If we understand it to claim that for any medium, x is its basic property if and only if x establishes the content of the medium, then it seems false. Why? Because there are media such as oil painting, where the basic ingredients of the medium do not establish its content. Oil-based paint is the basic property of oil painting, but it does not "establish" the content of the medium. You can paint anything—not only visible things but ultimate reality (remember Mondrian). So if first premise is supposed to be a thoroughly general principle for identifying the basic property of any medium, it appears questionable.

But perhaps we should understand first premise to say: "If x establishes the content of a medium, then x is its basic property." This enables one to hold that where a medium has definable content and x establishes it, then x is its basic property. But unless we have a clear understanding of what it is to establish the content of a medium, this at least looks controversial. For at a given time a medium may be used to portray certain subject matter—say religious figures—as a result of social factors, and yet we do not conclude that these social factors, which establish the content of the medium, are the basic properties of the medium.

But, be that as it may, Kracauer might respond that it is clear what we mean by establishing content when it comes to film—it means providing what we see—and, furthermore, what we see in film is there because of photography. If there was no photography, no photographic film would have any content whatsoever. If at this point you ask, "What about animated films?" then you have begun to appreciate the force of Kracauer's exclusion of animation from the domain of his theory.

Though the supposition that photography establishes the content of film has problems that we address shortly, let us grant Kracauer this premise momentarily in order to see how he uses it. Kracauer wants to establish that photography is the basic property of cinema because he believes that if you can determine the essence of film, then that will indicate the appropriate way in which to use the medium. He believes that essence implies function. In terms of aesthetic theory, this doctrine is often elaborated in terms of the notion of medium specificity, that is, the view that each medium has an inherent nature that dictates the range of possibilities available in that medium.[11] The nature of film is essentially photographic. So the range of genuine possibility—its proper scope and limitations—is photographic.

But this pushes the question of the nature of film back a step. For in order to determine the nature of film, one must establish the nature of photography. And this is something Kracauer tackles in the introduction to his book, which is entitled "Photography." In order to plumb the nature of a medium, Kracauer suggests that we listen to the conversation concerning the nature of the medium that has arisen during the course of its history (3). Listening to that conversation, Kracauer claims to discern two trends. There are those who favor the realist conception of photography, the view that it is the essence of photography to record reality. And there are those who favor the formative conception of photography, who see the photographer as inevitably involved in creatively shaping her or his subject matter through processes of selectivity. Proponents of the formative tendency maintain that photography does not merely record reality, but that it molds reality as well.

Kracauer agrees that both conceptions have claims to validity. But he also realizes that extreme versions of the realist and the formative conceptions tend to conflict. So, in effect, he proposes to combine the two tendencies in such a way that they turn out to be operationally compatible. The way to coordinate the two conceptions that Kracauer proposes is to say that it is the nature of photography to record and to reveal physical reality. The *recording* component of this formula evidently respects the realist conception of photography, while the *revealing* component acknowledges the claims of the formative conception, since revealing reality involves the creative activity of the photographer.[12]

What is perhaps interesting about the way that Kracauer strives to reconcile realist and formative claims is that the realist conception functions as a constraint on the formative conception. The creative activity of the photographer is endorsed so long as it is dedicated to revealing physical reality, rather than, say, to concocting reflexive abstractions or imaginary worlds. Realism is a necessary condition of photography and any exercise of the formative powers of photography must be in the service of realism rather than pure formal experimentation. The nature of photography is twofold—a matter of recording *and* revealing physical reality—with the realist half of this conjunction calling the tune.

Though one can ascertain Kracauer's grounds for isolating the two aspects of the nature of photography, I am not able to find any direct justification in the text for the proposal that the realistic tendency and the formative tendency be reconciled in the way he suggests. Why does Kracauer think that his formula is the right one? One could imagine other ways of reconciling the two tendencies. Why not suggest that the realist tendency be constrained by the formative tendency? This, in effect, is what the Soviet theorist Kuleshov advocates—proposing that editing (montage) is the central element of film and that the other elements of film should support its so-called natural effects and purposes.[13] Kracauer offers no explicit argument against this possibility. Nor does he have an argument to preclude the possibility that photography has a double nature that sometimes conflicts after the fashion of Jekyll and Hyde.[14]

However, if we extrapolate interpretively, perhaps something Kracauer says in another context has some bearing on why he believes the notion that photography records and reveals physical reality captures the nature of photography. Speaking of what justifies calling some film genres cinematic and others not, Kracauer suggests that we look to see which ones afford insight and enjoyment that are otherwise unattainable (37). Applying a principle like this to the present case, perhaps Kracauer thinks that because the formative tendency can be realized in other media, such as painting, and is, therefore, attainable in media other than photography, his formula—out of the alternatives—zeroes in on the way of coordinating the realist and formative tendencies that is uniquely photographic.

Furthermore, since Kracauer believes that the nature of photography survives in the nature of film, he is now in a position to conclude that the nature of film is to record and to reveal physical reality. And, moreover, Kracauer maintains that photography, because of its realist nature, has natural affinities for certain content: for the unstaged (real things and events); for the fortuitous (random events); for the indeterminate (objects and events bearing the possibility of multiple significance); and for endlessness (the photograph yields the impression that what it represents is part of a larger, "endless," spatiotemporal continuum) (18–20). Therefore, in so far as film inherits its nature from photography, it inherits these affinities as well. But since film adds movement to the still photograph, it also lays claim to an affinity all its own, namely, an affinity for the "the continuum of life, or 'the flow of life,' which of course is identical with open-ended life" (71).

The basic property of film is photographic—the capacity to record and reveal physical reality.[15] This disposes film to a certain roughly definable content—the recording and revealing of the unstaged, the fortuitous, the indeterminate, spatiotemporal endlessness, and the endless flow of life. But, of course, as mentioned earlier, film has other properties besides its putative basic property, photography. Kracauer calls them "technical properties." What can one say about these? On Kracauer's view they should be subservient to the basic property of film.

They should be used in the service of recording and revealing reality. Editing, for example, ideally functions to reveal aspects of the unstaged physical world, perhaps by showing us causal processes operating across great distances—as Vertov does by cutting between city lights and the dams from whence they derive their power in his paens to the electrification of the Soviet Union. Quite clearly, the technical properties of film stand to its basic property as the formative capacity of photography stands to its realist capacity. In both cases, the latter features constrain and direct the appropriate exercise of the capabilities of the former feature. Nor is this correlation accidental, since among the technical capacities of film are many of the major levers, like editing, for realizing formative effects upon that which is recorded.

As it is with the technical capacities of film, so it is with film genres. Film genres, especially in terms of their narrative structures, must be constrained and guided by the basic properties of film, its photographic nature and purposes. Not all the genres one finds in the historical corpus of films meet these criteria, however. Historical films, for example, employ costumes and are, as a result, apt to be stagey. So historical topics are, prima facie, unsuitable for film, unless the filmmakers can discover mitigating or compensating strategies to deal with the problem of staginess. Tragedies, Kracauer believes, present viewers with a narratively closed universe, where events transpire as the result of destiny. This is incompatible with the open-ended endlessness of the flow of life and with photography's affinity for what is accidental. Thus, tragedy is an unsuitable subject for films.

Similarly, Kracauer also maintains that detective films and films of intrigue traffic in narratively closed universes and, therefore, are, prima facie, uncinematic.[16] On the other hand, found narratives (e.g., *Nanook of the North*) and episodic narrative structures (*Paisan*) provide hospitable frameworks for showcasing the affinities toward which photography gravitates and, therefore, are presumptively cinematic.

In summary, then, Kracauer contends:

1. Photography is the basic property (element) of film. (Other properties, like editing, lens distortion, and sound, are technical properties, not basic properties.)
2. Any medium should emphasize the essential features (natural inclinations, affinities) of its basic element.
3. The essential feature of photography is its inclination for the straightforward recording and revealing of the visible world, especially in terms of the unstaged, the fortuitous, indeterminacy, and endlessness.
4. Therefore, film should emphasize the essential features of its basic element by recording and revealing the visible world, especially in terms of the unstaged, the fortuitous, indeterminacy, and endlessness (including the endless flow of life).
5. Where a medium possesses properties (elements) in addition to the basic elements, these should be deployed to emphasize the essential features (natural inclinations, affinities) of the basic element.
6. Film possesses technical properties and narrative (genre) structures in addition to its basic element.

7. Therefore, the technical properties and narrative structures of film should be deployed to emphasize the recording and revealing of the visible world, especially in terms of the unstaged, the fortuitous, indeterminacy, and endlessness (including the endless flow of life).

I call this argument the "medium specificity argument" since the second premise presupposes that media have essential (unique) features that determine what should (and, by implication, what should not) be emphasized when using the medium. The fifth premise is also a corollary to this idea. And, indeed, as we saw earlier, Kracauer's major reason for believing he has captured the essential feature of photography (in the fifth premise) may involve uniqueness claims about the medium.[17]

Let us go through this argument step by step. We have already encountered the first premise as the conclusion of a previous argument. Photography is said to be the basic element in film because it establishes the content of film. We have suggested that Kracauer might defend such a position by arguing that without photography film has no content at all, since what comprises film is the cinematography of pro-filmic events. Without photography, there is nothing to see in films and, therefore, no content.

This conclusion, however, may be precipitous. Consider the genre of avant-garde films called "flicker films," of which *Arnulf Rainer* by Peter Kubelka and *The Flicker* by Tony Conrad are perhaps the most famous. Such films can be made by alternating clear and opaque leader or black-and-white leader. No photography is necessary. Moreover, the fact that these films were made after Kracauer articulated his theory is irrelevant, since his claims are ontological, not historical.

Perhaps Kracauer would reject these counterexamples by claiming that they have no content. But this is not obvious. They are exercises in rhythm, and if rhythm is a content of music, why can't it function as content in film? Also, the films are interesting for the visual effects they engender. Why not count that as content? And, of course, critics have claimed that such films make reflexive comments about the nature of film. And that certainly sounds like content to me.

A second reply available to Kracauer might be to argue that these are really animated films and, therefore, outside the domain of his theory. But whether they are animated films is hardly self-evident; they are certainly not like paradigmatic cases of animated films. They are not cartoons. Here, Kracauer might respond: "Well, even if they aren't animated films, they are certainly not photographic films."

That's right but maybe irrelevant, since films indiscernible to these could be made photographically by taking close-shots of black walls at night and alternating them with clear leader. Would the content of these films—the rhythms, the visual effects, and the reflexive comments—be established by photography? Surely that is at least debatable. The content is not necessarily established by all and only photography because it can be fixed by the standard procedure for composing flicker films. Indeed, even with flicker films composed in the alternative way we have suggested, the content does not seem to be established by photography; rather, photography is merely a means of securing an other-than-photographic agenda.

Once again it must be emphasized that Kracauer's claims are not historical claims about films as he knew them but ontological claims about the nature of film *sub specie aeternitatas.* Admittedly, Kracauer did not envision computer-generated imagery. But it is possible to imagine computer-generated feature films of the striking verisimilitude of the stampede scene in *Jurassic Park.* Wouldn't such films be the kind of films that Kracauer intends to be talking about, since it is probably possible in principle to replicate the films he applauds by means of exclusively computer technology? And wouldn't the content of these computer-generated fascimiles have the same content as the originals? But in that case, the content of films—what we see—can be established without photography.

Here, Kracauer might say that these computer-generated fascimiles are not literally *photographic* films and, therefore, not relevant to his theory. But he calls his book a "theory of film," and it seems fair to expect the theory to encompass any technical expansion of the practice that viewers and filmmakers are willing to regard as a continuation of the same practice by other means (in the way that we are willing to consider various different technical processes photography). And certainly viewers and filmmakers are willing to count the stampede scenes in *Jurassic Park* as film. On the other hand, if Kracauer maintains that his theory only pertains, by stipulation, to the photographic technology of his own era, then we might wish to respond that then it is on its way to obsolescence, and irrelevant as a theory of film.

Of course, Kracauer might attempt to block my counterexamples by specifying what he means by "content" more narrowly than by the notion of "what we see." But one must be careful here. For if what Kracauer might have in mind as the relevant sense of content is precisely the unstaged, the fortuitous, the indeterminate, and endlessness, then his argument will beg the question in its first premise. After all, the commitment to such content is supposed to be the conclusion of his argument.

The second premise in the argument is the assertion of medium specificity: any medium should emphasize the essential feature of its basic element. This is an idea with a long history. Perhaps due to its long history, it appears obvious or even self-evident. But at the risk of sounding boorish, it seems worthwhile to ask why a medium should emphasize its essential feature. Since the principle is framed in terms of how a medium *should* be used, it must be apparent that media can be used in ways that do not emphasize their essential feature (supposing that they have one). But, despite this possibility, Kracauer contends that a medium should be used to emphasize its essential features.

What reasons can be given for this? Suppose a work of stone architecture fails to emphasize an essential feature—say weight—of its basic element or even hides it by appearing light and airy. Imagine that it leaves the impression of floating skywards toward heaven. What's the problem here, if the result is effective—if it is beautiful or thrilling?

Perhaps Kracauer and other proponents of the medium specificity principle think that such an outcome is impossible. Perhaps they believe that the medium specificity principle is a reliable predictor of what will be successful in a given medium—that there will be no successful results that do not abide by the principle. But then the medium specificity principle becomes an empirical hypothesis. And we will just have to wait and see whether or not successful films are all in accord with it.

Of course, if we simply attend to the pretheoretical record—the canon of films that are regarded as classics—then it would seem that informed viewers think that there have been successful films, like Cocteau's *Blood of a Poet,* which defy Kracauer's version of medium specificity. Moreover, if Kracauer tries to block this evidence by claiming that the informed viewers in question cannot be truly informed if they reach conclusions that deviate from his predictions, then, once again, he looks as though he is simply begging the question.

The problem here, as in so many medium specificity arguments, is that there is an ambiguity in the way that the medium specificity principle is treated. Is it supposed to be a conceptual or an empirical truth? At times, people like Kracauer seem to treat it as a conceptual truth. But it doesn't look like a conceptual truth. It's certainly not analytically true. And in fact the only putative grounds that proponents typically adduce for it seem to be empirical—that is, their claim that experience shows that all successful works of art abide by it. But in that case, it is not insulated from contestation. And with regard to every art form I know of, one can find some generally acknowledged, informed people (critics, artists, curators, publishers, and audience members) who will reasonably defend counterexamples to every reigning proposal about medium specificity.

The third premise of Kracauer's argument advances his conception of the nature of photography. It is of the essence of photography to record and reveal the visible world, especially in terms of the unstaged, the fortuitous, indeterminacy, and endlessness. As noted previously, this formulation attempts to coordinate the claims of the realist and formative conceptions of photography. By why should a friend of the formative conception agree to Kracauer's way of cutting the difference between the realist and formative conceptions? Why not suggest that the realist capacities of photography be subservient to the formative capabilities—that the realist powers of photography be devoted, for example, to the creation of imaginary beings and vistas of compelling verisimilitude?

My interpretive hypothesis was that Kracauer would answer this question by saying that the tension between these tendencies should be adjudicated in favor of effects that are uniquely attainable within the medium. Formative effects are achievable in other media, like painting, whereas photography has a unique purchase on visual reality. But this, of course, is once again just an invocation of the medium specificity principle. And, as such, its defender must explain why it makes any difference if a photographer makes a successful photograph that that success (e.g., Heartfield's "Adolf the Superman") has to be something attainable only in the medium of photography. That the photograph is successful should be all that counts.

Nor can the proponent of medium specificity block this possibility on a priori grounds. The matter of success is an empirical one. And if Kracauer attempts to invoke the medium specificity principle as an a priori truth, we may charge him with begging the question once again. That is, Kracauer can be faced with a dilemma: either the medium specificity principle can be held as an empirical truth or a concpetual truth. If it is held as an empirical generalization, it looks false; if it is held as a conceptual truth, that not only looks dubious, but it also in effect begs the question in the debate with rival views of photography.

With respect to the third premise, it is also worthwhile to comment on Kracauer's candidates for photography's natural affinities—the unstaged, the fortuitous, indeterminacy, and endlessness. Kracauer asserts that these affinities obtain; there is no demonstration, beyond citation of a few examples. I suspect that each affinity could be challenged, along with the very idea that media possess natural affinities. Moreover, what the affinities involve is very vague, which perhaps is what allows Kracauer's rather high-handed use of them when it comes to his evaluation of the various film genres.

But a more interesting feature of these so-called affinities from a logical point of view is that Kracauer never establishes that this is an exhaustive list. Thus, there may be more candidates for photography's affinities than the ones he enumerates. Thus, he has not logically precluded the possibility that there might be affinities that are more congenial to the formative persuasion and, indeed, to some of the genres and techniques that he disparages.

The fourth step in Kracauer's argument is a logically valid conclusion of the preceding premises. But, as such, it inherits all the problems that plague the medium specificity presuppositions that precede it. One can imagine a debate over Kracauer's conclusions here about how film should be used with someone like Kuleshov where Kuleshov, employing the medium specificity principle but favoring a different candidate (montage) as the basic element of film, would support a vision of film diametrically opposed to Kracauer's. How could Kracauer maneuver in such a debate? I suspect by either relying on false empirical generalizations or by begging the question by means of spurious a priori claims.[18]

The fifth premise in the argument is simply an extension or a corollary of the medium specificity principle—an application of the principle to the case where a medium has more than one element. The argument against it is of a piece with previous argumentation. Even supposing that photography is the basic element in film (something I would reject), we still need a reason why if in a given film (like *Ballet Mecanique*) emphasis on another element (say editing) is effective, though it does not emphasize photography, making that film should be illegitimate? I contend that Kracauer will not be able to advance a reason without incurring the dilemma rehearsed heretofore.

Premise 6 is true enough. Film does possess technical properties and narrative structures in addition to cinematography. But its combination with premise 5 yields a logically valid but false (or unsound) conclusion due to the problems that vex the fifth premise. Confronting the conclusion on its own terms, the problem is once again: Why should we sacrifice something like the breathtaking battle scenes in films like Visconti's *Senso*, Pontecorvo's *Burn!*, Walsh's *Captain Horatio Hornblower*, and Bondarchuk's *War and Peace* because the costumes make us aware they have been staged?

Indeed, we should also complain that Kracauer's conclusion is so vague in many of its central concepts—especially those pertaining to cinema's affinities—that it virtually guarantees the arbitrary use that Kracauer makes of them when he declares which films, genres, and deployments of techniques are uncinematic. Kracauer has not provided a firm theoretical foundation for determinig what films are cinematic, and, therefore, laudable. Rather, his theory is more like quicksand.

The Historical/Cultural Argument

So far we have been examining Kracauer's medium specificity argument. Kracauer develops this argument in the first section of *Theory of Film*. However, in his "Epilogue," entitled "Film in Our Time," where Kracauer discusses the importance of film, especially for contemporary society, he suggests another argument in favor of his conception of the cinematic. This argument rests on a diagnosis of culture in the age of science.

Kracauer begins by maintaining that, in large measure, we live in an era where religion and, putatively, ideology are disappearing. The result of this is that individuals experience the world as fragmented. What has brought this about is the rise of science. Science has destroyed the old gods. Moreover, science brings with it a distinct mode of thinking, one that relies on abstraction, and this penchant for abstraction further facilitates alienation, specifically alienation from the physical world and particular things. That is, science operates in terms of generalizations; the more we are engrossed in this mode of thinking, the more we are estranged from particulars.

Film, because of its supposed affinity for the physical world and for particulars, has a historic role or value in this context. Unlike past art, which transformed physical reality, film is a new art form, one that records and reveals physical reality. Thus of all the arts, film can function as an antidote to contemporary alienation from physical reality. Film, or at least cinematic film, enables us to get back in touch with particulars. Moreover, once we are back in touch with particulars, we will be in a position to evolve a new culture—not a return to religion and ideology, but a new framework that, apprised of the limits of science, will enable us to be at home in the world again. Given the awesome task that he attributes to film, it is perhaps no surprise that Kracauer falls into quasi-religious language, talking about film as the redemption of physical reality.[19]

The elements that comprise Kracauer's analysis should be familiar enough to intellectual historians. The fragmentation of modern life is a theme one finds almost everywhere, including in the works of Lukacs, Simmel, Benjamin and Heidegger. Indeed, for Heidegger, science is once again the culprit. Also, Kracauer's emphasis on the centrality of the particular is a recurring feature of Kantian and Neo-Kantian aesthetics and even predates them in the writings of Baumgarten. In the twentieth century, theorists as diverse as Adorno, Benjamin, Bergson, and Munsterberg champion the particular in various ways. In fact, Munsterberg develops a theory of film in the context of an aesthetics of particularity which, for Munsterberg, stands in contrast to scientific generality.[20] As with all these figures, including Kracauer, the determining background influence seems to have been Kant's decisive cleavage of the faculty of pure reason from that of aesthetic judgment.

But even if Kracauer stands in a definable lineage, he develops the aesthetics of particularity in his own fashion. Moreover, it supplies him, even if he is not explicitly aware of this, with a way of laying out and defending his theory of film without relying on the troublesome notion of medium specificity. For he can argue that the function of film today is set by the needs of contemporary society. Society's greatest need, given the rise of science, is the redemption of physical reality. That is a condition that requires urgent attention. Whatever features of film can serve this purpose are the ones that deserve emphasis.

Stating the case this way, Kracauer can pick out photography as the basic element of film without invoking the notion that film has a necessary essence. What directs our attention to the photographic element of film is its capacity to fulfill a contingently, historically situated function—

the task of redeeming physical reality. The approved use of film to record and reveal physical reality in terms of the unstaged, the indeterminate, the fortuitous, and endlessness does not follow here from film's putative status as essentially photographic, but from the fact that the primary role or value of film in our time is to function in a way that redeems physical reality. This value or role, albeit contingently motivated, serves in a fairly straightforward way to pick out photography as the relevant or basic element of film (for contemporary society) and to constrain and to guide the use of the articulatory processes of film (technical properties and narrative structures) at least for the duration of the current crisis of the dominance of scientific abstraction.

So, the core of the historical/cultural argument goes like this:

1. Due to the rise of science, modern society is alienated from the physical world and the experience of particularity.
2. If modern society is alienated from the physical world and the experience of particularity, then, all things being equal, any medium that can relieve that alienation should be used in a way that will enable it to do so.
3. Film can relieve the alienation from the physical world and the experience of particularity.
4. If film is to relieve the alienation from the physical world and the experience of particularity, then it must be used in such a way that its photographic element and its affinities are emphasized.
5. Therefore, film must emphasize its photographic element and its basic affinities (the unstaged, the fortuitous, the indeterminate, and endlessness).

This argument can then be continued, arguing that the technical properties and narrative structures of film should be subordinated to the purposes of the photographic element in order to fulfill the pressing social role of film—the redemption of physical reality for people lost in scientific abstraction.

We can ask at least two questions about the first premise: Is modern society alienated from physical reality and the experience of particularity? Is this the result of science? The first question is not easy to answer. How could you tell if a society is alienated from physical reality? Does driving a car put you in contact with physical reality or not? If not, why not? If it does so, since so many drive cars in first world societies (which I take it is, for Kracauer, the locus of modern society), then is alienation really so rampant? Perhaps Kracauer has something particular in mind that would discount counterexamples like this one. But then the burden of proof is on him to articulate it. Ironically, he rarely speaks in terms of abstractions less encompassing than "physical existence," "material reality," and so on.

Furthermore, even if we are amidst the crisis Kracauer adumbrates, has science brought it about? There aren't that many scientists in the population statistically and scientific knowledge does not pervade mass society. There are more people obsessed with alien abductions and satanic cults than those obsessed with quantum physics.

Moreover, pundits who believe in the crisis of abstraction have advanced other causes for it, such as bureaucracy and technology, including information technologies, a class to which film belongs. Indeed, few, I think, would endorse the end-of-ideology theme that Kracauer takes as given, and many who are sure that ideology is still alive and well might be disposed to attribute the alleged crisis of abstraction to ideology.

The question of whether science did it is especially problematic when it comes to Kracauer's third premise. For many nowadays who are disposed to agree with Kracauer that there is a crisis of abstraction would be prone to attribute it to the proliferation of information technologies, including both film and photography. We live in a mediated world, so the story goes, and you can't smell the roses if you are looking at a photograph of one.

Perhaps Kracauer would respond that the alienation from the physical world is only abetted by certain uses of film and photography, the ones that he regards as uncinematic and unphotographic. But certainly the case could be made that technological mediation in any form alienates us from the physical world, that is, if you believe that most of us are alienated from the physical world. Film, it might be said, tends, no matter how it is used, to estrange people from the flow of life, not to reimmerse them in it. (I raise this point not in order to endorse it, but only to remind the reader that if you believe that we are alienated from the physical world, particular things, and the flow of life, then you might still reject Kracauer's project of redemption because of a view of information technologies in general, which view, by the way, Kracauer has not bothered to foreclose.)[21]

Furthermore, before committing film to a crusade against abstraction, one might like to hear more from Kracauer about how film, even cinematic film, is supposed to secure this end. Why will seeing photographic pictures of particular things loosen the grip of scientific abstraction in the cases of those caught up in it. Is there some special psychological mechanism that will swing into operation here? Kracauer leaves such questions unanswered, which, in turn, leaves me skeptical.

Some aestheticians are apt to reject Kracauer's second premise—that if modern society faces a desperate situation, like the so-called crisis of alienation from the physical world, and, in addition, some artistic media can make a difference, then they should. Their grounds might be that art is and should be divorced from claims of social utility. I, however, am sympathetic to Kracauer's intuitions here. I see no genuine philosophical objection to placing art in the service of society. Nevertheless,

again, I would like to have a better account of the way in which a particular art, like film, can actually alleviate the putative malaise of abstraction as well as more compelling evidence that we are, in fact, in the
throes of such an epidemic.

Moreover, I should also note that Kracauer's suggestion that film
serve the needs of the modern world appears inconsistent with the dis-
paraging things that he has to say about film genres that persist because
they "cater to widespread social and cultural demands" (38). For isn't this
the grounds for Kracauer's historical/cultural defense of his conception of
cinematic films? Here Kracauer would probably respond that he is not
talking about catering, but ministering. But I suspect that his opponents
will charge that this is just another case of his begging the question.

In summary, Kracauer's *Theory of Film* is an ambitious attempt to defend
film realism—the doctrine that film should be realist because it is, in
essence, photographic. Kracauer maintains that in order to be authenti-
cally cinematic, film should be true to its photographic nature, which
brings with it an inherent commitment to realism. However, we have
seen that Kracauer's defense of this conclusion frequently relies on ques-
tion-begging assumptions that should be the results of his arguments
rather than their premises, hidden or otherwise. In this, Kracauer's attempt corresponds to a recurring tendency in classical film theory. For
the quest for the cinematic generally travels in a circle with theorists,
like Kracauer, discovering this or that nature of the cinematic by presupposing it from the start.

NOTES

1. Siegfried Kracauer, *Theory of Film: The Redemption of Physical Reality* (Oxford:
Oxford University Press, 1960). Page references to this book are to be found in the body of
my essay in parentheses. My source is the 1973 reprint of this book. For students interested
in reading more works by Kracauer, a useful guide is "Kracauer in English: A Bibliography,"
by Thomas Levin in *New German Critique*, no. 41 (Spring–Summer 1987).

2. For examples of some of Kracauer's earlier writings on film and mass culture, see
Siegfried Kracauer, *The Mass Ornament*, trans. Thomas Levin (Cambridge, Mass.: Harvard
University Press, 1995).

3. It should be noted that at present there is lively interest in Kracauer's early writings
on cinema among film scholars as well as a general interest in Kracauer's highly diversified
writings as cultural theorist, especially in relation to his contemporaries, such as Walter
Benjamin and T. W. Adorno. Some might even claim that these writings are more interesting than *Theory of Film*. Nevertheless, *Theory of Film* is an important landmark in the evolution of film theory as we now know it, and, therefore, still commands attention on its
own terms. For a taste of recent writings on Kracauer as a Weimar intellectual and an émi-
gré scholar, one place to start might be the *Special Issue on Siegfried Kracauer* presented by
New German Critique, no. 34 (Fall 1991). Of especial use for students in that issue is "The
English-Language Reception of Kracauer's Work: A Bibliography" by Thomas Y. Levin. Also
of interest is Dagmar Barnouw, *Critical Realism: History, Photography and the Work of
Siegfried Kracauer* (Baltimore, Md.: Johns Hopkins University Press, 1994).

4. In this assessment, I differ from Dudley Andrew, who finds the book "utterly transparent." Unlike Andrew, I think that *Theory of Film* only gives the appearance of clarity. With a little probing, it turns out to be a morass. See Dudley Andrew, "Siegfried Kracauer," in his book *The Major Film Theories* (Oxford: Oxford University Press, 1976), 106.

5. For biographical information about Kracauer, see esp. Martin Jay's "The Extraterritorial Life of Siegfried Kracauer," in idem, *Permanent Exiles: Essays on the Intellectual Migration from Germany to America* (New York: Columbia University Press, 1985). Also of interest in that volume are Jay's essays: "Politics of Translation: Siegfried Kracauer and Walter Benjamin on the Buber–Rosenzweig Bible" and "Adorno and Kracauer: Notes on a Troubled Friendship." For a more informal biographical account, see Leo Lowenthal, "As I Remember Friedel," *New German Critique*, no. 54 (Fall 1991).

6. Pauline Kael is very adept at demonstrating this. See Pauline Kael, "Is There a Cure for Film Criticism? Or: Some Unhappy Thoughts on Siegfried Kracauer's *Nature of Film*, " *Sight and Sound* 31, no. 2 (Spring 1962).

7. See André Bazin, *What Is Cinema?* trans. Hugh Gray (Berkeley: University of California Press, 1967), vol. 1.

8. Gotthold Ephraim Lessing, *Laocoon* (New York: Noonday, 1969). For a brief summary of this persuasion, see Noël Carroll, *Philosophical Problems of Classical Film Theory* (Princeton, N.J.: Princeton University Press, 1988).

9. The qualification "most probably" is introduced here in order to be sensitive to the fact that with particular cases Kracauer sometimes adduces compensating factors that insulate films that one might predict would be criticized on the basis of his theory from condemnation. Thus, the staginess of *The Cabinet of Dr. Caligari* is supposedly mitigated by underscoring a contrast between motion and motionlessness (61). As I have said earlier, I find Kracauer's ingenuity in incessantly discovering such mitigating circumstances and compensatory considerations suspiciously and lamentably ad hoc. Neverthless, since he finds so many special cases, it is safest to represent him as holding that ostensibly unsuitable cinematic content is only probable grounds for chastising a givem film. One must also cinch the case at hand by assuring oneself that there are no extenuating considerations.

10. Notice that although Kracauer repeatedly stresses that film finds its origins in photography, he does not use this to establish that photography is its basic element. Perhaps this is because he realizes that origin is irrelevant to essence. For example, if architecture originated in stone or wooden structures, that is nevertheless irrelevant to determining the essence of architecture, since other building materials, like steel and glass, became available to architecture after its origin.

11. For an examination of the medium specificity notion, see the first chapter of my *Philosophical Problems of Classical Film Theory*. Medium specificity theories of film appeared in Germany in the twenties, when Kracauer was a film reviewer. Indeed, one such theory that also claimed that film was realistic was propounded by Rudolf Harms, though Kracauer criticized it for other reasons. See Rudolf Harms, *Philosophie des Films: Seine aesthetischen un metaphysichen* (Zurich: Felix Meiner, 1926). For background information about early German film theory, consult Sabine Hake, *The Cinema's Third Machine: Writing on Film in Germany 1907–1933* (Lincoln: University of Nebraska Press, 1993).

12. It should be noted that the notion that film records and reveals reality may cause problems for the loose ways in which Kracauer characterizes "reality." Kracauer seems to think that talk about material reality and visible reality are interchangeable. But if we are talking about material reality, then revealing its nature (e.g., in terms of atomic structure) may be at odds with recording visible reality.

13. See Lev Kuleshov, *Kuleshov on Film*, trans. Ronald Levaco (Berkeley: University of California Press, 1975).

14. On pp. 12–13, Kracauer allows that determining the nature of certain media may be difficult, but then asserts that this is not the case for photography. Well, there's a knockdown, drag-out argument for you.

15. It is interesting to note that V. F. Perkins also develops a similar two-part approach to film that explicitly attempts to reconcile realist and formative tendencies. On his view, realism is a necessary condition for film as film and it constrains the range of formative effects. However, the range of formative effects for Perkins is not a matter of revealing reality but of making symbolic comments on it, where these comments are to be motivated by what is photographically plausible within the story world. It would be a nice question to consider how Kracauer would argue for the superiority of his theory against a competing theory as close to his own as Perkins' is. See V. F. Perkins, *Film as Film* (Baltimore: Penguin, 1972).

16. Probably Hollywood genre films, in general, tend to operate within narratively closed universes and, consequently, they would engender Kracauer's opprobrium. Perhaps this is the grounds for Heide Schlupmann's interesting suggestion that *Theory of Film* is a reaction to 1950s American films. See Heide Schlupmann's "On the Subject of Survival: On Kracauer's *Theory of Film*, " *New German Critique*, no. 54 (Fall , 1991): 121.

17. See Andrew Tudor's useful "Aesthetics of Realism: Bazin and Kracauer" for an alternative, thought compatible, way of setting out Kracauer's argument in *Theories of Film* by Andrew Tudor (London: Secker and Warburg in association with the British Film Institute, 1974), 84.

18. This is not said to defend Kuleshov's view, but only to point up problems with Kracauer's. In point of fact, I reject all medium specificity arguments, including Kuleshov's. For my arguments, see Noël Carroll, *Theorizing the Moving Image* (New York: Cambridge University Press, 1996).

19. For speculation on the religious sources of Kracauer's theorizing, see Miriam Hansen, "Decentric Perspectives: Kracauer's Early Writings on Film and Mass Culture," *New German Critique*, no. 54 (Fall 1991).

20. Hugo Münsterberg, *Film: A Psychological Study* (New York: Dover, 1970).

21. For the record, I should say that I am not convinced that modern society is alienated from the physical world, since I am so unclear about what such alienation would involve.

ANNOTATED BIBLIOGRAPHY

Kracauer, Siegfried. *From Caligari to Hitler: A Psychological History of the German Film.* Princeton, N.J.: Princeton University Press, 1947.

This is a pioneering work in the sociology of film. It claims to discern tendencies favorable to the rise of Nazism in German film prior to World War II. It is often criticized today for being overly selective and associative, for failing to attend to other non-German films that were popular with Weimar audiences, and for failing to note important differences between German films that were widely popular and those that were rather esoteric. However, it is a text that any prospective social critic of film needs to confront.

―――. *Theory of Film: The Redemption of Physical Reality.* New York: Oxford University Press, 1965.

This book, which is discussed at length in the essay by Noël Carroll in this anthology, is a major statement of the realist tendency in film theory. Along with the work of André Bazin, *Theory of Film* provided a credo for film realists in the sixties and seventies. However, with the advent of semiotics and newer forms of film theory, its influence has been largely eclipsed.

―――. *The Mass Ornament: Weimar Essays.* Ed. Thomas Levin. Cambridge, Mass.: Harvard University Press, 1995.

This is a collection of a number of Kracauer's works in social criticism before he left Germany. Of special interest to film scholars are the essays "Calico-World," "The Little Shopgirls Go to the Movies," "Film 1928," "Cult of Distraction," and "Photography."

Carroll, Noël. "The Cabinet of Dr. Kracauer," *Millennium Film Journal,* nos. 1–2 (Spring–Summer 1978): 77–85.

   This article presents a detailed criticism of Siegfried Kracauer's analysis of *The Cabinet of Dr. Caligari,* which is perhaps Kracauer's most famous discussion of a single film and the cornerstone of his book *From Caligari to Hitler.*

———. *Philosophical Problems of Classical Film Theory.* Princeton, N.J.: Princeton University Press, 1988.

   This book provides an overview of major trends in film theory prior to the advent of semiological film. As such, it is concerned with the problematic of many of the film theorists dealt with in this anthology.

Burch

"Spatial and Temporal Articulations" and "Editing as a Plastic Art"

Spatial and Temporal Articulations

The terminology a filmmaker or film theoretician chooses to employ is a significant reflection of what he takes a film to be.

The French term *découpage technique* or simply *découpage*[1] with its several related meanings is a case in point. In everyday practice, *découpage* refers to the final form of a script, incorporating whatever technical information the director feels it necessary to set down on paper to enable a production crew to understand his intention and find the technical means with which to fulfill it, to help them plan their work in terms of his. By extension, but still on the same practical, workaday level, *découpage* also refers to the more or less precise breakdown of a narrative action into separate shots and sequences *before filming.* French filmmakers, of course, are not the only ones to have a term for this procedure. Both English- and Italian-speaking filmmakers have a similar term for this final version of the script—called a "shooting script" in English and a *copione* in Italian—though they always speak of "writing" it or "establishing" it, thereby indicating that the operation the word describes is no more important in their minds than any other in the making of a film. A third French meaning of *découpage,* however, has no English equivalent. Although obviously derived from the second meaning of a shot breakdown, it is quite distinct from it, no longer referring to a process taking place before filming or to a particular technical operation but, rather, to the underlying structure of the *finished* film. Formally, a film consists of a succession of fragments excerpted from a spatial and temporal continuum. *Découpage* in its third French meaning refers to what results when the spatial fragments, or, more accurately, the succession of spatial fragments

Chapter 1 and the first section of chapter 3 from *Theory of Film Practice* by Noël Burch. English translation copyright © 1973 by Praeger Publishers, Inc. Reprinted by permission of Henry Holt and Co., Inc.

excerpted in the shooting process, converge with the temporal fragments whose duration may be roughly determined during the shooting, but whose final duration is established only on the editing table. The dialectical notion inherent in the term *découpage* enables us to determine, and therefore to analyze, the specific form of a film, its essential unfolding in time and space. *Découpage* as a structural concept involving a synthesis is strictly a French notion. An American filmmaker (or film critic, in so far as American film critics are interested in film technique at all) conceives of a film as involving two successive and separate operations: the selection of a camera setup and then the cutting of the filmed images. It may never occur to English-speaking filmmakers or English-speaking critics that these two operations stem from a single underlying concept, simply because they have at their disposal no single word for this concept. If many of the most important formal breakthroughs in film in the last fifteen years[2] have occurred in France, it may be in part a matter of vocabulary.

An examination of the actual manner in which the two partial *découpages*, one temporal and the other spatial, join together to create a single articulated formal texture enables us to classify the possible ways of joining together the spaces depicted by two succeeding camera setups and the different ways of joining together two temporal situations. Such classification of the possible forms of temporal and spatial articulations between two shots might seem to be a rather academic endeavor, but to my knowledge no one has previously attempted such a classification, and I believe that it may well open up some important new perspectives.

Setting aside such "punctuation marks" as dissolves and wipes, which may be regarded as mere variations on the straight cut, five distinct types of temporal articulation between any two shots are possible.

The two shots, first of all, may be absolutely continuous. In a certain sense, the clearest example of this sort of temporal continuity is a cut from a shot of someone speaking to a shot of someone listening, with the dialogue continuing without a break in voice-off. This is, of course, precisely what happens whenever a shot is followed by a reverse-angle shot. Although the term "straight match-cut," as is made clear later on in this chapter, refers more specifically to spatial continuity, it is also another example of absolute temporal continuity. If shot A shows someone coming up to a door, putting his hand on the doorknob, turning it, then starting to open the door, shot B, perhaps taken from the other side of the door, can pick up the action at the precise point where the previous shot left off and show the rest of the action as it would have "actually" occurred, with the person coming through the door and so on. This action could even conceivably be filmed by two cameras simultaneously, resulting in two shots[3] that, taken together, preserve an absolute continuity of action seen from two different angles. To obtain as complete a continuity in the edited film, all we would have to do is cut the tail of shot A into the head of shot B on the editing table.

A second possible type of temporal relationship between two shots involves the presence of a gap between them, constituting what might be called a *temporal ellipsis* or *time abridgment*. Referring again to the example of someone opening a door filmed by two cameras (or by the same camera from two different angles), a part of the action might be omitted when these two shots are joined together (in shot A someone puts his hand on the doorknob and turns it; in shot B he closes the door behind him). Even the most conventional films frequently use this technique as a means of tightening the action, of eliminating the superfluous. In shot A someone might perhaps start up a flight of stairs, and in shot B he might already be on the second or even the fifth floor. Particularly when a simple action such as opening a door and walking through it is involved, it might be emphasized that the ellipsis or abridgment can occur in any one of a large number of possible variations; the "real" action might span some five or six seconds, and the time ellipsis might involve the omission of anything from a twenty-fourth of a second to several seconds, and might occur at any point in the action. This is equally true in the case of absolute temporal continuity; the transition between shots may occur anywhere. A film editor might maintain that in both cases there is only one "right" point at which to make a straight match-cut or abridge the action, but what he really means is that there is only one place where the shot transition will not be consciously noticed by the viewer.[4] This may well be. But if we are seeking a film style that is less "smooth," that actually stresses the structures that it is based upon, a whole range of possibilities remains open.

This first type of temporal ellipsis involves, then, an omission of a time span that is not only perceptible but *measurable* as well. The occurrence and the extent of the omission are necessarily always indicated by a more or less noticeable break in either a visual or an auditory action that is potentially capable of being completely continuous. (A continuous temporal-auditory action, verbal or otherwise, occurring in conjunction with a discontinuous temporal-visual action, as in Jean-Luc Godard's *Breathless* and Louis Malle's *Zazie dans le Métro*, is, of course, not at all precluded.) In the previous examples of going through a door or going up a flight of stairs we become aware of the existence of a temporal discontinuity or gap as a result of the spatial continuity having been forcefully enough maintained to allow the viewer to determine mentally that some portion of a continuous action has been omitted and even enable him to "measure" the actual extent of the omission. (Temporal *continuity* can likewise only be measured relative to some other *uninterrupted* visual or auditory continuity.) Thus, if a shot transition takes us from one location to another, more distant one without there being any way of relating the two distinct spaces (such as a telephone or some other means of communication), the temporal continuity between them will remain indefinite unless it is preserved through the use of such clumsy devices as successive close-ups of a clock-dial or some convention such as cross-cutting, an emphatic alternation between two actions occurring in two distinct spaces.[5]

A third type of temporal articulation and a second type of abridgment are possible, the *indefinite ellipsis*. It may cover an hour or a year, the exact extent of the temporal omission being measurable only through the aid of something "external"—a line of dialogue, a title, a clock, a calendar, a change in dress style, or the like. It is closely related to the scenario, to the actual narrative and visual content, but it nonetheless performs a genuine temporal function,[6] for, even though the time of the narrative obviously is not the same as the time of the film, the two time spans can nevertheless be related in a rigorously dialectical manner. The reader may object that the boundary between the "measurable" ellipsis and the "indefinite" ellipsis is not clear. Admittedly a segment of time abridged in the process of splicing together two shots showing someone walking through a door can be measured rather accurately—namely, as that part of the action that we know must be gone through but do not see, whereas we are less capable of measuring "the time it takes to climb five flights of stairs." However, "the time it takes to climb five flights of stairs" still constitutes a unit of measurement, much as "one candle power" is the amount of light furnished by one candle; this is not at all the case, on the other hand, when we realize that something is occurring "a few days later," as in an indefinite ellipsis.

A *time reversal* constitutes another type of possible temporal articulation. In the example of someone walking through a door, shot A might have included the entire action up to the moment of going through the door, with shot B going back to the moment when the door was opened, repeating part of the action in a deliberately artificial manner. This procedure constitutes what might be called a *short time reversal,* or an overlapping cut, such as Sergei Eisenstein used so often and to such striking advantage—as in the bridge sequence in *October* (*Ten Days That Shook the World*)—and such as certain avant-garde filmmakers have used (see also François Truffaut's *La Peau douce* and Luis Buñuel's *The Exterminating Angel*). At this point, however, it is worth noting that time reversals, like time ellipses, are commonly used on a very small scale, involving the omission or repetition of only a few frames, as a means of preserving *apparent* continuity. The preservation of an appearance of continuity is, of course, what is always involved in any conventional use of time abridgment. What we are referring to now, however, no longer involves simple mental deception—that is to say, making an action that is not visually continuous convey a "spirit" of continuity—but the actual physical deception of the eye. When it comes to "match-cutting" two shots showing someone walking through a door, for perceptual reasons which are quite beyond the scope of this book, a few frames of the action may be omitted or repeated in order that the filmed action may seem more smoothly continuous than would have been the case had the shot been picked up *precisely* where the previous one left off.

The flashback is a more usual form of time reversal. Just as a time ellipsis can span either just a few seconds or several years, so too can a time reversal. The fifth and last type of temporal articulation thus is the *indefinite time reversal,* which is analogous to the *indefinite time ellipsis* (the exact extent of a flashback is as difficult to measure without outside clues as is the extent of a flashforward) and the opposite of a *measurable time reversal.* The reason why the flashback so often seems such a dated and essentially uncinematic technique today is that, aside from its use by Alain Resnais and in a few isolated films such as Marcel Carné's *Le Jour se lève* and Marcel Hanoun's *Une Simple histoire,* the formal function of the flashback and its precise relationship to other forms of temporal articulation have never been understood. Like the voice-over, the flashback has remained little more than a convenient narrative device borrowed from the novel, although both have recently begun to assume other functions.

But might not this inability to measure the exact temporal duration spanned by either flashback or flashforward point to some basic and previously overlooked truth? Are not jumps forward and backward in time really identical on the formal organic level of a film? Are there not ultimately, then, only four kinds of temporal relationships, the fourth consisting of a great jump in time, either forward or backward? Alain Robbe-Grillet obviously believes this is so, and in that sense, his and Resnais' *Last Year at Marienbad* perhaps comes closer to the organic essence of film than it is currently fashionable to believe.

Three types of articulation between the spaces depicted in two successive shots are possible—apart from, and independent of, temporal articulations, even though they have obvious analogies to them.

A first kind of possible spatial relationship between two shots involves the preservation of spatial continuity in a manner similar to that in which temporal continuity is preserved, *although this spatial continuity may or may not be accompanied by temporal continuity.* The door example in all three variations is an instance of spatial continuity; in each case, the same fragment of space fully or partially seen in shot A is also visible in shot B. Any change in angle or scale (matching shots, that is, taken from the same angle but closer or farther away) with relation to the same camera subject or within the same location or the same circumscribed space generally establishes a spatial continuity between two shots. That much is obvious. It seems to follow that there is only one other form of possible spatial articulation between two shots: spatial *discontinuity*—in other words, anything not falling into the first category. This discontinuity, however, can be divided into two distinct subtypes bearing a rather curious resemblance to the two distinct subtypes of time ellipses and reversals. While showing a space different in every way from the space visible in shot A, shot B can show a space that is obviously in close *proximity* to the spatial fragment previously seen (it may, for instance, be within the same room or other closed or circumscribed space). This type of spatial discontinuity has given rise to a whole vocabulary dealing with spatial orientation, and the fact that such a vocabulary should be necessary serves to emphasize how essentially different this type is from an obvious third possibility: complete and radical spatial discontinuity.

This vocabulary dealing with spatial orientation brings us to a key term, one of some concern to us here: the "match" or "match-cut." "Match" refers to any element having to do with the preservation of continuity between two or more shots. Props, for instance, can be "match" or "not match." On a sound stage one can often hear remarks such as "these glasses are not match," meaning that the actor was not wearing the same glasses or was not wearing glasses at all in a shot that has already been filmed and is supposed to "match" with the shot at hand. "Match" can also refer to space, as in eyeline matches, matches in screen direction, and matches in the position of people or objects on screen. There are also spatiotemporal matches, as in the door example, where the speed of movement in the two shots must "match," that is, must *appear* to be the same. To clarify this notion of "match" or "match-cutting," a brief history of how it developed is in order.

When, between 1905 and 1920, filmmakers started bringing their cameras up close to the actors and *fragmenting* the "proscenium space" that early cinema had left intact, they noticed that, if they wanted to maintain the illusion of theatrical space, a "real" space in which the viewer has an immediate and constant sense of orientation (and this was, and still remains, the essential aim for many directors), certain rules had to be respected if the viewer was not to lose his footing, to lose that instinctive sense of direction he always has in traditional theater and believes he has in life. This was the source of the concepts of eyeline match, matching screen direction, and matching screen position.

Eyeline match and matching screen direction concern two shots that are spatially discontinuous but in close proximity. When two shots show two different persons supposedly looking at each other, person A must look screen right and person B screen left, or vice versa, for if both look in the same direction in two successive shots, the viewer will inevitably have the impression that they are not looking at each other and will suddenly feel that he has completely lost his orientation in screen space. This observation on the part of the second generation of filmmakers contains a basic truth that goes far beyond the original goal of matching. Only the Russian directors, however (before Stalinism brought film experimentation to an abrupt halt), were beginning to glimpse what this really implied: that only what happens in frame is important, that the only film space is screen space, that screen space can be manipulated through the use of an infinite variety of *possible* real spaces, and that disorienting the viewer is one of a filmmaker's most valuable tools. We will come back to this idea later.

As a corollary to the eyeline match, filmmakers also discovered the principle of matching screen direction: someone or something exiting frame left must always enter a new frame showing a space that is supposedly close by or contiguous from the right; if this does not occur, it will seem that there has been a change in the direction the person or object is moving in.

It was also noticed, finally, that in any situation involving two shots preserving spatial continuity and showing two people seen from relatively close up, their respective screen positions as established in the first shot, with one of them perhaps to the right and the other to the left, must not be changed in succeeding shots. To do so risks confusing the viewer's eye, for he invariably will read any shift in screen position as necessarily corresponding to a shift in "real" space.

As the techniques for breaking down an action into shots and sequences were developed and refined, these continuity rules became more and more firmly fixed,[7] methods ensuring that they would be respected were perfected,[8] and their underlying aim, to make any transition between two shots that were spatially continuous or in close proximity *imperceptible*, became increasingly apparent. The introduction of sound brought an increased emphasis on film as an essentially "realistic" medium, an erroneous conception that soon resulted in what we might call the "zero point of cinematic style," at least in so far as shot transitions were concerned. The Russian experiments exploring an entirely different idea of *découpage* were soon considered outdated or at best only marginally important. "Jump cuts" and "bad" or "unclear" matches were to be avoided because they made the essentially *discontinuous* nature of a shot transition or the *ambiguous* nature of cinematic space too apparent (the overlapping cuts in *October* were viewed as "bad" matches, and the *découpage* of Alexander Dovzhenko's *Earth* was thought to be "obscure"). Attempting thus to deny the many-sided nature of the cut, filmmakers eventually had no well-defined aesthetic reason whatsoever for cutting from one shot to the next, often doing so for reasons of pure convenience, until by the end of the 1940s some of the most rigorous directors (Luchino Viscounti in *La Terra trema*, Alfred Hitchcock in *Rope*, Michelangelo Antonioni in *Cronaca di un amore*)[9] began wondering whether cuts were necessary at all, whether they should not be purely and simply eliminated or used very sparingly and endowed with a very special function.

The time has now come to change our attitude toward the function and nature of cinematic articulation, both between individual shots and in the film overall, as well as its relation to narrative structure. We are just beginning to realize that the formal organization of shot transitions and "matches" in the strict sense of the word is the essential cinematic task. Each articulation, as we have seen, is defined by two parameters, the first temporal, the second spatial. There are, therefore, fifteen basic ways of articulating two shots, that being the number of possible combinations of the five temporal types and the three spatial types of transitions. Each of these possibilities, moreover, can give rise to an almost infinite number of permutations, determined not only by the extent of the time ellipsis or reversal but also, and more importantly, by another parameter that is capable of undergoing an almost infinite number of variations too: the changes in camera angle and camera–subject distance (not to mention deliberate discrepancies in eyeline angles or matching trajectories, which are less easy to control but almost as important). I am not saying that these are the only elements that play a role in a transition between shots. But other elements such as camera and subject movement, frame content and composition, and the like can define only the particular nature of a given match and not the function of articulations in general. As regards the content of the film image, it may be interesting to know that a close-up of a man's expressionless face followed by a shot of a bowl of soup creates the impression that the man is hungry; but this relationship between the content of two shots is a *syntactical* one that merely helps us determine the *semantic* relationship between them. Although film remains largely an imperfect means of communication, it is nonetheless possible to foresee a time when it will become a totally immanent object whose semantic function will be intimately joined with its plastic function to create a *poetic function.* Although camera movements, entrances into and exits from frame, composition, and so on can all function as devices aiding in the organization of the film object, I feel that the shot transition will remain the basic element in the infinitely more complex structures of the future.

One of the possible forms that this overall organization of film articulations might take can already be foreseen, for the fifteen types of shot transitions can give rise to patterns of *mutual interference,* resulting in yet another controllable set of permutations. At the moment of transition, the articulation between two shots might seem to fit into any one of the five temporal categories and any one of the three spatial categories, but then something in shot B or some other subsequent shot might *retrospectively* reveal that the transition actually belongs in an altogether different temporal or spatial category, or perhaps even both. Examples of this procedure exist even in relatively conventional filmmaking. In a scene in Hitchcock's *The Birds,* Tippi Hedren, who has lingered too long at the home of the local schoolteacher, telephones her fiancé. The first shot shows her in a medium close-up. The next shot shows the teacher starting to sit down in an armchair, blocking part of the frame at the beginning of the shot. Because of the alternation between shots to which we have become accustomed in similar scenes, and more importantly, because of the absence of any other clue to the spatial orientation, we have the impression the camera is aimed at some other part of the set; hence there appears to be preservation of temporal continuity (Tippi Hedren continuing her conversation off screen) along with spatial discontinuity. When the teacher is finally seated, however, she reveals the part of the set in the background that she has previously blocked from view, and we see Tippi Hedren in a medium-long shot at the telephone. Spatial continuity had in fact been preserved as well (it is a matching shot from the same angle). Our first impression of the situation was an erroneous one, and we are belatedly forced to correct our initial misconception. This is a much more complex process of awareness, to say the least, than that implied in the "invisible" match. The exact nature of the relationship between the two shots remains vague for several seconds and becomes obvious only sometime after the transition has occurred. The variable duration of this interval may furnish another parameter.

Another frequently employed technique involves having a distant shot of someone followed by a closer one, with this second shot subsequently turning out to be occurring at some other time and perhaps even in some other place. Although this procedure is commonly used in flashbacks and time ellipses, it has hidden potentialities that allow more complex formal structures to be created (as in *Une Simple histoire*).

It is, however, important to note that this sort of disorientation presupposes a "coherent" spatial and temporal continuity, a previously created context built around immediately comprehensible relationships between shots.[10] A more systematic,[11] more structural use of the disorientation created by these "retroactive matches" would depend on establishing some sort of dialectical relationship between such matches and others that are immediately comprehensible, a dialectic in which the "deferred" match might perhaps still be an exceptional device but would no longer remain a gratuitous or merely stylistic "gimmick."

Still other possibilities can result from the nonresolution of these "open" matches, films that would have this very ambiguity as their basis, films in which the viewer's sense of "real" space would be constantly subverted, films in which he could never orient himself. Resnais' *Last Year at Marienbad* and Jean-Marie Straub's *Nicht Versöhnt*, especially in their use of indefinite time ellipses and reversals, already provide examples.[12]

I have just briefly outlined a set of formal "objects"—the fifteen different types of shot transitions and the parameters that define them—capable of rigorous development through such devices as rhythmic alternation, recapitulation, retrogression, gradual elimination, cyclical repetition, and serial variation, thus creating structures similar to those of twelve-tone music. None of this is as abstractly theoretical as might be imagined.

As early as 1931, Fritz Lang's masterpiece *M* was entirely structured around a rigorous organization of the film's formal articulations, starting with sequences in which each shot is temporally and spatially autonomous, with time ellipses and changes in location playing the obviously predominant role, then gradually and systematically evolving toward the increasing use of the continuity cut, finally culminating in the famous trial sequence in which temporal and spatial continuity are strictly preserved for some ten minutes. In the course of this progression a certain number of "retroactive matches" also occur, the most striking of which takes place when the gangsters leave the building in which they have captured the sadistic child-murderer. Lang repeats a shot, already used several times, of a housebreaker seen through the hole in the floor he has made to get into a locked bank. The thief asks for a ladder so he can climb out. A ladder is thrown down and he clambers out, only to discover that it is the police and not his gangster friends who are there waiting for him. We then realize that the time between the mob's departure and the arrival of the police has been completely skipped over in a time ellipsis, that instead of occurring immediately after the departure of the thief's pals this shot in fact happens a good deal later than we initially thought.

A more recent film, Marcel Hanoun's little-known masterpiece *Une Simple histoire,* is entirely structured around principles similar to the one I have been describing. Although these principles are arrived at in Hanoun's case in a purely empirical manner, they are nevertheless applied with utmost rigor. *Une Simple histoire* will be examined in detail in another chapter.

The contemporary film narrative is gradually liberating itself from the constraints of the literary or pseudo-literary forms that played a large part in bringing about the "zero point of cinematic style" that reigned supreme during the 1930s and 1940s and still remains in a position of some strength today. It is only through systematic and thorough exploration of the *structural* possibilities inherent in the cinematic parameters I have been describing that film will be liberated from the old narrative forms and develop new "open" forms that will have more in common with the formal strategies of post-Debussyian music than with those of the pre-Joycean novel. Film will attain its formal autonomy only when these new "open" forms begin to be used organically. What this principally involves is the creation of a truly consistent relationship between a film's spatial and temporal articulations and its narrative content, formal structure determining narrative structure as much as vice versa. It also implies giving as important a place to the viewer's disorientation as to his orientation. And these are but two of the possible multiple dialectics that will form the very *substance* of the cinema of the future, a cinema in which *découpage* in the limited sense of breaking a narrative down into scenes will no longer be meaningful to the real filmmaker and *découpage* as defined here will cease to be experimental and purely theoretical and come into its own in actual film practice. It is this cinema of the future that the following pages will hopefully help to bring forth.

NOTES

1. From the verb *découper*, "to cut into pieces."

2. As of 1966.

3. Two meanings of the word "shot" should be distinguished, depending on whether it is shooting or editing that is being referred to. During shooting a shot refers to whatever is filmed after the camera starts and before it stops; during editing it refers to whatever is included between two "cuts" or shot changes. Two words are in fact needed, but to my knowledge no language makes such a distinction.

4. See my remarks below on the "zero point of cinematic style."

5. That this is no more than a convention is quite amply demonstrated by an episode in the television series "The Man from U.N.C.L.E.," which consisted of two separate actions cross-cut together; on the one hand, we witnessed Ilya Kouriakin's misadventures as a prisoner of an Arab tribe, obviously extending over a period of several days, and, on the other hand, Napoleon Solo's adventures, taking place within a period of only a few hours.

6. This has only recently become apparent, principally because this kind of ellipsis has ceased to be systematically indicated by dissolves.

7. The principal ones have been mentioned here. Also worth mentioning is the rule about changing a camera angle by at least 30 degrees (or not at all), which stems from the perceptual nature of the matched-shot change (see Chapter 3).

8. Also worth citing: the cutaway, the rule of the median line, and the manner in which actors' movements can be slowed down or speeded up so that long shots and close-ups of the same subject match (see Chapter 3).

9. It is worth pointing out that this preference for prolonged shots was subsequently abandoned by all three directors, corresponding (in Antonioni's case at least) to an increased awareness of the extremely important function a shot change can fulfill.

10. The author refers readers to Eisenstein's concept of the "montage unit" as set forth in Vladimir Nizhny, *Lessons with Eisenstein,* trans. Jay Leyda and Ivor Montagu (New York: Hill and Wang, 1969), a book with which he was unfamiliar at the time of writing.

11. Bresson's *Une Femme douce,* which appeared just before the publication of this book, has a formal texture entirely based on this kind of match—and it indicates the limits inherent in a systematic use of "deferred" or "retroactive" matches.

12. Robbe-Grillet's *L'Homme qui ment (The Man Who Lies)* obviously goes much farther in this direction.

Editing as a Plastic Art

Thus far, I have examined the general nature of a filmed image and the articulations between such images without really considering what they actually look like. While still maintaining my "structural" approach, I might now examine both the image and the shot transition as concrete visual phenomena.

The Screen Image

I might first venture to point out how the way in which we see differs from the way in which a camera sees, an ambitious and somewhat risky endeavor, which many others, notably Karel Reisz in his excellent *Technique of Film Editing,*[1] have undertaken before me. However, since I am attempting to redefine the components of film form, I cannot avoid dealing with this particular problem, despite the difficulty involved.

We may approach it by considering a phenomenon that occurs as frequently in film as in real life: reflections on a glass surface. Let us see what the top of a pinball machine looks like when viewed from an angle. If the intensity of light on both sides of the sheet of glass is more or less equal, we will have no trouble making out what is taking place below it, and, if we are absorbed in a game in progress, we will see only that game; the glass will seem perfectly transparent. If, however, it should occur to us to examine the sheet of glass more objectively, we will notice that a reflection of the surroundings is superimposed on our view of the game going on underneath it, that both images are more or less equal in intensity, and that if the reflected image of the surroundings is at all complex the game in progress under the glass surface will now strike us as being practically "illegible." It is actually an unconscious mental process (selection) and a physiological process (focusing the eye) that enable us to differentiate successfully the two superimposed images, rejecting the one that does not interest us.

Let us now film this same situation without taking any special precautions. The resulting film image will show these two images superimposed, and when this superimposition is projected on the screen, we would succeed in eliminating the image that in principle does not interest us only with the greatest difficulty. The image of the game in progress beneath the glass would have become absolutely "illegible." If we wish to recreate the same effect we experienced watching the scene with the naked eye, we must attach a polarizing filter to the front of the lens to tone down the reflection or mask the reflected background, if this is possible.

Why is it impossible to distinguish between these two images once they have been captured on film and projected on a screen? This is because everything projected on a film screen has exactly the same intrinsic "reality," the same "presence." Once projected on the flat surface of the screen, the two superimposed images become one and indissoluble, mainly because the screen has only two dimensions and therefore any shape projected on it is equally "present," just as much "before our eyes" as any other shape. Even the parts of the image that are out of focus are perceived as quite distinct, visible, tangible entities, as what might be called "clumps of fuzziness." Another example might clarify this even further. Let us consider the following situation: while setting up a shot, a director of photography notices that there is a lamp or some other prop behind an actor, perhaps even several yards behind him, but just above his head. Even if the object in the background is going to be shown in such soft focus that its contours will be very indistinct, the director of photography will insist that the lamp be moved, because it will seem to be growing out of the actor's head. And he is quite right. Were we to be confronted with the same scene in life or were we to stand in the same place as the camera, we would not be at all disconcerted by the lamp; it would not strike us as being some monstrous excrescence; we would probably not even notice it. Yet, on the screen, this juxtaposition of objects would immediately leap to the eye, for when we view a screen we see everything at once; every form and every contour seems equally prominent visually (while sometimes we are completely oblivious to the head of a person sitting just in front of us and blocking as much as a fourth of that same screen!). Because of this fact, the problem of "legibility" arises more commonly and above all in more specific terms when we are observing a film image than when we are observing a real-life situation.

Our contention that all the elements in any given film image are perceived as equal in importance obviously runs counter to a fondly cherished notion of nineteenth-century art critics later embraced by a number of twentieth-century photographers: the belief that the eye explores a framed image according to a fixed itinerary, focusing first on a supposed "center of compositional focus" (generally determined by the time-honored "golden rectangle"), then traveling through the composition along a path supposedly determined by the disposition of its dominant lines. Eisenstein himself was quite taken with this notion, and the visual portion of his analysis of the introduction to the battle on the ice in *Alexander Nevsky* is based on this supposition. Such a conception is as outdated in art criticism today as composition according to the golden rectangle is in the art of painting. Even if the nineteenth-century eye did indeed see things in this way, the modern eye apparently does not. Any film image obviously includes some elements that call attention to themselves more strongly than others do, a case in point being that someone who is speaking will generally be noticed first. This is indeed true, but we are nonetheless also aware of the compositional whole, of which the person speaking is but a part, and we are aware in particular of the actual rectangular frame, even if the background of the image is uniformly black, white, or gray. For to "look" has to do with a mental process, whereas to "see" has to do with the physiology of the eye. And, when we view a film, as when we view a painting or a photograph, *seeing* is no longer dependent on *looking*, as is nearly always the case in a real-life situation; the selectivity involved in looking no longer affects the nonselectivity involved in seeing in the slightest.[2]

For all this to be the case, there is, however, one essential condition: the viewer must be seated at the proper distance from the screen. If he is too close, so close that his field of vision does not include the whole screen, his eyes must change focus as the centers of visual interest shift, and he will never be able to grasp the total visual effect created by the framed image. If, on the other hand, he is too far away, the image will be so schematic that he will see only these centers of interest, within a frame that is smaller than that seen in the view-finder by the filmmaker when he shot it (the view-finder image, we must remember, takes in the eye's whole field of vision), and the initial principles underlying the composition will thus be distorted (just as in painting, a particular composition cannot be successfully executed on every scale, each composition seemingly having a scale best suited to it). With these as well as other considerations being taken into account, it has been mathematically determined that the optimum viewing distance is approximately two times the width of the screen. The fact that under present circumstances it is quite impossible for every viewer in a theater to be at that precise distance from the screen (nor even within a reasonable approximation of it) does nothing to invalidate this principle, but simply indicates that the movie theaters of the future will have to be built differently.[3]

Once a filmmaker has become aware of the nature of the film image, as outlined here, what conclusions should he draw? First, to state the obvious, the frame must always be conceived of as a total composition. Yet the possible ways of composing any given shot are as various as the temperaments of individual filmmakers, and the problem of composition in general is beyond the scope of this book. On the other hand, a far smaller number of filmmakers are aware of, let alone concerned with, the possibility—or even the obligation, if they are at all sensitive to the imperative need to deal organically with the raw materials of filmmaking—of organizing the transitions, that is, the articulations between shots as a function of the total composition of each successive shot—thereby creating a structural framework capable of incorporating the formal elements discussed thus far as well as those to be dealt with in future chapters.

NOTES

1. Karel Reisz and Gavin Millar, *Technique of Film Editing* (New York: Hastings, 1967).

2. What is described here, however, is the "good gestalt" of an ideal viewer. Further research has shown that the filmgoer often tends to see filmed images very much as he sees life: unframed, *lumpen,* with the figures completely blotting out the ground. The pinball example is in fact an extreme case significant only on an elementary level.

3. These comments were written before the release of Tati's *Playtime.* Even if they still hold true for films in general, they are not applicable to Tati's film, the first in the history of cinema that not only must be seen several times, but also must be viewed from several different distances from the screen. In its form, it is probably the first truly "open" film. Will it remain an isolated experiment? Masterpieces somehow eventually assert their authority and become models.

Edward Branigan

To Zero and Beyond:
Noël Burch's *Theory of Film Practice*

> *"J'ai tout oublié, sauf que, puisqu'on me ramène à zéro, c'est de là qu'il faudra repartir."*
>
> [*"I've forgotten everything, except that, since I have been led back to zero, it's from there that I will have to set out again."*]
>
> —Deux ou trois choses que je sais d'elle
> [Two or Three Things I Know about Her]
> Jean-Luc Godard, 1967

"Zero" is perhaps the central metaphor driving Noël Burch's early film theory. Despite Burch's spectacular denunciations of his own early work, I would like to reexamine his first book, *Theory of Film Practice*, written in 1967, by analyzing the rhetorical strategies and concepts through which the book found an audience.[1] Burch's early methodology continues to exert an influence on contemporary film theory, most notably in the guise of neoformalism and some aspects of cognitivism and phenomenology as well as in the unique synthesis of semiotics, Marxism, and psychoanalysis that arose in the 1970s and is found in his other books.[2] I propose to focus on Burch's distinctive ways of talking about film since I believe that by considering film theory itself as a special kind of "rhetorical practice," Burch's theory of "film practice" will appear in a new and instructive light. The potency of rhetorical practice is announced with the first sentence of Burch's book: "The terminology a filmmaker or film theoretician chooses to employ is a significant reflection of what he takes a film to be" (3).

We might begin by asking what sorts of general questions a film theory seeks to answer. A film theory is an intricate system of propositions that seeks to explain the general nature of all films—their materials, determining features, designed traits, types of interactions with a spectator, and relationships to the world. A film theory is intricate and dense because these questions are not entirely independent of one another; in fact, one of the most important goals is to specify the precise ways in which these problems interweave. A theory does not examine the meanings of a particular film, but rather seeks to uncover the general mechanisms and processes at every level that allow all films to possess meanings for a spectator. How is it possible for a spectator to take, and make, meanings from watching films? How is it possible for a spectator to recognize characters, construct space and time, connect actions, discover patterns, experience emotions, make judgments, learn, and hope?

More exactly, we might say that a film theory undertakes to analyze how beliefs are formed about the creation of, and viewing of, film, namely, what one may come to believe about film as an existent artifact (definition, identity, ontology), how it may be understood and known (phenomenology, epistemology), its aesthetic principles, ideology, and presumed realism or truth. A particular theory of film is a way of talking—a way of posing and answering basic questions about existence and perception and evaluation—in order to constitute the object film. Now, one should keep in mind that the basic questions that arise about film, as well as about other objects in the world, depend largely on the ways in which we make use of various things in our world, that is, on the economic, political, and social circumstances in which we fashion (and make appropriate) our speech, purposes, ideas, and actions. Objects do not possess meanings, but rather are made meaningful. Since a "theory" is a response to our particular world, many of its claims will not be universal or timeless, but instead merely be a way of thinking carefully about how we currently use and value things. Thus when we undertake to analyze a way of talking and writing in a particular theory, we put on display a worldview—indeed, two worldviews: the view associated with the terms being analyzed and the view associated with the terms being used to conduct the analysis. A film theory, then, describes, but also circumscribes, what is to count as a film in a given world: what it is (to be) taken to be. A film theory is a performance and use of ideas to discover new, general categories and values; or perhaps, less grandly, to discover new kinds of properties in particular films. By struggling to reconfigure present films, a theory assumes an integral role in making new ones.

Noël Burch lays the groundwork for a firm connection of theory to practice by drawing a distinction between *seeing* and *looking*. Seeing is based on the physiology of the eye, and is automatic and "nonselective." Looking is based on various mental processes active in a perceiver, and is tied to attention and purpose; hence, looking is voluntary and "selective" (33, 34–35). A similar distinction holds between merely *recording* ambient sound and actually *hearing* its significance (91–92).[3] Burch argues that the camera and microphone are concerned only with seeing and recording, and that therefore, without the intervention of a filmmaker, the filmed image and the sound track may become jumbled, incomprehensible, or "illegible" (33, 34, 92). He asserts that the camera and microphone must inevitably flatten the world since the camera reduces three-dimensional space to two on the screen while the microphone renders all sound, including noise, equally prominent in a recording (92). As an illustration, Burch notes that two objects distant from one another but lying along the same line of sight may be seen on the screen as a single, monstrous, and absurd object in a single plane. Furthermore, two objects not lying along the same line of sight may nonetheless be seen as merged when one appears on a reflective surface near the other (32–34). These sorts of latent conflicts in the image and on the sound track threaten to overwhelm the spectator's efforts at making sense of a film by looking and hearing.

Burch's next move has far-reaching implications. He defines the machinery of cinema in terms of its effect on the perception of the spectator.

> [W]hen we view a film, as when we view a painting or a photograph, *seeing* is no longer dependent on *looking*, as is nearly always the case in a real-life situation; the selectivity involved in looking no longer affects the nonselectivity involved in seeing in the slightest.[4] (34–35)

For Burch the cinematic machine operates to open a definite and measurable separation between seeing and looking, recording and hearing. It is not that a spectator *may* see or look differently when engaging a film, but that he or she *must* see and look differently. Even if a spectator is only momentarily mistaken about, or confused by, an image or sound (and there will be many examples of these effects throughout the book), Burch finds it to be crucial evidence for his theory. A small, disconcerting moment in watching a film reveals the microfluctuations of perception upon which, or against which, other higher-order agencies of looking and hearing will work. One of Burch's main projects will be to catalogue the diverse ways in which a spectator may be subjected to abrupt though fleeting kinds of panic in watching a film. As we will discuss later, he will resolutely praise these disconcerting moments and elevate them to the status of an aesthetic principle.

Although Burch may have posed the separation between seeing and looking, recording and hearing, in terms that are too strong, three fundamental consequences follow for his theory. First, in order to understand what cinema is, it will be necessary to understand what cinema does. The key will be to investigate the dynamics of both seeing and looking, both recording and hearing. These, and related mental phenomena, are components of quite ordinary perceptual activities. Burch believes that film art derives from our everyday abilities, not from some extraordinary or heightened state of consciousness nor from some mystical connection that an artist possesses to the truths of the world. Just as spectator and filmmaker are drawn together because they share and work with the same set of perceptual resources, so theorist and filmmaker begin to approach one another because each may be seen to be speculating about and experimenting with perceptual laws.

Second, the split that is opened between nonselective and selective perceptual activities through the filmmaking process implies that the data encountered on the screen by the spectator are at least partially independent of, as well as logically and temporally prior to, the spectator's higher-order mental functions that are at work constructing scenes and meanings for the film. That is, data encountered on the screen have their own weight and need to be studied on their own terms. Put another way, bottom-up perceptual processes in a spectator (which produce, for example, a sense of edge, color, texture, depth, scale, shape, motion, aural pitch, etc.) are distinct from top-down cognitive processes (which make use of, for example, a spectator's memories, expectations, purposes, and schematic knowledge).[5] For Burch bottom-up processes are primary. He says that the material of film is always "refractory" (*réfractaire*), that the apparatus always stands apart from what is filmed, that there is an "inevitable gap" between the instruments of film and life (115, 120–121). He contends that "[f]ilm is made first of all out of images and sounds; ideas intervene (perhaps) *later*" (144; emphasis in *Praxis*, 206). For Burch the apparatus is already at work before it can 'record' and, a fortiori, the material of film must be experienced before it can be read or interpreted (151–153 and n. 6). In writings subsequent to *Theory of Film Practice*, Burch shifts his concern toward interpretation and the political implications of theory and film practice.

The fundamental difference between bottom-up and top-down processes and the priority assigned to bottom-up processes leads Burch to insist in the beginning sentences of chapter 3 that a filmed image as well as the transition to the next image are both "concrete visual phenomena" that should be studied in terms of "what they actually look like" to a spectator (32). Here Burch is extending his argument by making the point that even though film editing is not at all visible on the screen in the same manner as an image, and even though editing is as transient as certain momentary confusions a spectator may have about an image, it is nonetheless a visual "form" (4) susceptible to a phenomenological analysis. (Such an analysis will yield fifteen types of shot transitions; see ch. 1.) Moreover, he asserts that because of the formal similarity between film editing and the filmed image, the spatial and temporal articulations *between* shots should be organized by the filmmaker as a function of the compositions *within* the shots (35–36; and see Burch's discussion of "spatial recomposition" [38–39, 77]). Presumably there are still other elements of film—such as off-screen space (ch. 2), retrospective temporal matching (12–14), abstract rhythm (45, 67; chs. 4, 5), discomfort and aggression (ch. 8), chance (ch. 7), sound (ch. 6), fiction effects (chs. 9, 10), and narrative form—that, although not strictly visible, may assume visual form. Burch's ambition is nothing less than to forge a new interpretation of what cinema is (ontology) and what it ought to be (aesthetics) based on certain beliefs about how cinema is perceived (epistemology): "I am attempting to redefine the components of film form" (32). His efforts will lead to a theory that is built on a newly defined intermediate level of forms that result from differences and conflicts among various mechanisms of perception as the spectator seeks to make legible—seeks to comprehend and give meaning to—the data on the screen. The forms listed above are intermediate because they are not yet directly associated with specific ideas in a film nor are they reducible to their material or perceptible differences. They are of practical use to filmmakers and analysts without being confined to a single film.

In summary, Burch defines the object film by referring to the film experience of a spectator which, in turn, emerges out of ordinary visual, though not necessarily visible, forms defined primarily by bottom-up perceptual processes. These processes create, in effect, new intermediate 'materials' from the data on the screen that will acquire additional significance for a spectator when interpreted by selective, top-down procedures. Again, what is of the essence of film—what makes the medium of film unique—are its middle-level materials and forms, not the technical specifications of the filmmaking equipment, not the photographic qualities or (more generally) the pictorial qualities of its product, nor the (high-level) communicative 'intentions' of a filmmaker. Because the perceptual forms of film are distinct from the physical, the perceptible, and the expressive potential of film, Burch can declare that "the essential nature of the relationship between sound and image is due not to the difference between them, but rather to the similarity between them" (91). Sound and image (and, for that matter, editing and image) are strikingly different as physical and perceptible entities, yet as forms of mental phenomena they can perfectly well share and exchange certain tasks (e.g., creating, or else disrupting, a spectator's sense of space and time). Though arising from physical and perceptible differences on the screen, an intermediate film form has the power to collect and integrate disparate materials, to discover commonalities and create relationships in a fresh way, to achieve or undo perceived connections. In short, film form reworks our perception from the bottom up and rekindles our propensity to see (rather than to look). Film form makes meaning possible by making possible many meanings. In fact, as mentioned earlier, certain brief disconcerting moments, ambiguities, retrospective interpretations, hesitations, denials, misjudgments, uncertainties, and indeterminacies that arise in the viewing of film may serve to draw further attention to the constitutive power of form and hence, for Burch, such moments will become an important aesthetic goal for the medium in its effort to achieve an awareness of form. I refer to these exceptional kinds of disconcerting moments, in the spirit of Noël Burch's terminology, as "clumps of fuzziness" embedded within our viewing of film.

There is a third and final consequence for Burch of the split within the spectator between nonselective and selective perceptual activities. Since a spectator's experience of the film medium initially involves a sensing of form in its own right prior to, say, the assignment of thematic or symbolic or narrative significance, all forms are precisely equal. Burch asserts that

> everything projected on a film screen has exactly the same intrinsic "reality," the same "presence." . . . [B]ecause the screen has only two dimensions . . . any shape projected on it is equally "present," just as much "before our eyes" as any other shape. Even the parts of the image that are out of focus are perceived as quite distinct, visible, tangible entities, as what might be called "clumps of fuzziness." . . . [W]hen we view a screen we see everything at once; every form and every contour seems equally prominent visually. . . . [A]ll the elements in any given film image are perceived as equal in importance. (33–34)

Thus what cinema makes immediately "present" to the spectator, according to Burch, are data on the screen and their resultant form; it is not *the* world, or *a* world, or a *possible* world, or even a photograph (of something real) that is witnessed by the spectator, but rather, in the first instance, palpable form that is made manifest out of the effort to see. Eventually a 'world' or a putative 'communication' may come to exist for the spectator who looks, but only as constructed through the elaborate mediation of the film machine and subject always to qualification and perceptual context. (Indeed, a somewhat more extreme notion would maintain that what is called 'reality' is only what one has become familiar with, based on a conventional understanding, a social consensus, a given set of schemata.) Thus Burch stands with Rudolf Arnheim and Sergei Eisenstein in the formalist tradition of film theory as opposed to the realist tradition of André Bazin and Siegfried Kracauer. The formalists are keen to investigate the formative presence of the medium itself, as well as the influence of other mediations (e.g., the institution of cinema, economic context, language use, perception, interpretive schemata, the psyche, history, myth, ideology, patriarchy), while the realists prefer to search for a more direct or immediate causal link (e.g., a photographic link or a 'message from a human source'), or else to search for some basic resemblance between the medium's product and the world's presence. The formalists tend to probe the whole of the medium and to stress that the filmed image has nonvisible determinants while the realists tend to concentrate on a special part or parts of the medium that are capable of making present the world's visible presence of embodying human vision.

Burch, as we have seen, emphasizes the inherent equality of all forms in film, even clumps of fuzziness.[6] By drawing attention to an area of the image that is out of focus—and perhaps will never be identified as an object or as some confluence [!] of objects—and by inventing the vivid name "fuzzy clump," Burch has found a way to assert that some undefined thing in the image actually does have a tangible, distinct, and conspicuous quality to it, at least as a phenomenological form on the screen. For theorists in the formalist tradition, there is no a priori hierarchy that ranks the importance or usefulness of film devices. For example, the extreme long shot in long-take deep focus with improvisational camera movement has no more of a privileged access to the "real" than a rapid montage sequence, metaphorical superimposition, or stylized perfect view of the action. Nevertheless, hierarchies and typical uses of devices have been established for various modes and types of filmmaking. One mode, in particular, has long been dominant—classical Hollywood cinema.[7] This mode makes use of an enormous number of conventions and rules to constrain the possibilities for (and thereby, of course, also make possible) one particular approach to filmmaking (9–10). Burch refers to this mode as the "zero point of cinematic style" (6 n. 4, 11, 15, 42 n. 7, 46, 76, 110, 113, 124 n. 7). He invokes this description in a number of contexts throughout the book. I believe that by scrutinizing closely the word "zero," not only will we discover the explicit reasons why Burch finds this description useful but also, more important, we will discover how the description functions as a powerful metaphor to rhetorically and symptomatically bind together deeper strands of his theory, namely, to bind together his beliefs about the ontology, epistemology, aesthetics, ideology, and realism of film.

The classical cinema is the "zero point" for Burch not because it defies the basic equality of forms by creating a hierarchy, for every mode and every style deploy and organize form into a specific pattern or system of relationships (in a particular film, in a group of films). Rather, it is the zero point because it offers its forms to the viewer as "invisible" (110). It pretends that there is no impediment to looking, that the viewer sees clearly and effortlessly, that the world arrives naturally and instantly to one's attention (6, 11; cf. 32–33). Thus "zero" comes to stand for a state of transparency in the same way that one might say that reducing something (say, a stain left by sweat) to zero makes it vanish (say, by using a detergent).[8] What seems to vanish in the classical cinema is the presence of the cinematic machine, the materiality of data on the screen, the palpable existence of forms, and the labor of filmmaker and spectator. All these seem to vanish—are disincarnated—because of the use of an enormous number of "continuity" devices. For instance, an illusion of spatial continuity may be created through sound perspective and through matching screen direction, position, and movement by adhering to the 180-degree axis of action in selecting camera positions. An illusion of temporal continuity may be created through sound bridges, eyeline matches, cutaways, prop and lighting continuity, matches on action, and the 30-degree rule (9–11, 11 nn. 7 and 8, 37, 43, 46). For Burch the continuity style makes forms appear to disappear as if seeing the screen were like looking at the world through a window recently washed. He complains that we don't really see when we look at a film: "all these things that are on the screen, we non-read them as something which is elsewhere. We are continually displacing our perception of films into this sort of diegetic world."[9]

Transparency has the effect of greatly reducing or eliminating the viewer's perception of that definite and measurable separation between seeing and looking, recording and hearing, that Burch believes must necessarily exist when one attends to a film. Transparency tends to make perception static, and leaves the viewer passive and inert. Thus the word "zero" is useful again because it suggests inaction, a state of perceptual inertia where form seems to have disappeared and nothing really is at risk: when we look we simply see a world that is already obvious and comfortable. The classical cinema, by failing to provoke in the spectator new methods of seeing, cuts off one of the important avenues through which we may learn when we look. More ominously, it has been claimed that the illusion of continuity is intimately related to one or more of the following: perceptual "delusion" (7, 124); the ego's defense of "disavowal" and fetishism; the ego's defense of "misrecognition" within the mechanism of Freudian projection; the formation of human identity through a general form of "misrecognition" (*méconnaissance*) in the Lacanian mirror stage; and Marx's "false consciousness."

Perceptual inertia in the classical cinema entails that the spectator must always be oriented and directed (10) much as the trajectory of an aircraft is automatically controlled by an inertial guidance system. Continuity conventions ensure that the spectator does not lose his or her bearings in the story world while a consistent scenic space and time is being created out of a multiplicity of spatial and temporal articulations on the screen. "Zero" in this new, extended sense comes to signify a spectator's feeling of security, a (steady) state of orientation (9–10), or rather, a lack of disorientation, a feeling that no outside forces (which would produce an acceleration disrupting the equilibrium) are acting on one's body and sense of direction. Since a spectator's impression of being orientated through continuity devices is a fabrication, Burch believes

> that only what happens in frame is important, that the only film space is screen space, that screen space can be manipulated through the use of an infinite variety of *possible* real spaces, and that disorienting the viewer is one of a filmmaker's most valuable tools. (10)

Burch has two ideas in mind when speaking of "possible" real spaces. He is saying that from the standpoint of a filmmaker any number of real spaces, or fragments of real spaces, are equally available to be employed in the construction of a single shot that will be interpreted by a spectator as part of some illusory and unified story space. In addition, he is saying that from the standpoint of a spectator what should be seen as real is only what is on the screen; that is, what is on the screen may refer to many sorts of real and unreal spaces, rather than refer directly and immediately to only one space (e.g., a real one that was originally in front of the camera or else a fictional one that is in the story). Although screen space is manifestly present, there is no automatic or easy way for the spectator to discover a unique space in his or her world or imagination (even when watching the nonfictional film; see ch. 10). Screen space makes no unequivocal reference to that which is absent—to some other thing or space not present. And, though Burch concentrates on screen space, he no doubt means to include many other qualities arising from the data on the screen as being equally a fictional construction for/of the spectator (e.g., the spectator's sensation of time). In short, like serial music (99), film is a thoroughly plastic medium, multifarious and labile, neither defined nor determined by either a real world or a fictional diegesis.

Since the classical cinema, as Burch describes it, strives for (an illusion of) fixity and stability, it is not surprising that he will advocate a practice of disorienting the viewer (10, 13, 15, 44–45) in order to open up the screen to a broad new range of possibilities for meaning. He will celebrate, for example, the use of jump cuts as well as matches that are bad, ambiguous, unclear, or open (11, 14). He is especially intrigued throughout the book by the possibilities for retrospective—retroactive, deferred—matches (12, 13, 13 n. 11, 14, 19, 21, 22, 23, 28, 59, 78, 122, 128). These are matches that force the spectator to recall a previous shot and, then, to drastically reinterpret the nature of its space or time in light of a new shot; that is, the spectator is made to make a mistake in imagining his or her initial orientation.[10] All of the above sorts of matches are 'disfavored' in the classical cinema because they produce disconcerting moments (which I have previously labeled as 'fuzzy clumps' embedded within our viewing of film). Burch, however, appreciates such moments of disorientation—discontinuity, disruption, disorder, discomfort—because our abilities to see, and to see form, are being stimulated and actively revived. "[T]he conscious perception of form," Burch states, "is a liberating activity" (xix).

Disorientation, however, does not mean simple confusion or incomprehension. Rather, it is a signal for the spectator to adopt some new or different way of seeing. For example, Burch notes that

> Eisenstein has [in *Ivan the Terrible*] managed to create a very unusual sort of cinematic space: It exists only in terms of the totality of shots included in the sequence; we no longer have any sense of a surrounding space endowed with independent existence from which a sequence of shots has somehow been excerpted. Rather, we see a space that exists in the same many-faceted, complex way that Braque's [cubist painting of a] billiard table exists; we see a setting that is the sum total of all the perspectives of it embodied in the successive shots. (39, footnote omitted)

The general principles that provide the spectator with a sense of orientation (at the expense of other ways of seeing) may also function within the overall discursive organization of a text, notably within narrative organization. Burch holds that the nineteenth-century novel and theater prescribed a relatively fixed format for narrative (15, 149), which has come to be known as the "classical" narrative. This format is marked by such global features as economy, simplicity, proportion, linearity, continuity, clarity, order, harmony, balance, symmetry, unity, and closure.[11] In particular, the feature of closure has been emphasized by so many writers, including Burch, that it is often taken to stand for all of the many aspects of classical narrative. Here the word "zero" is again convenient: both the closed oval shape of the numeral for zero (0) and the vowel "o" that is stressed in the pronunciation of "zero" suggest a form of utmost simplicity, restriction, enclosure, completion, closure. Thus the feature of closure becomes emblematic of the "predetermined" and "symmetrical" structure that seems to characterize the plot of the classical narrative (where, for instance, the ending in some respect is seen to mirror the opening at the same moment that the ending resolves the latent conflicts and enigmas of the opening, returning the spectator to a state of stasis). The spectator for the classical narrative appears to become trapped within a sequence of scenes that are presented as inevitable and invariable events. Thus if the classical narrative is to be visualized as linear, then it is a line that under closure spirals back on itself, providing only the illusion of change.

I wish to pause for a moment from analyzing Burch's term the "zero point" in order to demonstrate that there is nothing inevitable or absolute about the ways in which the phrase itself may be *seen* to be metaphorical. For example, suppose we think of the bounded area of the numeral for zero (0) not as closed, but as open! Consider the following passage from Anaïs Nin's erotica, *Delta of Venus:* "Instead of having one sexual core, Elena's body seemed to have a million sexual openings, equally sensitized, every cell of the skin magnified with the sensibility of a mouth."[12] A mouth, a living cell, an ovum, a million sexual openings, a million zeros, z-eros, eros, Eros. Evidently, it is possible to assert a graphic similarity between the openness of a mouth and a "zero," and from there to construct a further series of connections, say, linking sensation, emotion, pleasure, ecstasy, and the feminine with the Freudian claim that for the male a woman's otherness/openness—her alleged "lack" due to castration ("hollowness" as another kind of zero-ness?)— produces a fear of castration and raises anxiety about her needs (a mouth has teeth). In fact, these sorts of connections have been offered by some theorists and critics, and even by some films (cf. the image of a woman's open mouth that ends Jean-Luc Godard's 1985 *Hail Mary* or the aggressive non sequiturs spun from the title in Peter Greenaway's 1985 *Zoo: A Zed & Two Noughts*). Is "zero," then, open or closed, or both? Or, perhaps, it is simply indifferent to the descriptions we may apply.

I don't believe that Noël Burch (at least in his first book) makes use of the zero metaphor to pursue "openness" in the above ways. Nevertheless, the lesson for us is that interpretation is not mechanical. The appropriate reach of a metaphor depends on making judgments about relevant contexts (and not all contexts depend on authorial "intention" or the denotation of a word, nor are all contexts known at any one time). Earlier I argued that a theory is a complex response to how objects are being used generally in a world—how we choose to speak, think, act, and value things in relation to a community at a given time. Words themselves are also objects to be used (in acceptable ways) in relation to other tangible and intangible objects. Thus interpreting a theory involves an effort to understand a theoretical use of words, a rhetoric, and the institutions that have sanctioned it, through employing still more words (metaconcepts) in a new rhetoric. What I am suggesting is that the basic connection between film theory and film practice (or between interpreting theory and interpreting film) needs to be posed in some way other than in a simple hierarchy that begins with a "filmmaker" on top whose ideas and impulses trickle down into a "film," which is then interpreted by a "critic/spectator," and finally, at the furthest remove from filmmaking, is explained by a "theorist." It would be more accurate, I believe, to posit a hierarchy that is sensitive throughout to the productive, and historically relative, forces of meaning that govern human action. Film is not something that can be defined and known free of all preconceptions and situations. Accordingly, such an approach would begin with the assumption that a film is always seen under (or conforms to) some "description" or process of naming that is correlated with a "rhetorical practice" of using and valuing objects and words in a world. This rhetorical practice, in turn, is derived from beliefs about human perception and "agency," and is filled out (filled in) by the "purposeful activity" of a spectator, theorist, and filmmaker.[13] In this latter hierarchy, theory and practice are located at the same place: both are engagements with a world of objects as perceived through the available materials and forms of intelligibility.

To return to our analysis of the "zero point," Burch contends that the classical narrative "contains a fundamental principle of alienation that degrades both filmmaker and spectator" (xix). The use of the word "degrades" betrays a strong, negative evaluation. The word "zero" has now assumed a normative and aversive sense; for example, when you call someone a "zero," you say that someone means "nothing" to you, or you wonder how someone could sink (or be) so "low," or you say that all is for "nought," you've hit "bottom." However, paradoxically, at the same moment that Burch is condemning classical narrative and classical style, he needs both of them to exist as neutral reference points against which to gauge other types of narrative organization and other types of film style. Mathematicians have claimed that "zero"—the empty set—functions as a crucial background for defining the other numbers. Also Gestalt psychologists and Russian formalists have insisted that a familiar background (starting point, baseline, norm) is required in order to make prominent and pertinent a foreground. Just as the meaning of a word in a language or in a rhetoric depends on its differential position with respect to certain other words (potential words that may substitute for it and actual ones that precede and follow it), Burch continually defines, refines, and makes use of a "classical paradigm" in order to take the measure of a great many "alternative" forms and styles.

Zero may be seen negatively or neutrally, but it may also be literally just another number in a vast mathematics. When zero is simply an integer along a scale, it assumes a positive role in Burch's aesthetic principles. This use of zero connects to Burch's notions of "parameter" (an independent variable in an equation), "permutation" (a fundamental change based on a rearrangement of elements in a set), and "serial music" (as in the exhaustion of a matrix of tonal possibilities), all of which depend on mathematical analogies (cf. 130, 134).[14] A parameter for Burch is any element or feature of cinema that is capable of being altered through repetition, modification, and variation (e.g., camera angle, sharpness of focus, shot duration, the extent of temporal ellipsis or reversal, patterns of mutual interference among shot transitions, image legibility, sound perspective, mismatched eyelines, distance and direction to objects *off* screen, camera movement in relation to character action, character entrances and exits, narrative flashforwards). In addition, Burch makes explicit use of some of Eisenstein's key concepts, such as dialectical form and organic fusion (see, e.g., 22 n. 2, 51; 12 l. 20, 13, 15 ll. 14–17, 45, 88, 99, 141, 157–158; chs. 4, 5, 6).[15] Here one might interpret dialectical interaction as a kind of conflictual organization where pairs of opposing parameters collide (xx, 23–24), annihilating each other (i.e., cancelling each other into zero; cf. Marx's dialectical law of "the negation of the negation") in order to create a new parameter which, however, already contains the seed of its own future destruction by another, soon-to-appear antithetical parameter (cf. the dialectical law of "the interpenetration of opposites"). "Form" in this scheme is the result of a series of radical and discontinuous (i.e., unpredictable) jumps based on the destruction or exhaustion of complete sets of polar elements (37, 40, 53, 56, 66–68, 82). By contrast, in classical cinema only certain elements from a set are selected for use (e.g., those promoting transparency and orientation) while 'unacceptable' elements appear only as "a gratuitous or merely stylistic 'gimmick'" (cf. 13, 46, 70). Moreover, an "open," alternative form unlike the closed form of the classical cinema does not gradually and continuously evolve toward, or serve, some final goal predicted by an initial state and ratified through closure (14–15, 38–40, 108–9). An open form, as conceived by Burch, strives to juxtapose elements in such a way (through interruption, disjunction, tension, contrast, counterpoint) that something entirely new, not present in either element, suddenly appears (cf. 39–40, 149–50, 160 n. 4).

Burch, perhaps, has joined the idea of dialectics with the permutations of serial music in an attempt to show that formal change in his aesthetics will involve fundamental transformations through ceaseless contradiction (cf. the dialectical law of "the transformation of quantity into quality"), rather than being merely a static and endless recombination of elements already present in a matrix (cf. 72, 143, 145). Hence also the considerable importance that Burch ascribes to the "sudden intrusion" of chance as a distinctly modern technique through which "the traditional integrity of the work of art is being challenged" (105, 110, 113, 115; ch. 7). The "zero" of dialectics, chance, and permutation is not to be the static, closed "zero" of classical cinema, where limits are imposed on parameters; where, for example, the 180-degree and 30-degree rules operate to restrict the parameter of camera position. For Burch, the forms of classical cinema are at best temporary and special cases of a more wide-ranging and open cinema.

Burch's fascination with the various kinds of discontinuities in film that produce disorientation in a viewer can be seen in two ways: as a rejection of stylistic transparency and as a positive step toward the ceaseless tensions of dialectics and alternative ways of seeing. Burch notes that "if we are seeking a film style that is less 'smooth,' that actually stresses the structures that it is based upon, a whole range of possibilities remains open" (6; 11, 12, 13, 15, 44, 66–67). He concludes chapter 1 by enumerating some of the ways that a filmmaker can open up classical cinema to new aesthetic possibilities:

> I have just briefly outlined a set of formal "objects"—the fifteen different types of shot transitions and the parameters that define them—capable of rigorous development through such devices as rhythmic alternation, recapitulation, retrogression, gradual elimination, cyclical repetition, and serial variation, thus creating structures similar to those of twelve-tone music. . . . It is only through systematic and thorough exploration of the *structural* possibilities inherent in the cinematic parameters I have been describing that film will be liberated from the old narrative forms and develop new "open" forms that will have more in common with the formal strategies of post-Debussyian music than with those of the pre-Joycean novel. (14–15; cf. 30, 40, 65, 67, 83 n. 4, 97–99, 107–8, 128)

Recall that previously we encountered an example of a small-scale "retrogression" in a device designed to momentarily disorient a spectator, the "retrospective match." The other serial music devices listed by Burch would also seem to have an anti-narrative or at least a nonclassical narrative purpose. That is, as spatial metaphors they seem more varied in shape than the supposed 'linear, irreversible progression' of the classical narrative; they seem to be more tabular and tangled than 'causal' (cf. 75–88). Burch urges a filmmaker to search for "[t]he form of a work" that "ensures its unity [through] . . . the greatest possible diversity" (xviii, xx; cf. 37). In short, traditional narrative causality should be challenged by other forms of organization that spur radically new ways of seeing and looking.

To summarize: the word "zero" functions as a complex metaphor pulling together many aspects of Noël Burch's theory. It points to four traits of classical Hollywood cinema: stylistic transparency, perceptual inertia, lack of disorientation, and narrative closure. It also renders a clear negative judgment on this mode of filmmaking. However, at the same time, paradoxically, "zero" carries the idea of the classical cinema as being simply a neutral, historical reference point while alluding also to very different, radical principles that challenge the classical cinema: a mathematics of serial music and a dialectics, both of which promise to be positive alternatives to the classical paradigm by impeding, making difficult, and prolonging our perceptual contact with a film. For Burch there exists a definite "beyond," an obverse side to the zero style, which perhaps in true dialectical fashion contests the zero style by emerging from within its very texture: an alternative is reached, but only by forgetting again and returning to zero.

I would like to suggest that the central metaphor of zero is like the palm of one's hand. A number of different, and even incompatible, senses of zero spread out like fingers. A reader need not be forced to "leap" from one sense to the other across the gap between the fingers; the reader need only trace a finger back into the palm and then trace a new course out along another finger.[16] In this way, the central metaphor of zero helps promote unity, scope, and pliancy among the propositions in Burch's theory.

There is a final quality of zero that needs to be examined. It is a quality that relates to the writing of film theory. This new sense of zero derives from our impression that "zero" refers to a state of (non)being that is nevertheless balanced precisely on the edge of "nothing" and "something": though presently "nothing," it (?) may soon be(come) "something." This special feeling for zero reflects our way of looking at things from a position of being alive and sentient; many of our perceptual and cognitive activities in life concern assessing conditions, forming and testing hypotheses, meeting thresholds, being expectant. This particular sense of zero says only that we know that nothing is known about a (non)state or (non)object. I refer to this as the "epistemic zero," which warns us about some limit or boundary to what is known.

Kenneth Burke believes that each term in a theoretical discourse possesses a relationship to that which is unknown and indeterminate.[17] He implies that there is a point at which the meaning of a term becomes undecidable and at that point the term will no longer be useful in making new distinctions or finer discriminations (though the term may possess other uses). This does not mean that what is unknown becomes forever unknowable or indeterminable; only that a limit about *what can be known* has been reached with a particular term within a given rhetoric. Burke argues as follows:

> A perfectionist might seek to evolve terms free of ambiguity and inconsistency (as with the terministic ideals of symbolic logic and logical positivism). But we have a different purpose in view. . . . We take it for granted that, insofar as men cannot themselves create the universe, there must remain something essentially enigmatic about the problem of motives, and that this underlying enigma will manifest itself in inevitable ambiguities and inconsistencies among the terms for motives. Accordingly, what we want is *not terms that avoid ambiguity,* but *terms that clearly reveal the strategic spots at which ambiguities necessarily arise.* . . . Since no two things or acts or situations are exactly alike, you cannot apply the same term to both of them without thereby introducing a certain margin of ambiguity, an ambiguity as great as the difference between the two subjects that are given the identical title. . . . Hence, instead of considering it our task to "dispose of" any ambiguity by merely disclosing the fact that it is an ambiguity, we rather consider it our task to study and clarify the *resources* of ambiguity. (xviii)

Burke's aim in dissecting "motives" is to study the basic forms of language, grammar, and thought as manifested in modes of action (xv, xxii). As we have discovered, theory is a form of language that is especially concerned with producing categories, redescriptions, and generalizations. Burke seems to imply that in constructing a theory a writer must be sensitive to the devices of uncertainty—to the ways in which a term is ambiguous or inconsistent. Or perhaps, one should say that uncertainty is a "medium" with its own machinery, materials, and forms. The "margin of ambiguity" postulated by Burke may be undesirable in many instances but in others may spur new expressions, ideas, and explorations.[18] Recall that Noël Burch insists that a filmed image may contain clumps of fuzziness which, though conveying uncertainty, are not to be overlooked since they are as vital and tangible as other forms, and presumably, equally charged with important possibilities for the future. Moreover, as indicated earlier, I believe that similar fuzzy clumps may be detected in stylistic features like the forms of editing (e.g., retrospective matching), and, in general, may be found in many sorts of brief disturbances or disconcerting moments experienced by a spectator while he or she is perceiving a film. When film is seen as a rhetoric, it will be seen to have inevitable ambiguities and inconsistencies about it, both in literal ways, as in parts of the image that are out of focus or are broken by a frame line, and in figurative ways, as in the uses we make of the image when watching—that is, when using our style and imagination from inside our world.

I believe that "fuzziness" extends to our comprehension of narrative, including classical narrative, and to the meaning of a film. It extends to the rhetoric of theoretical writing and to the interpretation of metaphor. In particular, I believe that Burch's metaphor of the zero point becomes for the reader no less tangible than a fine clump of fuzziness in an image. Burch's many senses of zero help us begin to imagine concretely how film is to us and what it ought to be, negatively and positively. His use of zero is a remarkable illustration of the public language that founds rhetorical practice. Nonetheless, in an epistemic sense of zero we may glimpse the edges of Burch's theory, the tensions and uncertainties in terminology. "Zero," then, does more than testify to a material practice of film theory: when we choose to think retrospectively, "zero" can be seen to allude to certain zero points found in prior film theories and as such it marks a point of departure for the next theory of film practice, for the next response we make to whatever it is that falls just out of sight in an image or a word.

NOTES

1. Burch's book, *Praxis du cinéma* (Paris: Éditions Gallimard, 1969), is derived from ten articles published in *Cahiers du cinéma* in 1967. It appeared in English in 1973 as *Theory of Film Practice*, trans. Helen R. Lane (New York: Praeger). It was reprinted by Princeton University Press in 1981. The English translation has omitted a seven-page "Conclusion"; and, inter alia, some of the film stills have been changed for the Praeger edition and simply omitted in the Princeton edition.

All page citations to Burch's book will be given parenthetically in the text and refer to the English translation; citations are identical for both English editions. Roman numerals in the text refer to Burch's "Preface to the English-Language Edition," which appears only in the Praeger edition. Translations are mine unless otherwise indicated.

Burch vigorously rejects his early work in the Praeger edition of the book (134 n. 12; xvi–xvii), in the "Foreword" to the Princeton edition, in "Beyond Theory of Film Practice: An Interview with Noël Burch," *Women & Film* 1, nos. 5–6 (June 1974): 20–32, and in other writings. Assessments of Burch's theory may be found in Annette Michelson's "Introduction" to the Praeger edition; Constance Penley, "Theory of Film Practice: Analysis & Review," *Women & Film* 1, nos. 5–6 (June 1974): 32–34; Robert T. Eberwein, *A Viewer's Guide to Film Theory and Criticism* (Metuchen, N.J.: Scarecrow, 1979): 176–85; Kristin Thompson and David Bordwell, "Linearity, Materialism and the Study of Early American Cinema," *Wide Angle* 5, no. 3 (1983): 4–15; and in ch. 4, "The Return of Modernism: Noël Burch and the Oppositional Program," of Bordwell's forthcoming study of the historiography of film style, *On the History of Film Style* (Harvard University Press), which is an elaboration of "The Power of a Research Tradition: Prospects for Progress in the Study of Film Style," *Film History* 6, no. 1 (Spring 1994): 59–79.

I would like to thank David Bordwell, Melinda Szaloky, and Charles Wolfe for their valuable advice and commentary on this essay.

2. On neoformalism and cognitivism, see, e.g., Kristin Thompson, *Breaking the Glass Armor: Neoformalist Film Analysis* (Princeton, N.J.: Princeton University Press, 1988), esp. ch. 1, 3–46, and David Bordwell, "A Case for Cognitivism," *Iris* 9 (Spring 1989): 11–40. See also *Post-Theory: Reconstructing Film Studies*, ed. David Bordwell and Noël Carroll (Madi-

son: University of Wisconsin Press, 1996). On phenomenology, see, e.g., Vivian Sobchack, *The Address of the Eye: A Phenomenology of Film Experience* (Princeton, N.J.: Princeton University Press, 1992); Allan Casebier, *Film and Phenomenology: Toward a Realist Theory of Cinematic Representation* (Cambridge: Cambridge University Press, 1991).

Burch's other books include *In and Out of Synch: The Awakening of a Cine-Dreamer,* trans. Ben Brewster (Aldershot, England: Scolar, 1991); *Life to those Shadows,* trans. Ben Brewster (Berkeley: University of California Press, 1990); *To the Distant Observer: Form and Meaning in the Japanese Cinema* (Berkeley: University of California Press, 1979); and *Marcel L'Herbier* (Paris: Éditions Seghers, 1973).

3. It seems to me that Burch's distinction between seeing (*voir*) and looking (*regarder*) is valid in general and that further important distinctions may be built on it (e.g., the separation of material and structure; the divergence between screen and story world; the differences among acting, focalizing, and narrating). However, I think that the names chosen in the translation to draw the distinction should be reversed since in English "seeing" concerns the experience of sight whereas "looking" involves directing or moving the eyes toward an object of sight: "Melinda saw the furniture" is different from "Melinda looked at the furniture" since she may have looked without seeing. The noun "look-see" may be understood as a causal contraction of these two sequential visual activities. Consider also the analogous difference between "seeing through" and "looking through" something. The former is mental and perceptive (e.g., seeing through a scheme); the latter is physical and perceptual (e.g., looking through a window). In addition, "seeing" is commonly used to describe mental activities and judgments other than sight (as seen by such locutions as "I cannot see you, because I'm seeing someone else" or "Oh, I see what you mean"). It is true that "looking" may denote a mental process: "Melinda was looking at the problem and didn't see the cup of coffee." Still when "looking" is opposed to "seeing" and applied to the same object, it is usually prior to and subordinate to "seeing": "Melinda was looking at the problem, but didn't see the point." The reversal of the normal order of "seeing" and "looking" in the English translation does, however, accurately reflect Burch's polemical point since he is arguing that certain formal, material, and perceptual features of film are more important (and thus should be seen to be higher-ranking and called "seeing") than various higher-order mental and interpretive activities that should be seen to be banal and illusory (and merely accorded the status of "looking").

The corresponding distinction Burch draws for auditory perception between a sonic experience and an attention to a sonic source should have been translated as "hearing" (*entendre*) and "listening" (*écouter*) rather than "hearing" and "recording." *Praxis*, 55, 134–35. See generally Edward Branigan, *Narrative Comprehension and Film* (London and New York: Routledge, 1992), 33–34, 38, 61–62, 101–2, 105, 141.

Michel Chion expresses Burch's distinction in the following way: "The question of listening [*de l'écoute*] with the ear is inseparable from that of listening [*de l'ouïr*] with the mind, just as looking [*du regard*] is with seeing [*au voir*]." It is interesting that Chion chooses to use the verbs for sight in exactly the opposite way from Burch. Note especially that Chion claims that from the standpoint of the actual perceiving of sound and of sight, the two forms of each are inseparable. I disagree. Cf. Chion, *Audio-Vision: Sound on Screen* (New York: Columbia University Press, 1994): 33, translation by Claudia Gorbman of *L'Audio-Vision* (Paris: Nathan, 1990): 31, with Edward Branigan, "Sound, Epistemology, Film," in *Film Theory and Philosophy,* ed. Richard Allen and Murray Smith (Oxford: Oxford University Press, forthcoming).

4. It is curious that in proposing a gap between seeing and looking when one views a film, Burch's formulation at the beginning of the sentence ("no longer dependent on") seems weaker than the formulation that appears at the end of the sentence ("no longer affects . . . in the slightest") since the final phrasing rules out *all* causal interactions between seeing and looking. In quoting Burch I have omitted a footnote in which he raises a number of questions about this strict formulation that may seriously undermine his argument. I have chosen to ignore the footnote since the arguments in his book take no account of it. The

unresolved tensions in the strict formulation are evident when Burch wrestles with the phenomenological similarities and differences between two devices, both of which may be used to elide space or time, a straight cut and a dissolve (see 41–42). The tensions are also evident when Burch considers whether it is logically possible to have a totally meaningless juxtaposition of shots and when he considers the role of "chance" (42–43, 70–73; ch. 7). Cf. discussion in the main text of my essay at note 5.

5. Although Burch speaks only of the "physiology" and the "focusing" of the eye (33, 34, 35) when defining his special notion of "seeing" (as opposed to "looking"), I think it is fair to render this idea in terms of the cognitive psychological concept of bottom-up (as opposed to top-down) perceptual processing. And, although Burch refers to the selectivity of "looking" as being "unconscious" (33), he may mean to include preconscious, and even conscious, mental activities. Further, although bottom-up and top-down processes are distinct and are located in separate areas of the brain, the interaction between the two processes may be much more complex than suggested by Burch's formulations (e.g., on 34–35 and 144, both quoted in the text). In addition, there may be "lateral" kinds of interactions among modules of the brain. On the distinction between bottom-up and top-down perceptual processing, see, e.g., Branigan, *Narrative Comprehension*: 37–38.

6. Burch's actual words are: "même les parties floues de l'image sont parfaitement . . . nettes, visibles, tangibles, en tant que matière: 'des paquets de flou', comme on dit." The phrase "des paquets de flou" suggests packets, bundles, or lumps of some material thing (*matière*) that is soft, blurred, dim, or fluffy. *Praxis*: 54 (Burch's suspension points).

Burch provides a detailed argument to demonstrate that the inherent and absolute equality of all the forms within an image, including any out-of-focus "clumps of fuzziness," is *not* affected by the fact that the spectator's eye may require time to explore an image or may be drawn more strongly to certain elements in an image (34–35). There is a close relationship between Burch's idea of phenomenological equality and his aesthetic imperative of organic fusion (cf. 88 and see my text below on organic fusion). Consider also Burch's query, "Are not jumps forward and backward in time really identical on the formal organic level of a film?" (8).

7. The locus classicus for the analysis of classical Hollywood cinema is David Bordwell, Janet Staiger, and Kristin Thompson, *The Classical Hollywood Cinema: Film Style and Mode of Production to 1960* (New York: Columbia University Press, 1985).

8. Burch's notion of the stylistic transparency of the classical cinema is reminiscent of Barthes' "zero degree of writing," which is "almost an ideal absence of style" that becomes neutral, colorless, transparent, blank, and empty. The comparison, however, is complex because Barthes' idea has many strata. Roland Barthes, *Writing Degree Zero*, trans. Annette Lavers and Colin Smith (Boston, Mass.: Beacon, 1970 [1953]): 5, 77.

9. Burch, "Beyond Theory of Film Practice," 25. Burch offers a compact summary of how the effect of transparency is obtained by the classical Hollywood cinema in *To the Distant Observer*, 18–23.

10. Burch seems to raise the possibility that a retrospective match—already a "fuzzy clump" in my terms—may not itself always be definite, that is, be located at a determinate point in the film, but instead may sometimes be 'diffuse,' that is, 'fuzzy' in still another way (120). In addition, a retrospective match may be ambiguous (12).

11. Burch does not discuss many of the features of either classical narrative or classical narration. Nor does he consider the special problems of comprehending a "fiction." For some of these details, see, e.g., David Bordwell, *Narration in the Fiction Film* (London: Methuen, 1985), e.g., on canonical story format (33–40); Branigan, *Narrative Comprehension*, e.g., on narrative schema (13–32); and Murray Smith, "Film Spectatorship and the Institution of Fiction," *Journal of Aesthetics and Art Criticism* 53, no. 2 (Spring 1995): 113–27. Narration for Burch would seem to reduce to one of three "camera roles": dictator, participant, or passive spectator (116–20, 146, 158, 161, 163); *In and Out of Synch*, 79–80.

12. Anaïs Nin, *Delta of Venus* (New York: Harcourt Brace Jovanovich, 1969): 129.

13. The hierarchy that I have proposed which relates film theory and film practice is based on the creation and use of sentences and meanings, not on identifying persons and ob-

jects. I have taken this approach for reasons similar to those stated by W. V. Quine in a related context: "Conceptualization is human, and of a piece with language. Our reification even of sticks and stones [!] is part of it. To ask what they really are, apart from our conceptualization, is to ask for truth without language." Note that for Nelson Goodman nonverbal labels, such as pictures, qualify as "language." *A Dictionary of Philosophy,* ed. Thomas Mautner (Cambridge, Mass.: Blackwell, 1996), "Quine, a philosophical self-portrait," 354. See generally Goodman, *Ways of Worldmaking* (Indianapolis: Hackett, 1978) and *Of Mind and Other Matters* (Cambridge, Mass.: Harvard University Press, 1984); David Bordwell, *Making Meaning: Inference and Rhetoric in the Interpretation of Cinema* (Cambridge, Mass.: Harvard University Press, 1989); and David Alan Black, "*Homo Confabulans*: A Study in Film, Narrative, and Compensation" (unpub. ms., 1996) and "'Correct Me if I'm Wrong . . .': Narrative Film and the Incredulous Response" (unpub. ms., 1994).

14. For an important discussion of Burch's notions of parameter and permutation, and their relationship to serial music and general aesthetic principles, see Bordwell, *Narration in the Fiction Film,* 274–89. Burch's book is strongly prescriptive. In this essay I examine only a few of the criteria that underlie Burch's normative judgments of films. For a concise and systematic statement of some of his aesthetic values, see Burch and Jorge Dana, "Propositions," *Afterimage* 5 (Spring 1974): 40–67.

15. In attempting to join dialectical change with evolutionary change (see, e.g., 66–67) as well as to join discontinuity with organic fusion, Burch has created a tension within his theory not unlike the tension that exists within Eisenstein's theory. See David Bordwell, *The Cinema of Eisenstein* (Cambridge, Mass.: Harvard University Press, 1993), chs. 3 and 5, 111–38 and 163–98, and "Eisenstein's Epistemological Shift," *Screen* 15, no. 4 (Winter 1975): 29–46. Perhaps a better metaphor for Burch's organic fusion than biological cell growth (143, 149) or the facets of a crystal (145) would be the fractal. Enormous complexity in a fractal is engendered by relatively simple structures whose regularities span and integrate many scales of action through a process of self-similarity.

16. I have borrowed the metaphor of the palm and fingers in order to describe the nature of a central metaphor from Kenneth Burke, who uses it to discuss certain of his terms that are applied to describe a variety of philosophical systems. Kenneth Burke, *A Grammar of Motives* (Berkeley: University of California Press, 1969), xxii.

A metaphor is a hybrid, like a griffin. Selecting a metaphor is a delicate and important task, in both writing and interpreting theory. If I had chosen a different metaphor to characterize Burch's rhetoric, I could have created a different feeling for the nature of his theory (and in that case the theory would become subject to a new description). Consider these alternatives to the human hand: the tentacles of a squid, the rays of the sun, the spokes of a wheel. I have imagined these three metaphors by projecting them from three basic explanatory images that have dominated Western philosophy: the Aristotelian notion of organism, the Neo-Platonic notion of mathematical abstraction and mind, and the modern scientific notion of physical materials and machines. Burch primarily develops images derived from the latter two metaphysical traditions (but cf. his use of "organic fusion"). In characterizing Burch's rhetoric, I have used an organic metaphor in order to stress that a rhetoric is based on the performance and use of words within a human community. See my discussion in the main text at note 13. On the three worldviews, see Hugh Kearney, *Science and Change: 1500–1700* (New York: McGraw-Hill, 1971).

17. The epistemic zero should be contrasted with an absolute zero, where we do not know that we do not know. It is worth noting that from a Freudian perspective, the epistemic zero would be the site of the unconscious. For psychoanalysis, meaning resides in what is contradictory, absent, and missing, what has been excluded, forgotten, repressed. In this scheme Burke's concept of ambiguity would probably be rendered as "ambivalence." These ideas may be extended further to cover the writing of film theory. Christian Metz argues that "[t]o be a theoretician of the cinema" one must cultivate "the kind of deliberate ambivalence [that is] like a pair of pliers, one pincer (voyeuristic sadism sublimated into epistemophilia) coming to meet the other in which the original imaginary . . . with the object [cinema] is retained." "The Imaginary Signifier," in *The Imaginary Signifier: Psychoanalysis and the*

Cinema, trans. Celia Britton, Annwyl Williams, Ben Brewster, and Alfred Guzzetti (Bloomington: Indiana University Press, 1982), "'Loving the Cinema,'" 15–16; cf. 79–80.

I would take Kenneth Burke's idea in yet another direction: I believe that a certain kind of indeterminate and nonspecific reference is a key feature of *fictional* reference (i.e., null or zero reference). See Branigan, *Narrative Comprehension,* 122–24 and ch. 7.

18. Burke's notion of a "margin of ambiguity" as well as my expanded concept of Burch's "fuzzy clump" and my idea of an "epistemic zero" should be compared to such constructs as "fuzzy logic" in philosophy (which is based on degrees of truth, not on degrees of probability of truth), the "prototype schema" (with its core and periphery) in cognitive psychology, and "non-discrete grammar" in linguistics. One might even inquire about the general status of knowledge itself: how certain must knowledge be to count as "knowledge"? W. V. Quine proposes that "[w]e do better to accept the word 'know' on a par with 'big', as a matter of degree. It applies only to true beliefs, and only to pretty firm ones, but just how firm or certain they have to be is a question, like how big something has to be to qualify as big." *Quiddities: An Intermittently Philosophical Dictionary* (Cambridge, Mass.: Harvard University Press, 1987), "Knowledge," 109. See also Nelson Goodman and Catherine Z. Elgin, *Reconceptions in Philosophy and Other Arts and Sciences* (Indianapolis: Hackett, 1988), ch. 10, "A Reconception of Philosophy," 153–66; and Ian Stewart, "Mathematical Recreations: A Partly True Story," *Scientific American* 268, no. 2 (February 1993): 110–12.

ANNOTATED BIBLIOGRAPHY

Burch, Noël. *In and Out of Synch: The Awakening of a Cine-Dreamer.* Trans. Ben Brewster. Aldershot, England: Scolar, 1991.
   A collection of historical and theoretical essays.

———. *Life to those Shadows.* Trans. Ben Brewster. Berkeley: University of California Press, 1990.
   A study of the impact of sociohistorical circumstances on film style in the first three decades of cinema.

———. *To the Distant Observer: Form and Meaning in the Japanese Cinema.* Berkeley: University of California Press, 1979.
   A detailed examination of the influence of Japanese society and culture in producing a national cinema opposed to the classical Hollywood cinema.

———. *Marcel L'Herbier.* Paris: Éditions Seghers, 1973.
   Analyses of the films of Marcel L'Herbier.

———. *Praxis du cinéma.* Paris: Éditions Gallimard, 1969. Translated as *Theory of Film Practice* by Helen R. Lane. New York: Praeger, 1973. Reprinted by Princeton University Press, Princeton, N.J., 1981.
   A general study of the theory and aesthetic principles of cinema.

Metz

"Identification, Mirror" and "The Passion for Perceiving"

Identification, Mirror

The All-Perceiving Subject

Film is like the mirror. But it differs from the primordial mirror in one essential point: although, as in the latter, everything may come to be projected, there is one thing and one thing only that is never reflected in it: the spectator's own body. In a certain emplacement, the mirror suddenly becomes clear glass.

In the mirror the child perceives the familiar household objects, and also its object par excellence, its mother, who holds it up in her arms to the glass. But above all it perceives its own image. This is where primary identification (the formation of the ego) gets certain of its main characteristics: the child sees itself as an other, and beside an other. This other other is its guarantee that the first is really it: by her authority, her sanction, in the register of the symbolic, subsequently by the resemblance between her mirror image and the child's (both have a human form). Thus the child's ego is formed by identification with its like, and this in two senses simultaneously, metonymically and metaphorically: the other human being who is in the glass, the own reflection which is and is not the body, which is like it. The child identifies with itself as an object.

In the cinema, the object remains: fiction or no, there is always something on the screen. But the reflection of the own body has disappeared. The cinema spectator is not a child and the child really at the mirror stage (from around six to around eighteen months) would certainly be incapable of "following" the simplest of films. Thus, what *makes*

From *The Imaginary Signifier: Psychoanalysis and the Cinema,* by Christian Metz, trans. Celia Britton, Annwyl Williams, Ben Brewster, and Alfred Guzzetti (Bloomington: Indiana University Press, 1982), 45–64. These excerpts translated by Ben Brewster originally appeared in *Screen* 16, no. 2 (1975): 14–76. Copyright © 1975 by the Society for Education in Film and Television.

possible the spectator's absence from the screen—or rather the intelligible unfolding of the film despite that absence—is the fact that the spectator has already known the experience of the mirror (of the true mirror), and is thus able to constitute a world of objects without having first to recognize himself within it. In this respect, the cinema is already on the side of the symbolic (which is only to be expected): the spectator knows that objects exist, that he himself exists as a subject, that he becomes an object for others: he knows himself and he knows his like: it is no longer necessary that this similarity be literally *depicted* for him on the screen, as it was in the mirror of his childhood. Like every other broadly "secondary" activity, the practice of the cinema presupposes that the primitive undifferentiation of the ego and the non-ego has been overcome.

But *with what*, then, does the spectator identify during the projection of the film? For he certainly has to identify: identification in its primal form has ceased to be a current necessity for him, but he continues, in the cinema—if he did not the film would become incomprehensible, considerably more incomprehensible than the most incomprehensible films—to depend on that permanent play of identification without which there would be no social life (thus, the simplest conversation presupposes the alternation of the *I* and the *you*, hence the aptitude of the two interlocutors for a mutual and reversible identification). What form does this *continued* identification, whose essential role Lacan has demonstrated even in the most abstract reasoning[1] and which constituted the "social sentiment" for Freud[2] (= the sublimation of a homosexual libido, itself a reaction to the aggressive rivalry of the members of a single generation after the murder of the father), take in the special case of one social practice among others, cinematic projection?

Obviously the spectator has the opportunity to identify with the *character* of the fiction. But there still has to be one. This is thus only valid for the narrative-representational film, and not for the psychoanalytic constitution of the signifier of the cinema as such. The spectator can also identify with the actor, in more or less "a-fictional" films in which the latter is represented as an actor, not a character, but is still offered thereby as a human being (as a perceived human being) and thus allows identification. However, this factor (even added to the previous one and thus covering a very large number of films) cannot suffice. It only designates secondary identification in certain of its forms (secondary in the cinematic process itself, since in any other sense all identification except that of the mirror can be regarded as secondary).

An insufficient explanation, and for two reasons, the first of which is only the intermittent, anecdotal, and superficial consequence of the second (but for that reason more visible, and that is why I call it the first). The cinema deviates from the theater on an important point that has often been emphasized: it often presents us with long sequences that can (literally) be called "inhuman"—the familiar theme of cinematic "cosmomorphism" developed by many film theorists—sequences in which only inanimate objects, landscapes, etc. appear and which for minutes at a time offer no human form for spectator identification: yet the latter must be supposed to remain intact in its deep structure, since at such moments the film *works* just as well as it does at others, and whole films (geographical documentaries, for example) unfold intelligibly in such conditions. The second, more radical reason is that identification with the human form appearing on the screen, even when it occurs, still tells us nothing about the *place of the spectator's ego* in the inauguration of the signifier. As I have just pointed out, this ego is already formed. But since it exists, the question arises precisely of *where it is* during the projection of the film (the true primary identification, that of the mirror, forms the ego, but all other identifications presuppose, on the contrary, that it has been formed and can be "exchanged" for the object or the fellow subject). Thus when I "recognize" my like on the screen, and even more when I do not recognize it, where am I? Where is that someone who is capable of self-recognition when need be?

It is not enough to answer that the cinema, like every social practice, demands that the psychical apparatus of its participants be fully construed, and that the question is thus the concern of general psychoanalytic theory and not that of the cinema proper. For my *where is it?* does not claim to go so far, or more precisely tries to go slightly further: it is a question of the *point* occupied by this already constituted ego, occupied during the cinema showing and not in social life in general.

The spectator is absent from the screen: contrary to the child in the mirror, he cannot identify with himself as an object, but only with objects that are there without him. In this sense the screen is not a mirror. The perceived, this time, is entirely on the side of the object, and there is no longer any equivalent of the own image, of that unique mix of perceived and subject (of other and I), which was precisely the figure necessary to disengage the one from the other. At the cinema, it is always the other who is on the screen; as for me, I am there to look at him. I take no part in the perceived, on the contrary, I am *all-perceiving*. All-perceiving as one says all-powerful (this is the famous gift of "ubiquity" the film makes its spectator); all-perceiving, too, because I am entirely on the side of the perceiving instance: absent from the screen, but certainly present in the auditorium, a great eye and ear without which the perceived would have no one to perceive it, the instance, in other words, which *constitutes* the cinema signifier (it is I who make the film). If the most extravagant spectacles and sounds or the most unlikely combination of them, the combination furthest removed from any real experience, do not prevent the constitution of meaning (and to begin with do not *astonish* the spectator, do not really astonish him, not intellectually: he simply judges the film as strange), that is because he knows he is at the cinema.

In the cinema the *subject's knowledge* takes a very precise form without which no film would be possible. This knowledge is dual (but unique). I know I am perceiving something imaginary (and that is why its absurdities, even if they are extreme, do not seriously disturb me), and I know that it is I who am perceiving it. This second knowledge divides in turn: I know that I am really perceiving, that my sense organs are physically affected, that I am not fantasizing, that the fourth wall of the auditorium (the screen) is really different from the other three, that there is a projector facing it (and thus it is not I who am projecting, or at least not all alone), and I also know that it is I who am perceiving all this, that this perceived-imaginary material is deposited in me as if on a second screen, that it is in me that it forms up into an organized sequence, that therefore I am myself the place where this really perceived imaginary accedes to the symbolic by its inauguration as the signifier of a certain type of institutionalized social activity called the "cinema."

In other words, the spectator *identifies with himself*, with himself as a pure act of perception (as wakefulness, alertness): as the condition of possibility of the perceived and hence as a kind of transcendental subject, which comes before every *there is*.

A strange mirror, then, very like that of childhood, and very different. Very like, as Jean-Louis Baudry has emphasized,[3] because during the showing we are, like the child, in a submotor and hyperperceptive state; because, like the child again, we are prey to the imaginary, the double, and are so paradoxically through a real perception. Very different, because this mirror returns us everything but ourselves, because we are wholly outside it, whereas the child is both in it and in front of it. As an *arrangement* (and in a very topographical sense of the word), the cinema is more involved on the flank of the symbolic, and hence of secondariness, than is the mirror of childhood. This is not surprising, since it comes long after it, but what is more important to me is the fact that it is inscribed in its wake with an incidence at once so direct and so oblique, which has no precise equivalent in other apparatuses of signification.

Identification with the Camera

The preceding analysis coincides in place with others that have already been proposed and I shall not repeat: analyses of *quattrocento* painting or of the cinema itself, which insist on the role of monocular perspective (hence of the *camera*) and the vanishing point that inscribes an empty emplacement for the spectator-subject, an all-powerful position which is that of God himself, or more broadly of some ultimate signified. And it is true that as he identifies with himself as look, the spectator can do no other than identify with the camera, too, which has looked before him at what he is now looking at and whose stationing (= framing) determines the vanishing point. During the projection this camera is absent, but it has a representative consisting of another apparatus, called precisely a "projector." An apparatus the spectator has behind him, *at the back of his head*, [4] that is, precisely where fantasy locates the "focus" of all vision. All of us have experienced our own look, even outside the so-called *salles obscures* [= cinemas], as a kind of searching turning on the axis of our own necks (like a pan) and shifting when we shift (a tracking shot now): as a cone of light (without the microscope dust scattered through it and streaking it in the cinema) whose vicariousness draws successive and variable slices of obscurity from nothingness wherever and whenever it comes to rest. (And in a sense that is what perception and consciousness are, a *light*, as Freud put it,[5] in the double sense of an illumination and an opening, as in the arrangement of the cinema, which contains both, a limited and wandering light that only attains a small part of the real, but on the other hand possesses the gift of casting light on it.) Without this identification with the camera certain facts could not be understood, though they are constant ones: the fact, for example, that the spectator is not amazed when the image "rotates" (= a pan) and yet he knows he has not turned his head. The explanation is that he has no need to turn it really, he has turned it in his all-seeing capacity, his identification with the movement of the camera being that of a transcendental, not an empirical subject.

All vision consists of a double movement: projective (the "sweeping" searchlight) and introjective: consciousness as a sensitive recording surface (as a screen). I have the impression at once that, to use a common expression, I am "casting" my eyes on things, and that the latter, thus illuminated, come to be deposited within me (we then declare that it is these things that have been "projected," onto my retina, say). A sort of stream called the look, and explaining all the myths of magnetism, must be sent out over the world, so that objects can come back up this stream in the opposite direction (but using it to find their way), arriving at last at our perception, which is now soft wax and no longer an emitting source.

The technology of photography carefully conforms to this (banal) fantasy accompanying perception. The camera is "trained" on the object like a firearm (= projection) and the object arrives to make an imprint, a trace, on the receptive surface of the film-strip (= introjection). The spectator himself does not escape these pincers, for he is part of the apparatus, and also because pincers, on the imaginary plane (Melanie Klein), mark our relation to the world as a whole and are rooted in the primary figures of orality. During the performance the spectator is the searchlight I have described, duplicating the projector, which itself duplicates the camera and he is also the sensitive surface duplicating the screen, which itself duplicates the film-strip. There are two cones in the auditorium: one ending on the screen and starting both in the projection box and in the spectator's vision in so far as it is projective, and one starting from the screen and "deposited" in the spectator's perception in so far as it is introjective (on the retina, a second screen). When I say that "I see" the film, I mean thereby a unique mixture of two contrary currents: the film is what I receive, and it is also what I release, since it does not preexist my entering the auditorium and I only need close my eyes to suppress it. Releasing it, I am the projector, receiving it, I am the screen; in both these figures together, I am the camera, which points and yet which records.

Thus the constitution of the signifier in the cinema depends on a series of mirror-effects organized in a chain, and not on a single reduplication. In this the cinema as a topography resembles that other "space," the technical equipment (camera, projector, film-strip, screen, etc.), the objective precondition of the whole institution: as we know, the apparatuses too contain a series of mirrors, lenses, apertures, and shutters, ground glasses, through which the cone of light passes: a further reduplication in which the equipment becomes a metaphor (as well as the real source) for the mental process instituted. Further on we shall see that it is also its fetish.

In the cinema, as elsewhere, the constitution of the symbolic is only achieved through and above the play of the imaginary: projection-introjection, presence-absence, fantasies accompanying perception, etc. Even when acquired, the ego still depends in its underside on the fabulous figures thanks to which it has been acquired and which have marked it lastingly with the stamp of the lure. The secondary process does no more than "cover" (and not always hermetically) the primary process that is still constantly present and conditions the very possibility of what covers it.

Chain of many mirrors, the cinema is at once a weak and a robust mechanism: like the human body, like a precision tool, like a social institution. And the fact is that it is really all of these at the same time.

And I, at this moment, what am I doing if not to add to all these reduplications one more whereby theory is attempting to set itself up? Am I not looking at myself looking at the film? This *passion for seeing* (and also hearing), the foundation of the whole edifice, am I not turning it, too, on (against) that edifice? Am I not still the voyeur I was in front of the screen, now that it is this voyeur who is being seen, thus postulating a second voyeur, the one writing at present, myself again?

On the Idealist Theory of the Cinema

The place of the ego in the institution of the signifier, as transcendental yet radically deluded subject, since it is the institution (and even the equipment) that give it this place, surely provides us with an appreciable opportunity the better to understand and judge the precise epistemological import of the idealist theory of the cinema that culminates in the remarkable works of André Bazin. Before thinking directly about their validity, but simply reading texts of this kind, one cannot but be struck by the great precision, the acute and immediately sensitive intelligence that they often demonstrate; at the same time they give the diffuse impression of a permanent ill-foundedness (which affects nothing and yet affects everything), they suggest that somewhere they contain something like a weak point at which the whole might be overturned.

It is certainly no accident that the main form of idealism in cinematic theory has been phenomenology. Bazin and other writers of the same period explicitly acknowledged their debt to it, and more implicitly (but in a more generalized fashion) all conceptions of the cinema as a mystical revelation, as "truth" or "reality" unfolding by right, as the apparition of what is (*l'élant*), as an epiphany, derive from it. We all know that the cinema has the gift of sending some of its lovers into prophetic trances. However, these cosmophanic conceptions (which are not always expressed in an extreme form) register rather well the "feeling" of the *deluded ego* of the spectator, they often give us excellent descriptions of this feeling and to this extent there is something scientific about them and they have advanced our knowledge of the cinema. But the *lure of the ego* is their blind spot. These theories are still of great interest, but they have, so to speak, to be put the other way around, like the optical image of the film.

For it is true that the topographical apparatus of the cinema resembles the conceptual apparatus of phenomenology, with the result that the latter can cast light on the former. (Besides, in any domain, a phenomenology of the object to be understood, a "receptive" description of its appearances, must be the starting point; only afterwards can *criticism* begin; psychoanalysts, it should be remembered, have their own phenomenology.) The *there is* of phenomenology proper (philosophical phenomenology) as an ontic revelation referring to a perceiving-subject (= "perceptual *cogito*"), to a subject for which alone there can be anything, has close and precise affinities with the installation of the cinema signifier in the ego as I have tried to define it, with the spectator withdrawing into himself as a pure instance of perception, the whole of the perceived being "out there." To this extent the cinema really is the "phenomenological art" it has often been called, by Merleau-Ponty himself, for example.[6] But it can only be so because its objective determinations make it so. The ego's position in the cinema does not derive from a miraculous resemblance between the cinema and the natural characteristics of all perception; on the contrary, it is foreseen and marked in advance by the institution (the equipment, the disposition of the auditorium, the mental system that internalizes the two), and also by more general characteristics of the physical apparatus (such as projection, the mirror structure, etc.), which although they are less strictly dependent on a period of social history and a technology, do not therefore express the sovereignty of a "human vocation," but inversely are themselves shaped by certain specific features of man as an animal (as the only animal that is not an animal): his primitive *Hilflosigkeit,* his dependence on another's care (the lasting source of the imaginary, of object relations, of the great oral figures of feeding), the motor prematurity of the child that condemns it to an initial self-recognition by sight (hence outside itself) anticipating a muscular unity it does not yet possess.

In other words, phenomenology can contribute to knowledge of the cinema (and it has done so) in so far as it happens to be like it, and yet it is on the cinema *and* phenomenology in their common illusion of *perceptual mastery* that light must be cast by the real conditions of society and man.

On Some Subcodes of Identification

The play of identification defines the cinematic situation in its generality, that is, *the* code. But it also allows more specific and less permanent configurations, "variations" on it, as it were; they intervene in certain coded figures that occupy precise segments of precise films.

What I have said about identification so far amounts to the statement that the spectator is absent from the screen *as perceived,* but also (the two things inevitably go together) present there and even "all-present" as *perceiver.* At every moment I am in the film by my look's caress. This presence often remains diffuse, geographically undifferentiated, evenly distributed over the whole surface of the screen; or more precisely *hovering,* like the psychoanalyst's listening, ready to catch on preferentially to some motif in the film, according to the force of that motif and according to my own fantasies as a spectator, without the cinematic code itself intervening to govern this anchorage and impose it on the whole audience. But in other cases, certain articles of the cinematic codes or subcodes (which I shall not try to survey completely here) are made responsible for suggesting to the spectator the vector along which his permanent identification with his own look should be extended temporarily inside the film (the perceived) itself. Here we meet various classic problems of cinematic theory, or at least certain aspects of them: subjective images, out-of-frame space, looks (looks and no longer the look, but the former are articulated to the latter).

There are various sorts of subjective image and I have tried elsewhere (following Jean Mitry) to distinguish between them.[7] Only one of them will detain me for the moment, the one that "expresses the viewpoint of the filmmaker" in the standard formula (and not the viewpoint of a character, another traditional subcase of the subjective image): unusual framings, uncommon shot-angles, etc. as, for example, in one of the sketches that make up Julien Duvivier's film *Carnet de bal* (the sketch with Pierre Blanchar, shot continuously in tilted framings). In the standard definitions one thing strikes me: I do not see why these uncommon angles should express the viewpoint of the filmmaker any more than perfectly ordinary angles, closer to the horizontal. However, the definition is comprehensible even in its inaccuracy: precisely because it is uncommon, the uncommon angle makes us more aware of what we had merely forgotten to some extent in its absence: an identification with the camera (with "the author's viewpoint"). The ordinary framings are finally felt to be non-framings: I espouse the filmmaker's look (without which no cinema would be possible), but my consciousness is not too aware of it. The uncommon angle reawakens me and (like the cure) teaches me what I already knew. And then, it obliges my look to stop wandering freely over the screen for the moment and to scan it along more precise lines of force that are imposed on me. Thus for a moment I become directly aware of the *emplacement* of my own presence-absence in the film simply because it has changed.

Now for looks. In a fiction film, the characters look at one another. It can happen (and this is already another "notch" in the chain of identifications) that a character looks at another who is momentarily out of frame, or else is looked at by him. If we have gone one notch further, this is because everything out of frame *brings us closer to the spectator*, since it is the peculiarity of the latter to be out of frame (the out-of-frame character thus has a point in common with him: he is looking at the screen). In certain cases the out-of-frame character's look is "reinforced" by recourse to another variant of the subjective image, generally christened the "character's point of view": the framing of the scene corresponds precisely to the angle from which the out-of-frame character looks at the screen. (The two figures are dissociable moreover: we often know that the scene is being looked at by someone other than ourselves, by a character, but it is the logic of the plot, or an element of the dialogue, or a previous image that tells us so, not the position of the camera, which may be far from the presumed emplacement of the out-of-frame onlooker.)

In all sequences of this kind, the identification that founds the signifier is *twice relayed*, doubly duplicated in a circuit that leads it to the heart of the film along a line which is no longer hovering, which follows the inclination of the looks and is therefore governed by the film itself: the spectator's look (= the basic identification), before dispersing all over the surface of the screen in a variety of intersecting lines (= looks of the characters in the frame—second duplication), must first "go through"—as one goes through a town on a journey, or a mountain pass—the look of the character out of frame (= first duplication), himself a spectator and hence the first delegate of the true spectator, but not to be confused with the latter since he is inside, if not the frame, then at least the fiction. This invisible character, supposed (like the spectator) to be seeing, will collide obliquely with the latter's look and play the part of an obligatory intermediary. By offering himself as a crossing for the spectator, he inflects the circuit followed by the sequence of identifications and it is only in this sense that he is himself seen: as we see through him, we see ourselves not seeing him.

Examples of this kind are much more numerous and each of them is much more complex than I have suggested here. At this point, textual analysis of precise film sequences is an indispensable instrument of knowledge. I just wished to show that in the end there is no break in continuity between the child's game with the mirror and, at the other extreme, certain localized figures of the cinematic codes. The mirror is the site of primary identification. Identification with one's own look is secondary with respect to the mirror, that is, for a general theory of adult activities, but it is the foundation of the cinema and hence primary when the latter is under discussion: it is *primary cinematic identification* proper ("primary identification" would be inaccurate from the psychoanalytic point of view; "secondary identification," more accurate in this respect, would be ambiguous for a cinematic psychoanalysis). As for identifications with characters, with their own different levels (out-of-frame character, etc.), they are secondary, tertiary cinematic identifications, etc.; taken as a whole in opposition to the identification of the spectator with his own look, they constitute secondary cinematic identification in the singular.[8]

"Seeing a Film"

Freud noted, *vis-à-vis* the sexual act,[9] that the most ordinary practices depend on a large number of physical functions that are distinct but work consecutively, so that all of them must be intact if what is regarded as a normal performance is to be possible (it is because neurosis and psychosis dissociate them and put some of them out of court that a kind of communication is made possible whereby they can be listed retrospectively by the analyst). The apparently very simple act of *seeing a film* is no exception to this rule. As soon as it is subjected to analysis it reveals to us a complex, multiply interconnected imbrication of the functions of the imaginary, the real, and the symbolic, which is also required in one form or another for every procedure of social life, but whose cinematic manifestation is especially impressive since it is played out on a small surface. (To this extent the theory of the cinema may some day contribute something to psychoanalysis, even if, through force of circumstances, this "reciprocation" remains very limited at the moment, the two disciplines being very unevenly developed.)

In order to understand the fiction film, I must both "take myself" for the character (= an imaginary procedure) so that he benefits, by analogical projection, from all the schemata of intelligibility that I have within me, and not take myself for him (= the return to the real) so that the fiction can be established as such (= as symbolic): this is *seeming-real.*

Similarly, in order to understand the film (at all), I must perceive the photographed object as absent, its photograph as present, and the presence of this absence as signifying. The imaginary of the cinema presupposes the symbolic, for the spectator must first of all have known the primordial mirror. But as the latter instituted the ego very largely in the imaginary, the second mirror of the screen, a symbolic apparatus, itself in turn depends on reflection and lack. However, it is not fantasy, a "purely" symbolic-imaginary site, for the absence of the object and the codes of that absence are really produced in it by the *physis* of an equipment: the cinema is a body (a *corpus* for the semiologist), a fetish that can be loved.

The Passion for Perceiving

The practice of the cinema is only possible through the perceptual passions: the desire to see (= scopic drive, scopophilia, voyeurism), which was alone engaged in the art of the silent film, the desire to hear which has been added to it in the sound cinema (this is the *"pulsion invocante, "* the invocatory drive, one of the four main sexual drives for Lacan;[1] it is well known that Freud isolated it less clearly and hardly deals with it as such).

These two sexual drives are distinguished from the others in that they are more dependent on a lack, or at least dependent on it in a more precise, more unique manner, which marks them from the outset, even more than the others, as being on the side of the imaginary.

However, this characteristic is to a greater or lesser degree proper to all the sexual drives in so far as they differ from purely organic instincts or needs (Lacan), or in Freud from the self-preservation drives (the "ego drives" that he tended subsequently to annex to narcissism, a tendency he could never quite bring himself to pursue to its conclusion). The sexual drive does not have so stable and strong a relationship with its "object" as do, for example, hunger and thirst. Hunger can only be satisfied by food, but food is quite certain to satisfy it; thus instincts are simultaneously more and less difficult to satisfy than drives; they depend on a perfectly real object for which there is no substitute, but they depend on nothing else. Drives, on the contrary, can be satisfied up to a point outside their objects (this is sublimation, or else, in another way, masturbation) and are initially capable of doing without them without putting the organism into immediate danger (hence repression). The needs of self-preservation can neither be repressed nor sublimated; the sexual drives are more labile and more accommodating, as Freud insisted[2] (more radically perverse, says Lacan[3]). Inversely, they always remain more or less unsatisfied, even when their object has been attained; desire is very quickly reborn after the brief vertigo of its apparent extinction, it is largely sustained by itself as desire, it has its own rhythms, often quite independent of those of the pleasure obtained (which seemed nonetheless its specific aim); the lack is what it wishes to fill, and at the same time what it is always careful to leave gaping, in order to survive as desire. In the end it has no object, at any rate no real object; through real objects that are all substitutes (and all the more numerous and interchangeable for that), it pursues an imaginary object (a "lost object") which is its truest object, an object that has always been lost and is always desired as such.

How, then, can one say that the visual and auditory drives have a stronger or more special relationship with the absence of their object, with the infinite pursuit of the imaginary? Because, as opposed to other sexual drives, the "perceiving drive"—combining into one the scopic drive and the invocatory drive—*concretely represents the absence of its object* in the distance at which it maintains it and which is part of its very definition: distance of the look, distance of listening. Psychophysiology makes a classic distinction between the "senses at a distance" (sight and hearing) and the others all of which involve immediate proximity and which it calls the "senses of contact" (Pradines): touch, taste, smell, coenaesthetic sense, etc. Freud notes that voyeurism, like sadism in this respect, always keeps apart the *object* (here the object looked at) and the *source* of the drive, that is, the generating organ (the eye); the voyeur does not look at his eye.[4] With orality and anality, on the contrary, the exercise of the drive inaugurates a certain degree of partial fusion, a coincidence (= contract, tendential abolition of distance) of source and aim, for the aim is to obtain pleasure at the level of the source organ (= "organ pleasure"[5]): what is called "pleasure of the mouth."[6]

It is no accident that the main socially acceptable arts are based on the senses at a distance, and that those that depend on the senses of contact are often regarded as "minor" arts (e.g., the culinary arts, the art of perfumes, etc.). Nor is it an accident that the visual or auditory imaginaries have played a much more important part in the histories of societies than the tactile or olfactory imaginaries.

The voyeur is very careful to maintain a gulf, an empty space, between the object and the eye, the object and his own body: his look fastens the object at the right distance, as with those cinema spectators who take care to avoid being too close to or too far from the screen. The voyeur represents in space the fracture that forever separates him from the object; he represents his very dissatisfaction (which is precisely what he needs as a voyeur), and thus also his "satisfaction" in so far as it is of a specifically voyeuristic type. To fill in this distance would threaten to overwhelm the subject, to lead him to consume the object (the object that is now too close so that he cannot see it anymore), to bring him to orgasm and the pleasure of his own body, hence to the exercise of other drives, mobilizing the senses of contact and putting an end to the scopic arrangement. *Retention* is fully part of perceptual pleasure, which is thereby often colored with anality. Orgasm is the object rediscovered in a state of momentary illusion; it is the fantasy suppression of the gap between object and subject (hence the amorous myths of "fusion"). The looking drive, except when it is exceptionally well developed, is less directly related to orgasm than are the other component drives; it favors it by its excitatory action, but it is not generally sufficient to produce it by its figures alone, which thus belong to the realm of "preparatives." In it we do not find that illusion, however brief, of a lack filled, of a nonimaginary, of a full relation to the object, better established in other drives. If it is true of all desire that it depends on the infinite pursuit of its absent object, voyeuristic desire, along with certain forms of sadism, is the only desire whose principle of distance symbolically and spatially evokes this fundamental rent.

The same could be said, making the necessary modifications of course, about the invocatory (auditory) drive, less closely studied by psychoanalysis hitherto, with the exception of writers like Lacan and Guy Rosolato. I shall merely recall that of all hallucinations—and what reveals the dissociation of desire and real object better than the hallucination?—the main ones by far are visual and auditory hallucinations, those of the senses at a distance (this is also true of the dream, another form of hallucination).

The Scopic Regime of the Cinema

Although this set of features seems to me to be important, it does not yet characterize the signifier of the cinema proper, but rather that of all means of expression based on sight or hearing, and hence, among other "languages," that of practically all the arts (painting, sculpture, architecture, music, opera, theater, etc.). What distinguishes the cinema is an extra reduplication, a supplementary and specific turn of the screw bolting desire to the lack. First because the spectacles and sounds the cinema "offers" us (offers us at a distance, hence as much *steals* from us) are especially rich and varied: a mere difference of degree, but already one that counts: the screen presents to our apprehension, but absents from our grasp, more "things." (The mechanism of the perceiving drive is identical for the moment but its object is more endowed with matter; this is one of the reasons why the cinema is very suited to handling "erotic scenes" that depend on direct, nonsublimated voyeurism.) In the second place (and more decisively), the specific affinity between the cinematic signifier and the imaginary persists when film is compared with arts such as the theater in which the audiovisual given is as rich as it is on the screen in the number of perceptual axes involved. Indeed, the theater really does "give" this given, or at least slightly more really: it is physically present, in the same space as the spectator. The cinema only gives it in effigy, inaccessible from the outset, in a primordial *elsewhere*, infinitely desirable (= never possible), on another scene which is that of absence and which nonetheless represents the absent in detail, thus making it very present, but by a different itinerary. Not only am I at a distance from the object, as in the theater, but what remains in that distance is now no longer the object itself, it is a delegate it has sent me while itself withdrawing. A double withdrawal.

What defines the specifically cinematic *scopic regime* is not so much the distance kept, the "keeping" itself (first figure of the lack, common to all voyeurism), as the absence of the object seen. Here the cinema is profoundly different from the theater as also from more intimate voyeuristic activities with a specifically erotic aim (there are intermediate genres, moreover: certain cabaret acts, strip-tease, etc.): cases where voyeurism remains linked to exhibitionism, where the two faces, active and passive, of the component drive are by no means so dissociated; where the object seen is present and hence presumably complicit; where the perverse activity—aided if need be by a certain dose of bad faith and happy illusion, varying from case to case, moreover, and sometimes reducible to very little, as in true perverse couples—is rehabilitated and reconciled with itself by being as it were undividedly taken in charge by two actors assuming its constitutive poles (the corresponding fantasies, in the absence of the actions, thus becoming interchangeable and shared by the play of reciprocal identification). In the theater, as in domestic voyeurism, the passive actor (the one seen), simply because he is bodily present, because he does not go away, is presumed to consent, to cooperate deliberately. It may be that he really does, as exhibitionists in the clinical sense do, or as, in a sublimated fashion, does that oft-noted triumphant exhibitionism characteristic of theatrical acting, counterposed even by Bazin to cinematic representation. It may also be that the object seen has only accepted this condition (thus becoming an "object" in the ordinary sense of the word, and no longer only in the Freudian sense) under the pressure of more or less powerful external constraints, economic ones, for example, with certain poor strippers. (However, they must have consented at some point; rarely is the degree of acceptance zero, except in the case of *victimization*, e.g., when a fascist militia strips its prisoners: the specific characteristics of the scopic arrangement are then distorted by the overpowerful intervention of another element, sadism.) Voyeurism which is not too sadistic (there is none which is not so at all) rests on a kind of *fiction*, more or less justified in the order of the real, sometimes institutionalized as in the theater or strip-tease, a fiction that stipulates that the object "agrees," that it is therefore exhibitionist. Or more precisely, what is necessary in this fiction for the establishment of potency and desire is presumed to be sufficiently guaranteed by the physical presence of the object: "since it is there, it must like it"; such, hypocritical or no, deluded or no, is the retrenchment needed by the voyeur so long as sadistic infiltrations are insufficient to make the object's refusal and constraint necessary to him. Thus, despite the distance instituted by the look—which transforms the object into a *picture* (a *tableau vivant*[7]) and thus tips it over into the imaginary, even in its real presence—that presence, which persists, and the active consent which is its real or mythical correlate (but always real as myth) reestablish in the scopic space, momentarily at least, the illusion of a fullness of the object relation, of a state of desire that is not just imaginary.

It is this last recess that is attacked by the cinema signifier, it is in its precise emplacement (*in its place,* in both senses of the word) that it installs a new figure of the lack, the physical absence of the object seen. In the theater, actors and spectators are present at the same time and in the same location, hence present one to another, as the two protagonists of an authentic perverse couple. But in the cinema, the actor was present when the spectator was not (= shooting), and the spectator is present when the actor is no longer (= projection): a failure to meet of the voyeur and the exhibitionist whose approaches no longer coincide (they have "missed" one another). The cinema's voyeurism must (of necessity) do without any very clear mark of consent on the part of the object. There is no equivalent here of the theater actors' final "bow." And then the latter could see their voyeurs, the game was less unilateral, slightly better distributed. In the darkened hall, the voyeur is really left alone (or with other voyeurs, which is worse), deprived of his other half in the mythical hermaphrodite (a hermaphrodite not necessarily constituted by the distribution of the sexes but rather by that of the active and passive poles in the exercise of the drive). Yet still a voyeur, since there is something to see, called the film, but something in whose definition there is a great deal of "flight": not precisely something that hides, but rather something that *lets* itself be seen without *presenting* itself to be seen, which has gone out of the room before leaving only its trace visible there. This is the origin in particular of that "recipe" of the classical cinema, which said that the actor should never look directly at the audience (= camera).

Thus deprived of rehabilitatory agreement, of a real or supposed consensus with the other (which was also the Other, for it had the status of a sanction on the plane of the symbolic), cinematic voyeurism, *unauthorized* scopophilia, is from the outset more strongly established than that of the theater in direct line from the primal scene. Certain precise features of the institution contribute to this affinity; the obscurity surrounding the onlooker, the aperture of the screen with its inevitable keyhole effect. But the affinity is more profound. It lies first in the spectator's solitude in the cinema: those attending a cinematic projection do not, as in the theater, constitute a true "audience," a temporary collectivity; they are an accumulation of individuals who, despite appearances, more closely resemble the fragmented group of readers of a novel. It lies on the other hand in the fact that the filmic spectacle, the object seen, is more radically ignorant of its spectator, since he is not there, than the theatrical spectacle can ever be. A third factor, closely linked to the other two, also plays a part: the *segregation of spaces* that characterizes a cinema performance and not a theatrical one. The "stage" and the auditorium are no longer two areas set up in opposition to each other within a single space; the space of the film, represented by the screen, is utterly heterogeneous, it no longer communicates with that of the auditorium: one is real, the other perspective: a stronger break than any line of footlights. For its spectator the film unfolds in that simultaneously very close and definitively inaccessible "elsewhere" in which the child *sees* the amorous play of the parental couple, who are similarly ignorant of it and leave it alone, a pure onlooker whose participation is inconceivable. In this respect the cinematic signifier is not only "psychoanalytic"; it is more precisely Oedipal in type.

NOTES

Identification, Mirror

1. "Le temps logique et l'assertion de certitude anticipée," *Ecrits* (Paris: Ed. du Seuil, 1966) 197–213.

3. "The Ego and the Id," in *Standard Edition of the Complete Psychological Works of Sigmund Freud* (London: Hogarth, 1953–66), (vol. 19) 26 and 30 (on "desexualized social sentiment"); see also (on the subject of paranoia) "On Narcissism: An Introduction," (vol. 14) 95–96, 101–2.

3. "Cinéma: Effets idéologiques produits par l'appareil de base," *Cinéthique* 7–8 (1970), 1–8 ("Ideological Effects of the Basic Cinematographic Apparatus," trans. Alan Williams, *Film Quarterly* 28, no. 2 [1974–75]: 39–47). "Le dispositif: Approaches métapsychologiques de l'impression de réalité," *Communications* 23 (1975): 56–72 ("The Apparatus," trans. Jean Andrews and Bertrand Augst, *Camera Obscura* 1 [1976]: 104–26).

4. [*Derrière la tête* means "at the back of one's mind" as well as "behind one's head."] See André Green: "L'Ecran bi-face, un oeil derrière la tête," *Psychanalyse et cinéma*, January 1, 1970 (no further issues appeared), 15–22. It will be clear that in the passage that follows, my analysis coincides in places with that of Green.

5. "The Ego and the Id" (vol. 19), 18; *The Interpretation of Dreams* (vol. 5), 615 (= consciousness as a sense organ) and 574 (= consciousness as a dual recording surface, internal and external); "The Unconscious" (vol. 14), 171 (psychical processes are in themselves unconscious, consciousness is a function that *perceives* a small proportion of them), etc.

6. "The Film and the New Psychology," lecture to the Institut des Hautes Etudes Cinématographiques (March 13, 1945), translated in *Sense and Nonsense* (Evanston, Ill.: Northwestern University Press, 1964), 48–59.

7. See section 2 of "Current Problems of Film Theory," *Screen* 14, nos. 1–2 (1973): 45–49.

8. On these problems, see Michel Colin, "Le Film: Transformation du texte du roman," unpublished thesis (Mémoire de troisième cycle, 1974).

9. *Inhibitions, Symptoms and Anxiety* (vol. 20), 87–88.

The Passion for Perceiving

1. See esp. *The Four Fundamental Concepts of Psycho-Analysis*, trans. A. Sheridan (London: Hogarth, 1977), 180 and 195–96.

2. "Repression" (vol. 14), 146–47; "Instincts and Their Vicissitudes" (vol. 14), 122 and 134 n.; "The Ego and the Id" (vol. 19), 30; "On Narcissism: an Introduction" (vol. 19), 94, etc.

3. More precisely: lending themselves through their peculiar characteristics to a perversion that is not the drive itself, but the subject's position with respect to it (*The Four Fundamental Concepts of Psycho-Analysis*, trans. Sheridan, 181–83). Remember that for Freud as well as for Lacan, the drive is always "componential" (the child is polymorphously perverse, etc.).

4. "Instincts and their Vicissitudes" (vol. 14), 129–30.

5. Ibid., 138.

6. Lacan, *Four Fundamental Concepts of Psycho-Analysis*, trans. Sheridan, 167–68.

7. See the paragraph with this title in Jean-François Lyotard's article "L'Acinéma," *Revue d'Esthétique*, nos. 2–4 (1973): 357–69.

Robert T. Eberwein

Christian Metz

The title of this anthology, *Defining Cinema,* offers an appropriate phrase to describe the enterprise of Christian Metz, who devoted so much of his theoretical work to explaining what "cinema" in fact was. In an interview in 1979, Metz suggested that "cinema studies . . . has three kinds of main entrances: the linguistic one (cinema as a discourse, history, or story, editing patterns); the psychoanalytic one; and the directly social and economic one" (Flitterman-Lewis, 9). Our survey and examination of some of the central documents in Metz's works demonstrate the extent to which the first and second of these entrances engaged his attention quite forcefully and productively.

I have been guided in determining which of Metz's essays or explorations to include in this anthology by the criteria of impact, significance, and representativeness. Although my selection of an excerpt from "The Imaginary Signifier" (1975) foregrounds (or privileges) Metz's psychoanalytic theory, I suggest how his argument connects in a coherent manner with his earlier linguistic endeavors. The following commentary positions Metz historically, explores his main ideas, and offers a contemporary perspective on his importance.

One way to begin to situate Metz historically is to refer to his review of Jean Mitry's *Esthétique et psychologie du cinéma* (*Les Structures,* 1963; *Les Formes,* 1965). In the two-part review, originally written in 1964 and 1965, Metz demonstrates impressively his own profound awareness of previous theoreticians. For example, reading the first of the reviews (as yet untranslated), "Une Étape dans le refléxion sur le cinéma," one finds Metz praising Mitry for the latter's ability to reconcile the conflicting approaches to cinema offered by cineastes and by theoreticians such as Béla Balázs, Rudolf Arnheim, S. M. Eisenstein, and André Bazin (14). In "Current Problems of Film Theory," the review of the second volume (1965; translated 1972), Metz gracefully integrates Mitry's comments on synchronous sound with earlier perspectives on synchronicity voiced by Arnheim (51). He accepts Bazin's conception of the theater's centrifugal space (63). And he seconds enthusiastically Mitry's view, which echoes his own, that "the cinema is a language, infinitely different from verbal language, but a language nevertheless, since it has in common with verbal language the unique and fundamental property of communicating a sense" (75).

In a sense, we can consider Metz's commentary here as a benchmark. He speaks as a young theorist (b. 1931), just beginning his impressive career, and as someone well aware of a theoretical tradition that his emerging work on the question of whether cinema is a language will extend and modify.

When the reviews of Mitry were republished in *Essais sur la signification au cinéma* (1972), Metz added footnoted commentary, supplementing his earlier observations with references to film theory and criticism he had read and written since the first appearance of the review. It is in the notes that one finds new names being mentioned: Roland Barthes, for one, and his conception of cinema's "third meaning" (étape 18); Jean-Louis Comolli, for another, in the context of a discussion of the famous Kuleshov effect (étape 26). More significant, Metz is now referring to his own work, to what he was attempting to achieve in *Language and Cinema* (Problems, 53), and to ongoing and as yet unresolved theoretical questions (Problems, esp. 80–81). The two republished reviews can be considered a kind of mapping of Metz's perspectives on the theoretical and critical tradition that had preceded him. The notes help clarify the issues that still intrigue him: language, certainly, and the nature of the spectator.

Almost twenty years later, we still see Metz positioning himself in relation to a theoretical tradition, but this time one that has been powerfully inflected by his own contributions. In "Images subjectives, sons subjectifs," one of the essays in *L'Énonciation impersonnelle, ou le site du film* (1991), Metz refers to Noël Burch's six fields of off-screen space, specifically the space in front of the screen, as he explores his own conception of voyeurism (127). In "Quatre pa dans les nuages," Metz good-naturedly acknowledges David Bordwell's reservations regarding his argument about enunciation in "Story/Discourse (A Note on Two Kinds of Voyeurism)" (180). And again and again, he cites approvingly Edward Branigan's *Point of View in the Cinema* (1984) as he explores the viewing experience.

I will have more to say about Metz from a historical perspective at the conclusion of this essay, specifically in regard to his current status in contemporary theory. But the preceding has been designed to suggest that at any point of his career, one sadly terminated by his death in 1993, we encounter a theorist very much aware of his own position in relation to a rich theoretical tradition.

To begin exploring his interest in linguistics and psychoanalysis, I want to turn to perhaps the first film theorist, one who preceded even Hugo Münsterberg: Vachel Lindsay. He foresaw film as being a kind of "Esperanto," a new language of picture-words and hieroglyphs (205). Metz employs the same term in *Film Language: A Semiotics of the Cinema* (1968; translated 1974) but with a decided difference. He rejects the possibility of cinema as Esperanto because the latter is a self-contained "system that is totally conventional, specific, and organized" (63).

Metz argued that cinema could be considered a *language* but not a *language system* like Esperanto or French or English. He derived the distinction between the two from Ferdinand de Saussure, the Swiss linguist whose views were assembled by his students in *A Course in General Linguistics.* Saussure called for a study of language along *synchronic* rather than *diachronic* lines (i.e., emphasizing language's existing structures rather than tracing its historical, evolutionary developments). He distinguished three aspects of linguistic experience: language in general, (*langage*), the universal capacity for utterance or discourse; language system, (*langue*), an articulated and organized system of communication; and speech itself (*parole*), the individual's realization, through verbal activity, of the potential inherent in his or her particular language system.

Metz offers three reasons why cinema is not a language system, like the French tongue, but language or discourse that itself includes various systems, *langage* rather than *langue*. First, unlike a language system, film lacks the *double articulation*: it has no *phonemes*, minimal units of sound, which combine into *morphemes* or *monemes*, minimal units of meaning.

Second, a shot of a tiger cannot be construed to be the cinematic equivalent of the *word* "tiger," as earlier theorists like Lev Kuleshov and V. I. Pudovkin had suggested. There are no morphemes and monemes, minimal units of meaning; the shot always gives us more than a word and is comparable, at least, to a sentence. A shot of a tiger says to Metz "Here is a tiger" rather than simply "tiger."

Third, the relation between the image of the tiger and the meaning we derive from the image is motivated. According to Saussure, in language systems the relation between the linguistic signifier (the acoustical image) and the signified (the meaning of the image, the referent to which it points) is not motivated but arbitrary; that is, "tiger" means something (members of the cat family residing in certain parts of the world) by virtue of a convention that has established a connection between the acoustical image and the meaning. The sign that results from an English-speaking individual's apprehension of the signifier/signified is part of our language system. But there is no reason why another sign could not have arisen to designate tiger. In fact, the signifier/signified construct for tiger could as easily have been "lion"—and vice versa—because of the arbitrary nature of linguistic meaning and the way in which concepts are joined to sound images.

Metz thinks cinema is truly a universal language rather than an individualized language system precisely because its images are always motivated. An image of a tiger on the screen actually resembles a tiger.

We see an image on the screen, and, on the denotative level, immediately apprehend the tight relationship between the signifier, the image of the tiger, and the signified.

Readers will recall Bazin's earlier suggestions about the relationship of the photographic image and the object presented as a "molding, the taking of an impression" (12). Robert Stam has in fact suggested that Metz's language-based work "remains marked by vestigial Bazinianism" (282). Metz asserts that "the signifier is coextensive with the whole of the significate [signified], the spectacle its own signification" (43); there is a "lack of distance between the significate and the signifier" (59); "the signifier is an image, the significate is what the image represents" (62). "[T]he image is first and always an image. In its perceptual literalness it reproduces the signified spectacle whose signifier it is; and thus it becomes what it shows" and "from the very first an image is not the indication of something other than itself [as the acoustical image "tiger" is] but the pseudopresence of the thing it contains." Films can present all sorts of subjects, and be either realistic or naturalistic, "but whatever the case, the film itself only shows whatever it shows" (76). "[I]mage discourse needs no translation . . . because, having no second articulation, it is already translated into all languages: The height of the translatable is the universal" (64).

One speaks more properly of cinema as language when images are put together to form a narrative. Throughout *Film Language* and *Language and Cinema* (1971; translated, 1974), Metz deals primarily with filmed narratives having plots, themes, characters, and so on. As he conceives it, "'cinematographic language' is first of all the literalness of a plot" (99). Although the images we see convey reality to such an extent that there is virtually no distance between the signifier and the signified, these images are nonetheless distinct from the external reality to which they point; that is, mere reality itself does not give us a narrative—only a work of art can do that. In this sense cinema is language "to the extent that it orders signifying elements within ordered arrangements different from those of spoken idioms—and to the extent that these elements are not traced on the perceptual configurations of reality itself (which does not tell stories). Filmic manipulation transforms what might have been a mere visual transfer of reality into discourse" (105).

Within this discourse, Metz identifies five cinematographic codes that convey messages to the viewer: "the visual image, the musical sound, the verbal sounds of speech, sound effects, and the graphic form of credits" (*Language,* 16). The total semiotic study of a film would operate on two levels: one analyzing everything the signifying codes embody with respect to psychological, sociological, cultural, and aesthetic meaning; and one examining the cinematic manner by which the codes are presented to us.

Metz believes that, historically speaking, all the "specific signifying procedures" were established or codified for cinema by 1915. The semiotician can thus point to such aspects of cinematic language as camera movements, double exposures, optical effects, dissolves, fades, pans, close-ups, tracking shots, parallel and alternate montage, and can raise diachronic or evolutionary considerations—that is, who uses which of these for the first time; or the semiotician can discuss these in synchronic terms, and analyze a film or group of films to understand how these aspects of cinematic language are used to present the *diegesis*—Metz's term for the "sum" of all narrative elements of "a film's denotation" (98).

Essentially the semiotician explores the nature of the image as sign and the way images are ordered in the narrative as a whole. To understand how Metz approaches the first of these activities, observe his discussion of a common setting in gangster films, in which the represented image shows a waterfront area at night, with such aspects as docks, wet pavements, and the like. Using a model proposed by Roland Barthes in *Mythologies*, Metz suggests that here the actual image we see—the material on the screen—be considered the *signifier of denotation*. The signified, or meaning of the image, would be "the scene represented (dimly lit, deserted wharves, with stacks of crates and overhead cranes . . .)" (97). The product of this signifier/signified relationship is a sign. Now this *sign* becomes in turn the signifier of a *connotative* relationship; that is, the image and its denotative meaning (docks and wharves presented in a particular way) constitute the "signifier of connotation" that has as its signified "an impression of anxiety and hardness." In other words, Metz posits a two-stage process viewers go through when watching: first reading the image for its denotative content; and then considering what the image suggests connotatively.

This two-stage process, as he presents it, has potential value for viewers who wish to analyze the distinction between denotation and connotation in given images. Let us take an image from *Citizen Kane*—the scene in the Thatcher Library where Thompson sits at the desk about to read Thatcher's memoirs. The signified of denotation is the scene represented: certain lighting effects and interiors that are read on the level of the signified as meaning cavernous room, high ceilings, a beam of light falling on the table, the clanging of a door as Thompson is left alone. The denotative construct signifier/signified acting as a sign becomes the signifier of a larger connotative meaning in this way. The scene represented suggests the mystery (the lighting and the strange room) and foreboding (the ominous clang of the door) that we could associate with a tomb. In terms of the diegesis, this connotative meaning is not inappropriate, since in fact Thompson is trying to unearth a mystery buried in the past.

Metz points out that if any aspect of the dock scene were changed in respect to its manner of filming, the whole process of signification would be altered. The scene photographed in bright light rather than at night would take away from the eeriness. Similarly, in our example from

Kane, consider how the connotation of the scene would be changed if the library were brightly lighted. In other words, in both cases the setting would still be the same (denotatively a dock area or a library room) but the connotation would be different (elimination of frightening suggestions and associations). That is, the way the image is delivered to us through the photographic medium affects its meaning, its signification.

Turning to a consideration of the ways in which the images are assembled in the diegesis, we encounter a distinction borrowed from linguistic theory between a *paradigm* and a *syntagm.* As Metz uses these terms, paradigm refers to "a class of elements, only one of which figures in the text"; syntagm, to "a set of elements which are co-manifest in the same fragments of texts, which are already next to one another before any analysis" (164–65). Perhaps a linguistic example will explain his meaning here. In linguistics we can speak of a paradigm or class containing all the possible forms of a particular word—"love," for example ("love," "loves," "loved," and so on). Looking at a line of prose or verse with the word in it, such as "she loves good weather," we would say that we discover the verb "loves" in a syntagmatic relationship with the pronoun "she" and the phrase "good weather" used as direct object. If another form of "love" had been drawn from the paradigm, the meaning of the utterance could be different; if the line read, "she loved good weather," the inference we draw might be that she no longer does. The point is that the speaker draws out of the paradigm the form of the word that best suits the particular communication he or she desires to make. Once the word has been taken from the paradigm and entered into communication, we speak of it as a syntagm.

In general, Metz denies that there are paradigms of images as such in the way that there are paradigms of the forms of a given word like "love." Instead, there are paradigms of cinematic signifying codes that we can consider when examining how images are ordered in the films. For example, he discusses transitions between scenes in a film and says that the alternatives "fade" and "dissolve" constitute a paradigm. I see no reason why we cannot also add the possibility of "straight cut" as well. Thus the paradigmatic category for "conjunction of two sequences" would include three possibilities: cut, dissolve, fade. When any one of these occurs as a link between sequences, we call it a syntagm—an element from a paradigmatic category observed in active relation to another element.

By far the most important aspect of *Film Language* is Metz's attempt to define the very nature of narrative units in film, what he calls his *grande syntagmatique*—or the large syntagmatic system. Essentially he proposes to describe narrative discourse in terms of cinematic language; that is, each type of image, scene, and sequence can be defined and assigned a particular name. Here he suggests that there exist eight syntagms in the major paradigm of elements that permit the structuring of denotation. When making a film, a director must decide how all the shots and scenes will be assembled. Metz uses a linguistic model to conceive of the process by which the director utilizes a particular kind of cinematic discourse. As in the operation of language, an individual who wishes to communicate draws his or her utterance from the potentialities, the "deep structures" of possible utterances and constructions open to him or her as a speaker of a given language. Similarly, Metz says that the director draws from a paradigm of eight syntagmatic categories available, an "outline of the deep structure of the choices that confront the filmmaker for each one of the 'sequences' of his film" (123).

The first type, from the paradigm of denotative structures, is the *autonomous* segment, which is constituted by one shot. This can be extended, as in the long take or sequence shot encountered in Italian neorealist films and in *Citizen Kane* (the scene in the boardinghouse when Mrs. Kane signs over Charles to Thatcher); or it can be short, even subliminal, as in one-shot interpolations and inserts. Metz lists four such inserts: the *nondiegetic* insert, which shows something external to the action directly represented; the *subjective* insert, which presents an image conceived of in relation to a character—a dream or memory; a *displaced diegetic* insert, which is an image related to the main action but not made dominant (showing only one image of the pursued in a sequence covering the activities of the pursuers); and the *explanatory* insert, which uses a close-up or camera movement to give viewers better sight of a detail.

The remaining seven types of narrative syntagms are autonomous segments made up of more than one shot: "autonomous segments having more than one minimum segment" (124). Note carefully that single autonomous shots are combined to form segments having more than one shot.

Types 2 and 3 are nonchronological and do not posit any temporal relationship between their units. In type 2, we see *parallel montage,* or syntagms in which "montage brings together and interweaves two or more alternating 'motifs,' but no precise relationship (whether temporal or spatial) is assigned to them—at least on the level of denotation" (125). The third type or *bracket syntagm* (previously called frequentative syntagm by Metz), includes sequences in which a particular activity is described: "a series of very brief scenes representing occurrences that the film gives as typical samples of a same order of reality, without in any way chronologically locating them in relation to each other" (126). There is no alternation of images, as in type 2, but rather a series of actions depicting related facts. For example, in *The Godfather* (1972), we could cite the series of shots indicating the activities of the Corleone "family" when the members have gone underground. The viewer senses that the events are happening at the same general time, but has no way of knowing precisely the exact order in which the events occur; for example, one cannot tell precisely when the spaghetti meal takes place in diegetic time.

The remaining five syntagms are all chronological: "the temporal relationships between the facts that successive images show us are defined on the level of denotation (i.e., literal temporality of the plot, and not just some symbolic, 'profound' time)" (127). In type 4, the *descriptive syntagm*, the chronological element is construed as being simultaneous, as when in an establishing sequence the camera shows us in various shots spatially related elements coexisting at the same moment. Metz's example is of a landscape in which we see separate shots of a tree, a stream near the tree, and a hill beyond. We could also mention the opening of *Citizen Kane*, which presents the descriptive syntagm; the shots of the chain-link fence, "Xanadu," the lighted window, and so forth, combine to give us a single moment of reality as the camera picks out details that establish and locate the estate and property as belonging to a common space.

Types 5 through 8 are *narrative syntagms* in which there occurs an actual passage of time, consecutiveness. In type 5, the *alternate narrative syntagm*, the director switches from scene A to scene B to scene A, and so on, as in a sequence where we watch the pursuer and the pursued alternately. In each diegetic element (A or B) time is consecutive; but we are to understand that A and B occur simultaneously, as in the old-time thriller device of switching from shots of a hapless woman tied to the railroad tracks to shots of the approaching train.

Metz conceives of the sixth syntagm as the *scene*, most typically appearing in conversations in which time flows consecutively and in which there are no temporal breaks. A common example is dialogue between two characters using the shot-reverse shot-shot pattern as the camera shows us the speaker, the listener, the speaker, and so on. But we could include any scene as long as there is no break in time and as long as it is constituted by *more than one shot*: for example, the point at which we pick up Kane's speech in Madison Square Garden with the cuts from Kane to his son, to Leland, and to Gettys—one scene in which time passes consecutively and in which we have more than one shot.

The remaining two syntagms are more complex, and are called "sequences proper." Type 7, the *episodic sequence*, "strings together a number of very brief scenes, which are usually separated from each other by optical devices (dissolves, etc.) and which succeed each other in chronological order" (130). Metz offers the famous breakfast table sequence in *Citizen Kane* as an example. The six scenes there are linked by swing dissolves and, with amazing economy, create a sequence that indicates the deterioration of Kane's marriage. We could also mention from the same film the episodic sequence in which Thatcher follows the career of Kane by reading the headlines of various newspapers.

The last type of syntagm, the *ordinary sequence*, covers a single action but does so with spatial and temporal breaks. What we see are the elements in the particular action that have *not* been omitted: "the sequence is based on the unity of a more complex action . . . that 'skips' those portions of itself that it intends to leave out and that is therefore apt to unfold in several different locations (unlike the scene)" (132). Metz's example is that of an escape sequence in which our real time does not coincide with the diegetic time, as it does in a scene. Instead, we might watch a sequence lasting ten minutes in which an action understood to be lasting two hours takes place—for example, the two hours it takes for men to tunnel out from a prison. The omission in no way interferes with the unity of the action: "one encounters diegetic breaks within the sequence . . . but these hiatuses are considered insignificant—at least on the level of denotation—and are to be distinguished from those indicated by the fades or by any other optical device between two autonomous segments" (132). Another example we could mention here is the Odessa Steps massacre in *Potemkin*. Although the massacre takes seven minutes at the most of our time, the implication is that a much longer diegetic time is involved.

Metz applies his syntagmatic categories directly to a relatively unknown film by Jacques Rozier, *Adieu Philippine* (1961). Ideally, readers of Metz should be able to view the film in order to see and understand how he makes practical use of his categories to analyze a film completely. My own reaction after seeing the film several times is that some of his assignments of segments to various syntagmatic categories are highly debatable. There are times when the decisions seem somewhat arbitrary, and other times when they seem incorrect by his own standards.

Nonetheless, the method of examining a film on this basis does have the potential merit of helping us talk about the construction and pattern of the film's structure in objective, formal terms. For example, Metz shows how two events represented in the film have the same syntagmatic pattern: (1) hero has liaison with girl A, who later returns secretively to her companion, girl B; (2) hero has liaison with girl B, who later returns secretively to her companion, girl A. It helps to be able to say that both are episodic sequences, and, as such, underline in their parallel structure the parallel activities of the characters. When we have such terms at our fingertips, we are able to facilitate our discussion of film considerably, just as we can by using Noël Burch's spatiotemporal articulations. As is evident in the selection from Burch reprinted here, these help us describe film's formal relations with greater economy and precision.

In addition, as Metz suggests, one using the syntagmatic categories can determine whether films of a given period display a certain tendency to use particular syntagms more than those of other periods. Such historical analysis need not be limited to confirming the obvious— the frequency of alternate narrative syntagms in the silent period, the reliance on sequence shots using deep focus in the 1940s, and so on. In fact, the application of the categories might be an effective way to *test* the validity of exactly such assertions about what kind of structural tendencies dominate filmmaking during a given period. Used intelligently, this or a similar codification of syntagmatic categories could provide a means of distinguishing structural differences between genres or within the works of a given director. In this connection, it becomes not only a historical tool, but an important means of bringing precision to that most elusive topic, directorial style.

To be fair, though, one must note that Metz himself was not a supporter of the auteur theory. He told *Cinéthique*: "I do not consider the film-maker as a creative individual at all. . . . As far as I am concerned, the film-maker is only an effect of the text, the effect of the textual system of the films he has made" (210–11).

In *Language and Cinema,* the next major contribution of Metz to the discussion of film semiotics, he continues the same exploration of film from a semiotic perspective, but with some notable differences. First, he acknowledges the incompleteness of *Film Language,* suggesting that perhaps he "overestimated" the importance of the *grande syntagmatique* as a code in relation to all cinematic material. Although he rejects criticism that accuses him of privileging that code in respect to other aspects of cinema, he says he should have said more about the other operative codes (189). *Language and Cinema* is, in fact, the complementary volume to *Film Language* in that it provides a basis for understanding how one kind of code (the *grande syntagmatique*) fits in with other possible codes.

In *Language and Cinema* Metz describes a code as "a system of differentiations" (29) and "a generally coherent system" (61); codes are "systematically homogeneous units" (35). "[G]*eneral cinematic codes*" are "systemic processes . . . to which may be attributed those processes which not only characterize the big screen, but which in addition are . . . common to all films. Opposite the general cinematic codes, *particular cinematic codes* include those elements of signification which appear only in certain types of films" (62). The "filmic" is his term for "all the traits which appear in film (i.e., in the messages of the cinema)"; the "cinematic" refers to "certain filmic facts which are supposed to play a part . . . in one or more of the codes specific to the cinema" (47).

For example, in terms of the codification of shots, vast panning shots are general, since they can appear in any film, but "certain types of long shots are common only to the Western, certain types of camera movements only to the German expressionist school, etc." (62). When we try to define a particular genre, what we do essentially is indicate which particular and noncinematic codes figure most prominently. Again, in reference to westerns, "what characterizes the classic film of the West, and it alone, is a certain number of selections that are made from among these codes, and the arrangement of those elements into a quite definite overall configuration resulting from interaction between the cinematic and extra-cinematic options. This configuration is thus a textual system" (121).

Clearly this conception of codes and genres presupposes a stable relationship between the codes and their elements and what they signify. This presupposition seems complemented by Metz's following assertion: "What is called reality—i.e., the different prefilmic elements—is nothing more than a set of codes, that set of codes without which this reality would not be accessible or intelligible, such that nothing could be said about it, not even that it is reality" (103).

Although hardly an idealist's view of reality (it is, after all, "nothing more than a set of codes"), this conception still figures a kind of confidence in the coherence of the pre-filmic. As we saw in his earlier discussion of the image, Metz again displays an affinity to André Bazin, even though their theoretical agendas are quite different. Both see film as describable in terms of its meaningful relation to reality. Although Metz does not rely on the kind of literal or metaphoric phrases used by Bazin to explore the significatory relation between film and reality, the logic of his position is certainly close to Bazin's: the semiotician's ability to map codes must be in part a function of film's mimetic relationship to a reality that itself "is a coherent system."

There is a marked shift in emphasis in Metz's next major work of theory, one that signals his choice of a new entrance to film studies: psychoanalysis. But the semiotic cast and concern with signification still dominate this choice. What has happened is that in his attempt to explain the full range of signification involved in the experience of film, Metz finds that linguistics needs to be supplemented. Signification, the relation between the signifying image and its signified, cannot be understood simply in terms of codes analogically derived from linguistics. The very experience of viewing—the psychological and physical phenomena involved with projection of images and their reception—demands a different model to explain it, one that also involves examination of signification.

Jacques Aumont, Marc Vernet, and others have argued that "it was only by Metz's gradual progression from working on film devices to working on the spectator that the linguistic heritage was further complemented by the psychoanalytic illumination that gained more and more acceptance after his *Imaginary Signifier*" (143). In other words, they posit a continuity between the two entrances we saw mentioned in the interview, linguistics and psychoanalysis. The link between them is semiotics, the study of signification.

One of the chief influences on Metz at this time is the French psychoanalyst Jacques Lacan. But he should not be considered *the* major influence. Four years after writing "The Imaginary Signifier" Metz insisted in an interview: "I am not a Lacanian. There is a misunderstanding about my position, because I borrow some concepts from Lacan's work. . . . What was interesting for me was to take . . . certain concepts which I think are helpful for me in studying cinema. . . . [C]ertain of his ideas do concern me very closely: metaphor, metonymy, Imaginary, Symbolic" (Flitterman-Lewis, 8). Others who are important for Metz as influences on the conception of "The Imaginary Signifier" are Jean-Louis Baudry, and, as before in his study of signification, Roland Barthes.

The primary metaphor controlling "The Imaginary Signifier" is that of the mirror, drawn from Lacan. Briefly, Lacan considers the human subject with reference to three orders or phases: the *mirror,* the *symbolic,* and the *real.* The *mirror* phase refers to the experience of the pre-Oedipal infant, aged six to eighteen months, as it encounters its reflection in a mirror and assumes (mistakenly) that the image of wholeness and completeness it sees there (sometimes with its mother) represents reality. The *symbolic* refers to that aspect of the subject's experience involving the acquisition of language, particularly as it passes through the Oedipal phase and comes to terms with the fact of sexual difference. Here desire for the mother must be repressed; this repression of desire occurs specifically in and through language. The individual is thus positioned in relation to the primacy of the Phallus, the complex signifier that points not only to the male's possession of the penis and the female's lack of one, but also to a structure controlling how we speak and how we are spoken to in gendered relationships. The *real* refers to that which exists for the individual functioning as a subject in language as a signifier among other signifiers.

Metz draws on both Lacanian and Freudian theory to explain the nature of signification within cinema and the relationship of the spectator to the cinematic signifier. We are able to watch and understand films because we have passed through the mirror stage. Since as infants we identified with an imaginary image and took it for reality, as older beings we are able to identify with a fiction on the screen and take it for reality. Absent to the object we watch, we observe an image that stands in for an absent object. The cinematic signifier is thus "imaginary" (44).

Metz connects our desire to watch (scopophilia) with constitutive drives in our makeup. As opposed to an instinct like hunger, which must be satisfied by a real object (food), our drive to see can be satisfied by a substitute. Like the fetish which, for Freud, serves as a surrogate or substitute for the missing penis perceived by the male to be lacking in the female, the image on the screen is part of a fetishistic viewing structure in that it substitutes for and is taken for something else, the absent reality.

In a later section of the essay not included in the selection reprinted here, Metz develops even more thoroughly the relationship between the fetish and viewing. Essentially he argues that the very structure of denial and affirmation implicit in the discovery of sexual difference (the female lacks a penis) is psychically connected with the spectator's ability to believe in the validity of the image and the absent reality it signifies (69–71).

Moreover, the scopophilic drive confirms our inherent voyeurism and desire to watch unobserved. Metz also connects this with infantile development, specifically the primal scene experience. That is, the infant is understood by Freud to have witnessed its parents having sexual intercourse; hence, Metz's claim for the "Oedipal" nature of the signifier (64).

In addition to infantile experience in accounting for our interaction with the screen, Metz also considers the physical conditions of viewing. The inherent tendency to accept and identify fictions is enhanced by the manner in which we receive the images; they seem to come from us (the camera is behind us) and to be projected on us (we become a "second screen" [48]).

Emerging from this psychoanalytically inflected conception of signification is an emphasis on the complexity of viewing. Metz explores this issue further in "The Fiction Film and Its Spectator" (1975). Here he considers and refines the well-known analogy with viewing a film and dreaming. Specifically he turns to Freud's conception of the daydream, which is less than a dream in terms of the operation of the censorship and the other elements attributed to the dream work such as condensation and displacement. Metz argues that the fiction in and of the film combines with our "impression of reality" as well as with our dreamlike experience of the film to "meet": "a meeting which is possible only around a pseudo-real (a diegesis): around a *place* consisting of actions, objects, persons, a time and a space . . . but which presents itself . . . as a vast simulation, a non-real real" (141). That is, we must acknowledge: (1) the presence of the imaginary in our processing of the absent images we allow to serve as signifiers of presence; (2) the imaginary nature of the "fiction" itself—a made-up story; and (3) our imaginary daydream-like relation to the fictional world.

Metz explores some of the implications of the model generated by this hypothesis in "Story/Discourse (A Note on Two Kinds of Voyeurism)" (1975). Here as in "The Imaginary Signifier" Metz considers the nature of identification, but now from a different perspective. Because of the spectator's identification with the projective camera (called "primary" as opposed to the "secondary" identification that obtains with the characters), the "story" seems to come of itself, or more to the point, from the spectator: "by watching the film I help it to be born, I help it to live, since only in me will it live" (93). But our identification with the story and with the camera that releases the story tends to obscure our awareness of "discourse." Metz argues that the discourse, or "enunciation," necessarily effaces itself so that the imaginary relationship between spectator and fiction will not be disturbed.

There are ideological implications in this division that are hinted at by Metz but explored more fully by theorists like Jean-Louis Baudry. Essentially, any disguising effected by the discourse can have ideological ramifications since the enunicative operation of the film will, as Baudry explains, give the viewer a sense of primacy in terms of the viewing situation, making the viewer think himself or herself in command because of identification with the camera. But under such circumstances, we are less capable of denying the possibly problematic content of the images that seem to come from us and that are positioned perspectivally for us exclusively. Thus, given our practice of accepting as "true" or as "natural" the fiction represented in the film, if the agenda of the fiction film is politically conservative or reactionary (Baudry's particular fear), then the very "imaginary" identification that characterizes the operation of the apparatus contributes to the moral and political delusion of the spectator.

The final essay collected in *The Imaginary Signifier* (one-half of the volume), "Metaphor/Metonymy, or the Imaginary Referent" (1975), extends Metz's exploration of signification to specific rhetorical figures, considered in relation to their cinematic operation. This study is also inflected by his interest in psychoanalysis. Roman Jakobson had earlier suggested that film can be said to operate by a principle of metonymy (achieved by the associative framings and shots around an object) and metaphor (effected by the substitution of one visual object understood to stand in for another). According to Jakobson: "Ever since the productions of D. W. Griffith, the art of the cinema, with its highly developed capacity for changing the angle, perspective and focus of 'shots,' has broken with the tradition of the theater and ranged an unprecedented variety of synedochic 'close-ups' and metonymic 'set-ups' in general. In such pictures as those of Charlie Chaplin, these devices in turn were superseded by a novel, metaphoric 'montage' with its 'lap dissolves'—the filmic similes" (1114–15).

In some ways this essay provides a counterpart to Metz's agenda in *Language and Cinema*. In the earlier work he wants to define what is cinematic and filmic and to identify various codes operating in film in addition to the *grande syntagmatique*. In this essay, his aim is to clarify and validate the use of terms like metaphor and metonymy, and, in the process, distinguish them from related pairings like syntagm and paradigm, condensation and displacement, figure and trope. In so doing, he again effects a synthesis of his linguistic and psychoanalytic perspectives. And, as a subsidiary achievement, he offers a necessary corrective to the sometimes uninformed application by theorists of Jakobson's terminology.

Metz develops a complex four-part taxonomy of potential figural relationships (189–90). One example of his thinking will have to suffice as an indication of his interests here. He considers the scene in *Citizen Kane* in which Susan leaves Xanadu. The scene begins with Raymond describing her departure and then a process shot of the cockatoo followed by her departure: "An ultra-rapid dissolve ushers in the close-up of a shrieking cockatoo (a little textual trauma: nothing had led us to expect it) which immediately flies away where it was perched, revealing Susan who is crossing it hurriedly to leave Xanadu (the metonymic pretext . . . is extremely thin). It is the metaphor of flying away—which applies to Susan also" (271–72). Metz continues to explain how this metaphor is an example of condensation, Freud's term for the activity by which the dream work superimposes elements in the unconscious. The cockatoo as a textual element becomes a visual means of embodying not only Susan's departure but also Kane's rage.

Metz continued to explore the issues of metaphor and metonymy. In an interview in 1989 with Michel Marie and Marc Vernet, Metz explained that his recent work on jokes related directly to his work in *The Imaginary Signifier*, especially the essay on metaphor and metonymy (281). (Metz also noted that the work had been refused by two publishers [280].)

In "The Impersonal Enunciation, or the Site of Film" (1987; translated 1991), Metz returns to questions about the nature of enunciation and the spectator. Recalling his earlier statement regarding the linguistic and psychoanalytic entrances to cinema studies, one is struck by the extent to which neither approach in itself seems to be dominant. Rather, Metz appears now as an extraordinary synthesizer of these approaches, of reception theory, and of his own contributions to that point. Notably, he refers constantly to Branigan's work on *Point of View in the Cinema*.

Metz asks again how we receive the film: Who speaks it? How do we process it? His provisional answer is to expand the concept of the text itself: "the source [of the film] and the target [the spectator], considered in their literal transcription, are not roles, but *parts of texts*, aspects or configurations of the text. . . . Source and target are rather *orientations*, vectors in textual topography" (763). Again, "the source and target . . . are not the enunciator and the addressee, who are fictitious people; . . . they are . . . directions (belonging to the geography of the film), orientations discovered by the analyst" (765). To explore this thesis, Metz discusses such elements as films within films, first-person narrations, and framings that replicate the operations and positioning of the camera.

I want to conclude by considering Metz in the context of contemporary theory. Sandy Flitterman-Lewis's assessment is certainly accurate: "Metz's founding work in cinemasemiotics and psychoanalytic film theory not only shaped the critical practice of a generation, it redefined the very landscape of cinema studies" (Tribute, 3). Anyone who has taught (or taken) a class in film theory knows how discussion of Metz's theory helped us see where we had been and where we might go in the future. His writings represented a significant break with earlier theory and have become in turn the corpus of ideas to which those who follow have to react. He has truly been the defining presence for this generation of film theorists.

But without question, his semiotically based linguistic and psychoanalytic explorations have generated reservations, qualifications, or outright dissent. Specific problematic areas have been the absence of a political agenda, his apparent obliviousness to issues of gender, and his use of psychoanalysis.

The first salvo in regard to his lack of a political stance appeared in a 1972 review of his work in *Cinéthique*. The editors observed: "we are obliged to note that at the present juncture an *ideological* discussion of the assumption and development of semiology of the cinema seems alien to his practice" (210–11). It is not unfair to suggest that the kind of active politicizing of theory characterizing the work of his contemporaries at *Cahiers du Cinéma* and *Tel Quel* did not occur.

The problem of gender that affects Metz's critical reception arises inevitably with any form of psychoanalytic theory grounded in Freudian and Lacanian hypotheses. The Oedipus complex, its connection to vision and its privileging of the male as the point of entry to analysis in Freud, as well as the primacy of the Phallus as a signifier in Lacan offer profound problems for feminist theory. A typical kind of objection is voiced by Patrice Petro as she cites Jacqueline Rose's argument: "Metz's psychoanalytic reading of visual perception and, specifically, his use of the concept of disavowal to describe the ways in which cinema achieves its impression of reality failed to address the problem or the difficulty of sexual difference" (74).

The most sustained and thoughtful critique of his psychoanalytic theory has been offered by Noël Carroll. He finds Metz's thesis regarding film and the daydream in particular "altogether without proof" (47). But, from a more general perspective, Carroll questions the appropriateness of the application of psychoanalysis to film in the first place on the basis of such concerns as the extent to which viewers are really deluded and the incongruity in applying a method presupposing irrationality to a subject that is not in itself irrational (32–52).

In a section presenting a tribute to Christian Metz at the 1994 meeting of the Modern Language Association, Linda Williams, who had studied with him, offered an impressively balanced and moving estimate of him while striking a perfect, elegiac note. Acknowledging that by 1994 Metz's direct influence had lessened perceptibly, Williams concluded: "Christian Metz pioneered the confessional mode of theory, of exploring the theorist's own unconscious desires. He admitted to what film journals would later call guilty pleasures. . . . I would argue that we should reread Metz today to confront again, in a somewhat different mode, pleasures that no longer be regarded as guilty" (6).

NOTE

The discussion of Metz's linguistic-based theory draws significantly on my earlier treatment of this issue in *A Viewer's Guide to Film Theory and Criticism* (Metuchen, N.J.: Scarecrow, 1979).

WORKS CITED

Aumont, Jacques, Alain Bergala, Michel Marie, and Marc Vernet. *Aesthetics of Film*. Trans. and rev. Richard Neupert. Austin: University of Texas Press, 1992.

Barthes, Roland. *Mythologies*. Trans. Annette Lavers. New York: Hill and Wang, n.d.

———. "The Third Meaning." *Image-Music-Text*. Trans. Stephen Heath. New York: Hill and Wang, 1977.

Baudry, Jean-Louis. "Ideological Effects of the Basic Cinematic Apparatus." In *Film Theory and Criticism*. 4th ed. Trans. Alan Williams; ed. Gerald Mast, Marshall Cohen, and Leo Braudy. New York: Oxford University Press, 1992: 203–312.

Bazin, André. "The Ontology of the Photographic Image." *What Is Cinema?* Trans. Hugh Gray. Berkeley: University of California Press, 1971: 9–16.

Bordwell, David. *Narration in the Fiction Film*. Madison: University of Wisconsin Press, 1985.

Branigan, Edward R. *Point of View in the Cinema*. New York: Mouton, 1984.

Burch, Noël. *Theory of Film Practice*. Trans. Helen R. Lane. New York: Praeger, 1973.

Carroll, Noël. *Mystifying Movies: Fads and Fallacies in Contemporary Film Theory*. New York: Columbia University Press, 1988.

Cinéthique. "*Cinéthique on langage et cinéma.* " Trans. Diana Matias. *Screen* 14, nos. 1–2 (Spring–Summer 1972): 189–213.

Flitterman-Lewis, Sandy. "The Cinematic Apparatus as Social Institution—An Interview with Christian Metz." *Discourse* 1 (Fall 1979): 7–37.

———. "Tribute to Christian Metz." *Discourse* 16, no. 3 (Spring 1994): 3–5.

Jakobson, Roman. "The Metaphoric and Metonymic Poles." In *Critical Theory since Plato*. Ed. Hazard Adams. New York: Harcourt Brace Jovanovich, 1971: 1113–16.

Lacan, Jacques. "The Mirror Stage as Formative of the I." *Écrits A Selection*. Trans. Alan Sheridan. New York: Norton, 1977: 1–7.

Lindsay, Vachel. *The Art of the Moving Picture*. New York: Liveright, 1970.

Marie, Michel, and Marc Vernet. "Entretien avec Christian Metz." *Christian Metz et la théorie du cinéma*. Paris: Méridiens Klincksieck, 1990. *Iris* 10 in France. [*Iris* 6, no. 1 in the United States]: 270–96.

Metz, Christian. "Answers from Christian Metz." *Cinéthique on langage et cinéma.* " 208–210.

———. "Current Problems of Film Theory: Jean Mitry's *L'Esthétique et psychologie du cinéma, Vol. II.* " Trans. Diana Matias. *Screen* 14, nos. 1–2 (Spring–Summer 1972): 40–87.

———. *L' Énonciation impersonnelle, ou le site du film*. Paris: Méridiens Klincksieck, 1991.

———. "Une étape dans la réflexion sur le cinema." *Éssais sur la signification au cinéma*. Tome II. Paris: Éditions Klincksieck, 1972.

———. "The Fiction Film and Its Spectator." Trans. Alfred Guzzetti. *The Imaginary Signifier*: 99–147.

———. *Film Language: A Semiotics of the Cinema*. Trans. Michael Taylor. New York: Oxford University Press, 1974.

———. "The Imaginary Signifier." Trans. Ben Brewster. *The Imaginary Signifier*: 1–87.

———. *The Imaginary Signifier: Psychoanalysis and the Cinema*. Trans. Celia Britton, Annwyl Williams, Ben Brewster, and Alfred Guzzetti. Bloomington: Indiana University Press, 1982.

———. "The Impersonal Enunciation, or the Site of Film." Trans. Béatrice Durand-Sendrail with Kristen Brookes. *New Literary History* 22 (1991): 747–72.

———. *Language and Cinema*. Trans. Donna Jean Umiker-Sebeok. The Hague: Mouton, 1974.

———. "Metaphor/Metonymy, or The Imaginary Referent." Trans. Celia Britton and Annwyl Williams. *The Imaginary Signifier*: 149–314.

————. "Story/Discourse (A Note on Two Kinds of Voyeurism)." Trans. Celia Britton and Annwyl Williams. *The Imaginary Signifier*: 89–98.

Mitry, Jean. *Esthétique et psychologie du cinéma. 1. Les Structures.* Paris: Éditions Universitaires, 1963.

————. *Esthétique et psychologie du cinéma. 2. Les Formes.* Paris: Éditions Universitaires, 1965.

Münsterberg, Hugo. *The Film: A Psychological Study.* New York: Dover, 1970.

Petro, Patrice. "Feminism and Film History." In *Multiple Voices in Film Criticism.* Ed. Diane Carson, Linda Dittmar, and Janice R. Welsch. Minneapolis: University of Minnesota Press, 1994: 65–81.

Stam, Robert. "Film and Language: From Metz to Bakhtin." In *The Cinematic Text: Methods and Approaches.* Ed. R. Barton Palmer. New York: AMS Press, 1989: 277–301.

Williams, Linda. "Vision and Visuality in the Film Theory of Christian Metz." MLA Convention, Div. on Film, San Diego, December 28, 1994.

ANNOTATED BIBLIOGRAPHY

Andrew, Dudley. *Concepts in Film Theory.* Oxford and New York: Oxford University Press, 1984.

Andrew positions Metz helpfully within the context of contemporary critical issues and problems.

Aumont, Jacques, Alain Bergala, Michel Marie, and Marc Vernet. *Aesthetics of Film.* Trans. and rev. Richard Neupert. Austin: University of Texas Press, 1992.

Many of Metz's ideas receive thoughtful and illuminating treatment.

Flitterman-Lewis, Sandy. "The Cinematic Apparatus as Social Institution—An Interview with Christian Metz." *Discourse* 1 (Fall 1979): 7–37.

This invaluable interview presents a wide-ranging array of views in the less formal context of a conversation rather than the written essay. Metz emerges as person, not just a theorist.

Metz, Christian. *Film Language: A Semiotics of the Cinema.* Trans. Michael Taylor. New York: Oxford University Press, 1974.

Metz offers his theory of cinema semiotics and the *grand syntagmatique.*

————. *The Imaginary Signifier: Psychoanalysis and the Cinema.* Trans. Celia Britton, Annwyl Williams, Ben Brewster, and Alfred Guzzetti. Bloomington: Indiana University Press, 1982.

This collection brings together Metz's most important psychoanalytically inflected essays.

————. *Language and Cinema.* Trans. Donna Jean Umiker-Sebeok. The Hague: Mouton, 1974.

Metz explores the issue of codes and extends his examination of signification in the cinema.

Contributors

DUDLEY ANDREW is Angelo Bertocci Professor of Critical Studies at the University of Iowa, where he directs the Institute for Cinema and Culture. He has lectured and written on topics in film history (especially French and Japanese cinema), film theory, and literary theory. His books include *The Major Film Theories* (Oxford, 1976), *André Bazin* (Oxford, 1978), *Kenji Mizoguchi* (co-authored with a brother, Paul Andrew, 1981), *Concepts in Film Theory* (Oxford, 1984), *Film in the Aura of Art* (Princeton, 1984), *Breathless* (Rutgers, 1987), and *Mists of Regret: Culture and Sensibility in Classic French Film* (Princeton, 1995). He has also recently edited *The Image in Dispute: Art and Cinema in the Age of Photography* (Texas, 1997). Among other awards, he has received the Guggenheim Fellowship and a three-year Interpretive Grant from the NEH for a project on French culture between the Wars.

ANDRÉ BAZIN, barred from the teaching profession because of a stammer, directed a ciné-club during the Occupation and began to make a living as a film critic after the war ended. In his all-too-brief career (he died in 1958), he wrote over two thousand pieces for daily, weekly, and monthly periodicals. In 1951, he co-founded *Cahiers du Cinéma*, the most influential of all film journals, where he shaped the taste of the New Wave generation. A frequent presence at film festivals, Bazin affected the cinema through his close friendship with such directors as Renoir, Rossellini, and Buñuel.

EDWARD BRANIGAN is a professor in the department of film studies at the University of California–Santa Barbara. He is the author of *Narrative Comprehension and Film* (Routledge, 1992) and *Point of View in the Cinema* (Mouton, 1984), as well as general editor (with Charles Wolfe) of The American Film Institute Film Readers series (Routledge). He has received two teaching awards including a UCSB Distinguished Teaching Award.

NOËL BURCH was born in San Francisco in 1932, emigrated to France in 1951, received a degree in filmmaking from the French film school I.D.H.E.C., and became a French citizen in 1970. As a filmmaker, theorist, educator, and translator, he has exerted an important influence on film studies in a number of works that have been translated into several languages. They include *In and Out of Synch* (1991), *Life to those Shadows* (1990), *To the Distant Observer* (1979), *Marcel L'Herbier* (1973), and *Theory of Film Practice* (1973).

NOËL CARROLL is the Monroe C. Beardsley Professor of the Philosophy of Art at the University of Wisconsin–Madison. His books include *Philosophical Problems of Classical Film Theory, Mystifying Movies, The Philosophy of Horror, Theorizing* the Moving Image, A Philosophy of Mass Art (forthcoming) and *Interpreting the Moving Image* (forthcoming). He has also co-edited, along with David Bordwell, *Post-Theory: Reconstructing Film Studies.*

ROBERT T. EBERWEIN is a professor of English at Oakland University, where he teaches film theory, history, and appreciation. Among his publications are *Film and the Dream Screen* (1984) and *A Viewer's Guide to Film Theory and Criticism* (1979), as well as essays in *Wide Angle* and the *Journal of Popular Film and Television.* He is currently writing a book on the use of film and video in sex education.

SERGEI M. EISENSTEIN (1898–1948) was the most important filmmaker to emerge from the cinema of the Soviet Union and its most influential theorist of montage. He completed seven feature films during the course of his career: *Strike* (1925), *Battleship* Potemkin (1926), *October* (1928), *Old and New* (1929), *Alexander Nevsky* (1938), and *Ivan the Terrible,* Parts I and I (1944–1946). He was also a prolific author of treatises on film technique and aesthetics.

VANCE KEPLEY JR. is professor of film in the department of communication arts at the University of Wisconsin–Madison. He is the author of *In the Service of the State: The Cinema of Alexander Dovzhenko* (Wisconsin, 1986) and several essays on Soviet cinema.

SIEGFRIED KRACAUER was born in 1889. Trained as an architect, he worked as a journalist covering cultural affairs in the Weimar Republic. Among his many publications are *Orpheus in Paris: Offenbach and the Paris of His Time, From Caligari to Hitler, Theory of Film,* and *History: Last Things before the Last.* An anthology of his Weimar Essays has been recently edited by Thomas Y. Levin and published by Harvard University Press under the title *The Mass Ornament.* Kracauer died in 1966.

PETER LEHMAN is a professor in the department of media arts at the University of Arizona. He is author of *Running Scared: Masculinity and the Representation of the Male Body* and editor of *Close Viewings: An Anthology of New Film Criticism.* He is co-author of three books with William Luhr: *Authorship and Narrative in the Cinema, Blake Edwards,* and *Returning to the Scene: Blake Edwards,* Vol. 2.

CHRISTIAN METZ (1931–1993) taught at the École des Hautes Etudes en Sciences Sociales in Paris and published major theoretical studies of film. The most significant translated works include *Film Language: A Semiotics of the Cinema* (1974), *Language and Cinema* (1974), and *The Imaginary Signifier: Psychoanalysis and the Cinema* (1982).

Index